EXPOSING SATAN'S PLAYBOOK

PERRY STONE

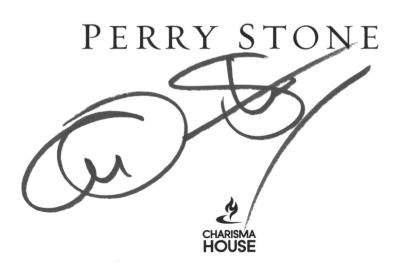

CHARISMA
HOUSE

Most CHARISMA HOUSE BOOK GROUP products are available at special quantity discounts for bulk purchase for sales promotions, premiums, fund-raising, and educational needs. For details, write Charisma House Book Group, 600 Rinehart Road, Lake Mary, Florida 32746, or telephone (407) 333-0600.

EXPOSING SATAN'S PLAYBOOK by Perry Stone
Published by Charisma House
Charisma Media/Charisma House Book Group
600 Rinehart Road
Lake Mary, Florida 32746
www.charismahouse.com

Cover design by Justin Evans
Design Director: Bill Johnson

Visit the author's website at www.voe.org.

Library of Congress Cataloging-in-Publication Data
Stone, Perry F.
  Exposing Satan's playbook / Perry Stone. -- 1st ed.
      p. cm.
  Includes bibliographical references (p.   ).
  ISBN 978-1-61638-868-3 (trade paper) -- ISBN 978-1-61638-869-0
(e-book)
  1. Spiritual warfare. I. Title.
  BV4509.5.S84735 2012
  235'.4--dc23
                          2012024127

While the author has made every effort to provide accurate telephone numbers and Internet addresses at the time of publication, neither the publisher nor the author assumes any responsibility for errors or for changes that occur after publication.

First edition

12 13 14 15 16 — 9 8 7 6 5 4 3 2 1
Printed in the United States of America

Contents

INTRODUCTION

❦ ❧

I T WAS IN the early 1970s, and my father, Fred Stone, was pas-
toring the Fillmore Avenue Church of God in Northern Virginia. One evening Dad received a phone call at home from
a woman whose last name was Hall. She had been looking in the
phonebook for a Full Gospel church. When Dad answered, she got
right to the point. Her husband "worked for the government," and
she was looking for a minister who believed in healing prayer to
go and pray for him. Dad, not knowing the family, consented to
go, as he believed in the power of prayer and had witnessed several dramatic healings during his ministry. Dad went to the hospital, prayed a very energetic prayer for the man (named Bill), and
shortly the man was released from the hospital, free of cancer by
a touch from the hand of a merciful God. The family joined the
church and became faithful followers of Christ.

Dad and Bill became very close friends. Dad learned that Bill worked for the Central Intelligence Agency (CIA) in an *unmarked* building in Northern Virginia. Bill could speak seven languages and had worked in Russia and the Middle East. Years earlier he had been sent to Saudi Arabia to warn King Faisal that the Russian spies had infiltrated the Saudi government and were secretly brainwashing a mentally challenged nephew to assassinate the king. Despite the warning, in 1975 the nephew, Faisal bin Musaid, assassinated the king.

One afternoon Dad received a call from Bill. His voice sounded urgent: "Preacher, can we get together later this evening? Something has happened, and I am very disturbed." Dad and Bill set up a meeting at a local restaurant. Sitting at a back table, Bill said, "Preacher, something has happened that is going to create a national crisis in the Nixon administration." Bill proceeded to inform Dad of a break-in at the Watergate Complex where the Democratic National Committee Headquarters was located. There had been wiretaps on the phones, and *Bill had personally heard tape recordings of several conversations.* (He never said which tapes or where they came from.)

Dad never discussed this with anyone until after Bill's *apparent* death. (Dad actually thought Bill's funeral was staged—an unopened coffin—and that Bill had been sent to a foreign country.) Dad never shared the details of what Bill said that afternoon until about twenty years after the Watergate scandal cost Nixon his presidency.

According to Bill, information revealed there was a plan in place by the opposing political party to try to "hurt Nixon's reelection bid." The plan was to *damage* Nixon by using the controversial Vietnam War and making him appear to be incompetent, and, as a result, the war was going badly. Without going into details, an official in a very high position with links to American military planning for the Vietnam War was promised a very high and lucrative position in the new administration if he would assist in the strategy. This man was copying the bombing raids and other information of the United States in Vietnam—which were secret plans—and handing over the information to an agent linked to the Russian embassy in Washington. The Russians were then transferring the plans to the Vietnamese leaders. Part of the break-in was linked to a belief that the Russians may have compiled personal information on the man who was stealing the plans and were actually blackmailing him to hold him as a hostage by claiming that if the information the CIA had about him was released, he would (in that day) lose his job in the government. Before information of the Watergate break-in was reported in the *Washington Post*, Bill told Dad, "What I have heard is so damaging that if the American people who love this nation knew, it would negatively impact the future of the Democratic Party." The evidence Bill heard and saw proved there were active Socialists and Communists in America working within the system against American forces in the war to discredit the president. He stated, "It proves the higher-ups in the party are pro-Socialist, and some are Communists in their ideology." Bill predicted that Nixon would be the brunt of the news stories and would be forced to step down in embarrassment. Several days later the news broke across Northern Virginia of the break-in and spread like wild fire throughout the world. There are more details (that my father suggested I never share), but I think you get the picture. *You cannot win a war when the enemy knows your battle plans!* However, what if you knew your enemy's strategies? How would that change the outcome of your conflicts?

Now switch the scene. You have been a Christian for several years, and by using Scripture and practical daily experience, you have discovered how your archenemy thinks and works. You are a *strategy soldier* and understand your strengths and weaknesses and where, in the future, you could be vulnerable. You have discovered the need to close the front and back doors of your life—the *front door* being the things that people see, and the *back door* being the secret entrances that the enemy often uses to avoid being detected, the secret things.

On a particular day you walk into a restaurant alone for a quick lunch. The restaurant is packed, and you are seated at a table near the bar. Being a former alcoholic, you must mentally resist a slight churning in the pit of your stomach to order a drink. But because you are armed with the knowledge of the danger of the substance, the fiery dart (Eph. 6:16) entering your mind is immediately quenched by the knowledge of the danger and the fact that your desires have been changed!

After sitting down, suddenly you look up, and a woman whom you haven't seen in years walks up to you. Your heart skips a beat. Before your life with Christ, she was a woman you were living with, and you spent so much time partying that you can't recall most events that occurred on those drunken weekends. Her eyes meet yours, and immediately she moves toward you. There she is— dressed in her normal seductive attire—and you have to make a choice. A voice whispers, "Man, this is your chance. Just get with her one more time. It's been a few years, and you can always repent later."

Then another voice vibrates inside your spirit and says, "You know this is no good. She is a seducer and will do whatever she can to seduce you. Greet her and excuse yourself for the men's room, or call a friend and tell him you need to see him!" The thought comes, "Run as Joseph did when Potiphar's wife desired to have an affair with him." (See Genesis 39:11–12.)

Had this same scene unfolded a few months after your conversion to Christ, as a newborn infant in the faith, you probably would have submitted to the pressure building inside of your mind. This time is different. You now understand the *playbook of the enemy.*

You have been armed with important, soul-saving knowledge. Thus you greet the woman, and immediately you begin to tell her how your life has been changed by the power of the Lord. She was not expecting your testimony, and being uncomfortable, she immediately says, "Good to see you again," and goes her way. By using a spiritual strategy, you overcame a possible attack of the enemy, "…by the word of [your] testimony" (Rev. 12:11).

PRE-ATTACK DOWNLOADS

In our computer age we speak of downloading a song, message, or movie. The information is stored on a hard drive at a company or ministry, but it must be accessed and transferred to your information system—a computer, iPod, iPad, smartphone, or other electronic device. Within seconds the information is received through a download.

At times I have been praying or studying when suddenly a new and exciting thought for a message, book, or article is *downloaded* into my mind and spirit. The information was always available in the spirit realm, but it was necessary for me to tap into the Spirit of God and gain access to the revelation and information that will assist me in the spiritual battle.

How would, or could, your life change if you could acquire advance knowledge of planned mental, physical, and spiritual attacks against you or your family—a *pre-attack download*? In this book, *Exposing Satan's Playbook,* we will expose the questions Satan hopes you never ask and the strategies he hopes you never discover that give you valuable information the adversary does not want you to know. Spiritual knowledge is like sharpening a sword for a battle or finding shelter in a rock fortress during a storm. It is a strong shield that stops flying arrows and a weapon that defeats strategies assigned against you.

Many of the questions we answer in this book are questions

that believers often have in the back of their minds but are often hesitant to discuss. Some can be controversial or even difficult to answer, and they require intensive research. However, if we can expose the playbook of the enemy, we have a far better opportunity to win every spiritual conflict and enter each spiritual battle with confidence.

CHAPTER 1

WHEN A PROPHETIC WORD
BECOMES A WEAPON OF WAR

I T IS ONE of the most dramatic true stories I have ever heard. Pastor Robert Kimberling, who now pastors the East Point Church of God in East Point, Florida, related to me that in 1985 he and his wife were assigned to a church in Lemmon, South Dakota. The church clerk, Vallie Bishop, informed the new pastor that one of their senior members, Liz Brockwell, lived forty miles away in Bison and was unable to attend church as she was elderly. She requested the pastor to visit her. Pastor Kimberling did set up a visit, and when he and his wife arrived at the house, Liz met them and informed them they would be staying for lunch as she had an important story to tell them. She then began to relate a remarkable incident.

It was in 1928; Liz, her husband, Adam, and two daughters

were working hard to keep their ranch. The now famous Dust Bowl was blowing top soil away, preventing a harvest. Her husband had been diagnosed with tuberculosis and was dying at a sanitorium in Rapid City, South Dakota. At that time the doctor called Liz and told her to bring a suit for her husband on her upcoming weekend visit, because he would probably die that weekend. Liz took Adam's suit from the old trunk, hung it on a clothes line to briefly freshen it, but she could not bring herself to pack it.

Another challenge was that the family's only cow had a large sore with maggots surrounding the wound. The cow was unable to stand and walk. On this day Liz took a small bit of grain and some water and was attempting to hand-feed the dying cow, hoping to keep it alive a little longer. Suddenly she felt a strong whirlwind. It was not the normal "dust devil" that she had witnessed numerous times. It felt supernatural, and when she turned to see what was occurring, to her shock a man, which was actually an angel from the Lord, stepped out of the wind and said, "Your husband, Adam, will not die. He will return home, father a child (daughter), and live to see his family raised." The angel said, "As a sign, this cow will walk into the barnyard under its own power and live."

Liz was amazed and responded, "If this happens, I will sell this cow and give the money to missions."

The angel the immediately spoke these words, "Liz, there are no IFS in God's plan!"

Later that day her brother pulled up in the yard to shoot the cow with a rifle to put it out of its misery. Simultaneously the cow got up and walked into the barnyard. Liz's father then ran into the kitchen shouting, "It's a miracle, it's a miracle!"

"Woman, You Are Crazy"

That weekend Liz returned to Rapid City without the suit. Her doctor met her and became angry, rebuking her and telling her that her husband was dying soon. Her reaction was cemented in the revelation of the angel. She related the story, and the doctor screamed, "Woman, you are crazy." She held fast to the promise despite the fact that her husband still lay in the bed. However, two weeks later, Adam left the sanitorium healed, fathered another daughter, and lived to see his family raised. In fact, Adam outlived the doctor who predicted his death. Liz did sell the cow and gave the income to world missions for evangelism![1]

Once this word was revealed that Adam was going to be healed, nothing could pull that promise away from Liz, including any circumstances she witnessed at the hospital. This word from the angel is considered a *prophetic word*, which is a word that reveals an event or situation that will occur in your future. Just as a biblical prophecy is an advanced revelation of a coming event before it transpires, any promise from God concerning events in your future is a *prophetic word*. In this case Liz knew her husband would live and not die and that the dying cow would revive and live. The seven words "There are no ifs in God's plan" were a life-changing revelation for her, and should be for all believers as well.

FIGHTING WITH A PROPHETIC WORD

When Paul wrote to Timothy, he revealed an amazing and important spiritual concept that we must expound upon, as it can be a true weapon of war that the enemy does not want us to understand. Paul said:

> This charge I commit to you, son Timothy, according to the prophecies previously made concerning you, that by them you may wage the good warfare.
> —1 TIMOTHY 1:18

Timothy was a young minister who had accompanied Paul during his second missionary journey to Lystra (Acts 16:2). Paul circumcised Timothy to avoid a conflict with Jewish believers, as Timothy's father was a Greek (v. 3). This young minister was well loved in the early church, including in the area of Iconium (v. 2). He was blessed with strong faith that was handed down from his grandmother, Lois, and his mother, Eunice (2 Tim. 1:5). Paul addressed Timothy as "faithful...in the Lord" (1 Cor. 4:17), and because Timothy mentored under Paul, Paul called him "[my] son" (1 Tim. 1:18).

Paul had spent three years at Ephesus working in a very wicked city, yet this church had become a strong church among the early churches and is listed as one of the churches Christ addressed in Revelation (Rev. 2:1–7). Paul had commissioned Timothy as the lead pastor of Ephesus, and in his letter to Timothy, he gave him important instructions.

The situation was this. Timothy was a young man, and there were many elders in Ephesus who for some reason were not pleased with such a young minister. Paul reminded Timothy not to rebuke an elder (1 Tim. 5:1). It seems the pressure from the opinions of some had caused Timothy to become intimidated with a spirit of fear.

Paul wrote, "God has not given us a spirit of fear, but of power and of love and of a sound mind" (2 Tim. 1:7). The common Greek word for *fear* in the New Testament is *phobos* (i.e., Rom. 8:15) and alludes to being afraid of the possibility of something bad. It is the root of the word *phobia*. The Greek word for *fear* that Paul used in 2 Timothy 1:7 is *deilia*, which means "timid."[2] Timothy was not fearful of his elders or congregation, but he was becoming timid or *intimidated* by comments and opinions concerning his ministry. Paul reminded his spiritual son that God had not given him this feeling of being timid but desired him to have a "sound" (disciplined or self-controlled) mind.

Paul reminded Timothy of two important spiritual weapons that would help him overcome his situation. First he told Timothy, "Stir up the gift of God which is in you through the laying on of my hands" (2 Tim. 1:6). The original Greek word for "stir up" is a reference to rekindling a fire that is about to go out. It can read "to kindle up the gift."[3] In the first letter Paul instructed Timothy not to "neglect the gift that is in you" (1 Tim. 4:14), and in this second letter he said to stir it up and get a fire burning—a fresh zeal for God! The word *gift* in both references is *charismata* in Greek and can allude to the nine gifts of the Spirit (1 Cor. 12:7–10) or to a specific gift imparted from the Lord and transferred to a person through the laying on of hands, as Paul did with Timothy (2 Tim. 1:6).

A POWERFUL WEAPON

The second weapon for defeating mental strongholds is a spiritual weapon available in your own life. Paul told the young pastor to war with the prophecies that went before him! Paul gave Timothy a "charge" (1 Tim. 1:18), which is more of a term used for a military commander giving an order to a soldier. Paul is not saying, "I have some good advice," but "I have an order I want you to follow!"

Paul reminded Timothy that "prophecies...went before" him (KJV). This indicated that Timothy was given prophetic words concerning God's will for his life that were confirmed by the Holy Spirit and that revealed God's will for Timothy was the pastoral assignment at Ephesus. It was common in the early church for apostles with spiritual gifts to operate in a vocal gift and give a word of prophecy concerning God's will for a minister. As an example we read the phrase, "It seemed good to the Holy Spirit, and to us..." (Acts 15:28). In Acts 13, as Paul and others were praying and fasting, the Holy Spirit instructed the church leaders to send Paul and Barnabas on a missionary journey (vv. 2–4). There were even warnings of coming famines and warnings of coming danger that were received through a Holy Spirit–inspired utterance (Acts 11:28; 21:11).

5

Paul's instruction was for Timothy to war with the prophetic words he had received! He was making it clear to Timothy that this battle was not against flesh and blood or against elders who thought he was too young and inexperienced. It was a spiritual battle against Timothy's mind to challenge the call of God on his life and the will of God for his ministry. Timothy could submit to the words of others and become timid and ineffective, allowing the fire to die and the zeal to cease. However, by publicly reminding the congregation that it was the Holy Spirit Himself through an inspired utterance who assigned Timothy to his position, this truth became a weapon to be used to battle the fear and intimidation attacking the young pastor!

THE WEAPON OF PROPHETIC WORDS

Most believers have heard great instructional teaching on the importance of knowing the written Scriptures and of using the Word of God as the "sword of the Spirit" (Eph. 6:17). Believers quote various passages as a promise and assurance of victory in the time of spiritual, physical, or emotional conflict. We see this concept at work in the life of Christ when He was tempted forty days by the adversary. The "tempter" came (Matt. 4:3) and began mentally harassing Christ, attempting to make Him question who He was and His relationship with God. Satan told Christ that if He really was the Son of God, He could turn stones to bread and jump from the pinnacle of the temple and not be injured. Satan also told Jesus that if He bowed to the him, Satan he would give Him power over the world's kingdoms (vv. 1–11). In each of the three "temptations" Christ immediately quoted scriptures to counter the assault. All three scriptures are found in the Torah, the five books written by Moses in the wilderness.

The quote Christ gave to the adversary	The original passage in the Old Testament
"Man shall not live by bread alone, but by every word that proceeds from the mouth of God" (Matt. 4:4).	Deuteronomy 8:3
"You shall not tempt the LORD your God" (Matt. 4:7).	Deuteronomy 6:16
"You shall worship the LORD your God, and Him only you shall serve" (Matt. 4:10).	Exodus 34:14

A *prophetic word* is a special inspired message or word that a person receives in his or her inner spirit after a season of fasting and extended prayer or, at times, through an inspired utterance from Scripture and occasionally confirmed by a vocal gift from another believer. There have been strong *prophetic movements* among Christians in various nations that encourage individuals to prophesy over each other, giving words from the Lord at times about as fast as a person pumping gas into a gas tank. I want to use discretion and wisdom when saying this, but some of these movements are filled with what I call "cereal saints," meaning they are full of flakes and nuts. Many times they are stepping out in faith to speak but have a hit-or-miss ratio of about 50 percent that are accurate and 50 percent that are wrong, which is about the same percentage of an alleged psychic who attempts to predict someone's future!

I was blessed to be raised with and around great men and women of God who prayed hours each day, fasted extensively, and would never open their mouths and say, "The Lord said…" until they had a true burning inspiration from the Holy Spirit. My own father commonly would receive special inspired messages, including words of knowledge and warnings for individuals, and in my lifetime I never saw him *miss the mark* when giving a prophetic word to a person. He was so accurate that it created an awesome presence and fear of the Lord among those in the congregation. A second personal observation about those alleging to give a word is that the "word" often is a word of great, future blessing and prosperity without the requirement for a life of sacrifice or holiness. Throughout the Bible true prophets would call out those in sin and rebuke those in arrogance and pride and give warnings while weeping at the same time. A true prophetic word is not just for edification, exhortation, and comfort (1 Cor. 14:3), but throughout the Bible, including the New Testament, a word can bring an advance warning.

JUDGING A PERSONAL WORD

If a person claims to have received a word from the Lord to give to you, the first important point is to "recognize those who labor among you, and are over you in the Lord and admonish you" (1 Thess. 5:12). Is the person respected in the church and in the body of Christ, or is he or she a rebel on the loose and a self-appointed prophet who left a church in a negative manner because the "pastor wasn't spiritual enough"? At times pastors detect arrogance and pride and a wrong spirit, and this is why this lone ranger prophet or prophetess was removed from the assembly of the saints! So the first point is not to accept a word just because a person claims, "The Lord told me thus and so…" Know something about the person's reputation and character.

The second point is to examine if the word agrees 100 percent with the inspired Scriptures. Never, and I do mean never, will a word from the Holy Spirit contradict the Bible. The Lord will never tell a person to suddenly leave his or her companion for another "more spiritual" individual, because marriage is a covenant. (Some have done this in the name of "the Lord told me to.") The Lord would never permit a person, in the name of Christian liberty, to participate in substances that cause drunkenness and addiction to an individual, for "drunkards" cannot "inherit the kingdom of

God" (1 Cor. 6:10). God is not the author of confusion, nor is He the author of most church splits where individuals are hurt, offended, and quit serving God because of the confusion and distrust created when people divided their loyalty. God is the author of "peace…in all the churches" (1 Cor. 14:33).

The third point is that a prophetic word must agree with your spirit and will only confirm what you already know. Because vessels are human and subject to fallibility, prophetic words are to be *judged* by other mature and older people within the church, as it is written: "Let two or three prophets speak, and let the others judge" (1 Cor. 14:29). The Greek word for "judge" here is *diakrino*, which can mean to "separate thoroughly" and implies the ability to dissect what was spoken and see if it is a correct statement. The root word *krino* is a legal term meaning to make a decision on the basis of the information presented, similar to the informed decision a jury makes after hearing the pertinent information.[4]

When you tell a person giving you a prophetic word that you are going to judge the message by sharing it with other mature believers, you will be able to tell if that speaker has the right spirit. A humble sincere person will agree, but the "prophets" who speak out of their own spirits will become angry that you would even question their spiritual integrity and authority!

PROPHETIC WORDS CREATE SPIRITUAL BATTLES

The biblical, prophetic signs of the end times indicate that our generation is witnessing the fulfillment of many pre-apocalyptic predictions penned by the ancient Hebrew prophets. During major prophetic cycles there will always be an increase in spiritual warfare, especially warfare between angels of God and angels of the wicked one. For example, when the time arrived for God to bring

Israel out of Egyptian bondage, there was a clash between the God of the Hebrews and the idols of the Egyptians (Exod. 4–12). The prophet Daniel experienced a supernatural warfare in the heavens above Babylon between angels of God and a prince spirit from Persia—a strong demonic entity that was attempting to block the releasing of a prophetic revelation Daniel was receiving from God concerning Israel's future (Dan. 10). When the time arrived for God to bring the Jews back from seventy years of Babylonian captivity, resistance arose from inside Samaria with the governor resisting the rebuilding of the walls of Jerusalem. (See the books of Ezra and Nehemiah.)

Zechariah the prophet actually saw a vision of Satan himself standing at the altar in Jerusalem attempting to prevent the progress of the Jews in rebuilding the temple (Zech. 3:1–2). Angels announced the birth of Christ as shepherds and wise men made their way to worship the future king (Matt. 2:9–11; Luke 2:13–20). Shortly after the wise men departed Bethlehem, Herod commissioned Roman soldiers to kill all infants under two years of age within the area of Ramah—a ten-mile radius of Bethlehem (Matt. 2:16–18). These events and others indicate that during major prophetic seasons there is an increase in satanic, demonic activity.

The truth is that if Satan could stop a prophecy from God from coming to pass, he could accuse God of being untruthful and a liar. I personally believe that the behind-the-scenes reason the adversary initiated the Jewish holocaust was a satanic attempt to destroy the Jewish people before they could return to their original land and reestablish Israel—because Israel must be a nation with Jerusalem as the capital when the Messiah returns to earth (Ps. 102:16; Isa. 66:8).

A spiritual conflict is often initiated when a prophetic word concerning a person's future is made public. After Samuel anointed David as the future king of Israel, David's own brothers viewed him in a negative manner (1 Sam. 17:28–29), and David was thrust into new battles. He had defeated a bear and a lion and afterward took on the giant Goliath (1 Sam. 17). Yet this anointed young man would spend about thirteen years being chased like a hunted animal through the Judean wilderness by his jealous father-in-law who was attempting to kill him (1 Sam. 18–28). He experienced one battle after another and eventually came to Ziklag, where the entire city was burned and the enemy captured the wives, daughters, sons, and spoils of David and his six hundred mighty men (1 Sam. 30). This was the lowest moment of his life, but David "encouraged himself in the LORD his God" (v. 6, KJV) and received a prophetic instruction to "pursue, for you shall surely overtake them and without fail recover all" (v. 8). David was certainly a threat to Israel's and God's enemies, and the word that he would be the next king set the kingdom of darkness on alert to prevent the prophecy of his kingship from coming to pass—but God won and the enemy failed!

Christ is another example. From age twelve (Luke 2:42) to thirty (Luke 3:23) we know Christ lived in Nazareth in Galilee (Matt. 2:23), but little is known about His activity. He was being kept in reserve in this private mountain setting prior to His public ministry. However, after His public baptism at age thirty, He immediately encountered Satan and was tempted for forty days (Luke 4:1–13). Notice that the battle began shortly after Christ's baptism when the heavenly voice announced, "This is My beloved Son, in whom I am well pleased" (Matt. 3:17; 4:1). Prophetic revelation can attract spiritual conflict, as prophetic revelation often deals with the future of a person or a nation. Through a vocal prophetic announcement the spiritual powers are alerted to the person's assignment, as was the case in the announcement at the baptism of Christ.

The fact that a battle often ensues when you receive revelation of your destiny, revealing God's purpose for your life, must not intimidate you from receiving encouragement, edification, and direction through the written and spoken Word. God often makes His will known to bring you confidence and to impart a weapon for you to use in defeating the enemy's questions thrown at your mind.

Warring With the Prophecies

The purpose of a biblical promise or a prophetic word is to give you *something solid to hold on to while you are waiting for the promise to come to pass.* Timothy was reminded to war with the prophecies, to remind himself and others that it was a word from the Lord that brought him to where he was. When Timothy became discouraged, he could always go back to the word of the Lord and have confidence that everything would work out well in the end because he was in the perfect will of God.

Many years ago I had a wonderful dream of a little girl named Amanda, who told me in the dream that she was the daughter I would have one day. I told my wife who, unknown to us, was pregnant at that time. However, we were blessed with a beautiful son and not that little girl. Eleven years passed, and my wife was thirty-nine. She became pregnant, but seven weeks into the pregnancy she lost the baby. We were crushed, because I felt strongly the dream of the girl was a word from the Lord. Despite the warnings of doctors and the fact Pam was about forty, we prayed and believed the Lord, and she became pregnant again. In the seventh month we received a negative report, and Pam was put on complete bed rest. I told Pam, "You are carrying the little girl I saw years ago, and she was perfect and not sick or deformed, so I am fighting this battle with the word of the Lord and not the word of man!" I felt simple faith and confidence because of what *I had seen* in the Spirit years go. On August 2, 2001, our healthy and very bright daughter, Amanda, was born.

Another biblical example is in Acts 27–28, which tells of when Paul was sent to Rome in a ship during the worst storm season the Mediterranean experiences each year. The apostle attempted to warn the ship's captain of impending danger, but the warning fell on deaf ears. As the ship entered the heart of the sea, a violent storm struck, and the sun and stars were hidden under dark clouds for fourteen days. The men began throwing out excessive baggage, and eventually the ship began breaking up near some quicksand off the coast of an island. Paul and the prisoners had to swim or float on broken boards to the shore. Before the shipwreck Luke, the writer of Acts, had written, "All hope that we would be saved was finally given up" (v. 20). When this great man of faith wrote that all hope was gone, you can rest assured that ship was going to sink!

However, in the darkest part of the crisis an angel of the Lord appeared to Paul and told him the ship would be ravaged, but not one person would die. All would survive if they would follow the angel's instruction (vv. 23–26). As the boat began breaking, there was an order to kill all the prisoners lest they escape (v. 42). *I am certain Paul found it necessary to remind the Lord of the angelic prophecy that no lives would be lost!*

In the end not only did Paul and the entire crew and prisoners survive on an island, but also Paul won the entire island of barbaric people to Christ through the miracles he performed in Christ's name (Acts 28).

The first battle instruction is to recall and dwell on the promises from the Bible for your victory and the promises given through the inspiration of the Holy Spirit that come through prayer and encouragement from believers. The last thing you should do is to forget the Word of the Lord and the prophetic words He has spoken to you! *The purpose of God's words is to give you a foundation on which to stand when everything is shaking and an anchor to outlast the storm you are in.*

Beware of the Fads
of Spiritual Warfare

Being from a Full Gospel background, I was raised to believe the Bible "from cover to cover" and to believe that Christ is the same "yesterday, today, and forever" (Heb. 13:8). Part of our foundational belief was (and is) that there is a real world of angels and demonic spirits that are in a continual battle for this planet and its inhabitants. This is called *spiritual warfare*, and this belief has produced thousands of books and messages on the subject. The concept of warring "against principalities, against powers, against the rulers of the darkness of this age, against spiritual hosts of wickedness in the heavenly places" (Eph. 6:12) has given the body of Christ much-needed truth over the centuries, but it has also produced some of the oddest fads related to warring against demonic spirits.

There are several fads I have observed over the years. The first is the idea of flying in a small plane high in the clouds and rebuking the prince spirits in the atmosphere. The idea is that by going up into the realm of their rule (the heavens—wicked spirits in heavenly places, Eph. 6:12) a believer has greater authority over them. To a young, immature believer this may have some logic. But use the mind the good Lord gave you and ask yourself, "If Jesus spoiled principalities and powers and gave us authority over them, how did He do it without an airplane?" The answer is that He conquered the enemy through His shed blood, death, and resurrection. We read:

> Having wiped out the handwriting of requirements that was against us, which was contrary to us. And He has taken it out of the way, having nailed it to the cross. Having disarmed principalities and powers, He made a public spectacle of them, triumphing over them in it.
>
> —Colossians 2:14–15

While it is true that these types of spirits rule from the heavenly realm and that Satan is the prince of the power of the air (Eph. 2:2), it is also true that the throne of God sits far above these spirits in the third heaven (2 Cor. 12:2). Christ today is seated "far above all principality and power" (Eph. 1:20–21). When we pray to God, it is not necessary to get in a plane and go up thirty-five thousand feet to be closer to the enemy's heavenly headquarters! David taught that a person can never escape God's presence: if he ascended into heaven, God was there; if he made his bed in hell, God was even there. The Lord dwells in the sea, on the mountains, and covers the entire earth (Ps. 139:7–10). If God, who sits high above all demonic powers, can hear your prayer on earth, then Satan can hear your rebuke on earth!

One man said he was flying with a prayer team and commanding the prince spirits to "come down from their high places, and be cast to the earth!" I thought, "Who does he think he is, Michael the archangel?" That is the job of Michael in the middle of the Great Tribulation, when he wars against Satan and his angels and casts them to the earth (Rev. 12:7–10). Following Michael's heavenly war, we read that Satan "has come down to you, having great wrath, because he knows that he has a short time" (v. 12). It is far better for stronger spirits to remain in the atmospheric heaven instead of being cast down to the earth. When this future expulsion does occur, all hell breaks loose on the entire globe. In reality, God can hear you pray anywhere and at anytime, and the enemy can hear your verbal rebuke anywhere and at anytime. Some will remind us that we are to "cast down the stronghold of the enemy," which is true. However, that verse is dealing with mental strongholds and personal imaginations that battle against the knowledge of God. (See 2 Corinthians 10:3–5.)

For those who believe in the prayer language of the Holy Spirit, there was a charismatic fad that swept through North America years ago in which some were told to pray in a "war tongue" and scream out in other tongues to the enemy. Again, this may seem very spiritual, but examine the Scripture related to speaking in other tongues. There are various reasons for speaking with tongues or, as some call it, the prayer language of the Spirit. Paul makes it clear that "he that speaketh in an unknown tongue speaketh not unto men, but unto God," and the individual doing the speaking "speaketh mysteries" (1 Cor. 14:2, KJV). Paul also said that "no man understandeth him" (the one speaking in tongues).

The same ministers who instruct believers to yell in tongues in a "war tongue" at the enemy will often teach that one of the important reasons for praying in tongues is that Satan and his kingdom cannot understand the language being spoken. Thus there is the contradiction. Why yell at the enemy in tongues if he can't even understand what is being said? There is no Bible support whatsoever for speaking in tongues in a war tongue or a battle tongue. The purpose of speaking in tongues, or a prayer language, is for a sign to the unbeliever (1 Cor. 14:22), to edify and spiritually build up the believer (v. 4), to build faith in the believer (Jude 20), and to assist the believer in praying the will of God when we are uncertain of God's will or uncertain how to pray (Rom. 8:26–28). As I will show you, our daily war is a war of the mind and the flesh. There are times when a believer will engage in deep intercession in the language of the Holy Spirit, but this intercession is to God and not to Satan.

THE REAL WARFARE

There are three New Testament references using the word *warfare*. Two of them deal with the warfare of a believer (2 Cor. 10:4; 1 Tim. 1:18). In 2 Corinthians 10:4 Paul says that the "weapons of our warfare are not carnal but mighty in God for pulling down strongholds." Paul then adds that these strongholds are imaginations and mental darts that exalt themselves against God's knowledge in our lives (v. 5). When you consider why a person has never received Christ, it is often because that person is stuck with certain ideas or thoughts contrary to the knowledge of God, thus the stronghold becomes an imagination that paints an image contrary to God.

Paul also used the word *warfare* when he told Timothy to resist fear by using the prophetic word spoken over him to fight a good war (1 Tim. 1:18). Paul used the word *warreth* in 2 Timothy 2:4 (KJV), alluding to keeping your life free from the clutter and cares of life. James speaks of "desires for pleasure that war in your members" (James 4:1). Peter then adds, "Abstain from fleshly lusts which war against the soul" (1 Pet. 2:11). From these verses we see that the real battle is with the mind, with the lust of the flesh, and with cares of this life attempting to choke off the Word of God by using mental strongholds.

It is important to look at the word *warfare* as used in 2 Corinthians 10:4. The Greek word is *strateia* and is where we derive the English word *strategy*. It is a word used in military service when a leader and his soldiers search out the strategy of their adversary before going to battle. The adversary may set out a well-laid plan against you, even from the time of birth, to destroy or disrupt God's will for your life. Just as the enemy makes a plan of assault, *you* must set out a plan for defeating the enemy's plans *before* the battle intensifies.

Plans are established by counsel; by wise counsel wage war.
—PROVERBS 20:18

Wisdom is better than weapons of war; but one sinner destroys much good.
—ECCLESIASTES 9:18

Three Parts to Satan's Strategy

The New Testament writers reveal a three-pronged strategy of the enemy designed against every person. The first step is to keep *spiritual blinders* on the eyes of the person. Paul referred to the god of this world who had blinded people to see the gospel (2 Cor. 4:4). Paul was not referring to physical scales that cover the eyes from light, but to a spiritual blindness that prevents a person from receiving understanding.

The second phase that is often linked with the first is to keep a person in *spiritual ignorance* (2 Cor. 2:11), especially concerning the subtle devices and deceptions of the enemy. You will always remain in bondage if you do not believe you are in bondage.

This leads to Satan's third phase, which is *deception*. Christ and the apostles warned of deception in the last days as one of the signs of the time of the end.

To remove spiritual blindness requires light, or illumination from the Word of God. Ignorance of spiritual truth produces scales that cover the understanding in men's minds, thus opening the door of deception. We must do more than say to a sinner, "What you are doing is wrong," or "If you keep doing that you will die lost!" We must give them solid, sound biblical proof as to why we are warning them. When growing up in a strict Full Gospel church in the 1970s, I knew what we *didn't believe in doing* but not what we *believed doctrinally*. The emphasis was always on the *you don't do this* instead of the *you should do*. Thus, when our youth went to college and returned, they lacked foundational teaching in order to be a light in the darkness.

If the adversary can't keep you blinded, he will keep you dumb or ignorant—just enough light to keep you from tripping, but just enough ignorance to keep you from total deliverance. If he cannot keep out the light and you become educated in spiritual truth, then he will plan a trap of deception as his third phase strategy.

One of the prime examples of deception was years ago when a married bishop of a large congregation engaged in a long-term extramarital relationship with a younger woman in his church. The woman told him she thought they were sinning and the adulterous act was wrong. He in return allegedly convinced her that he was an *archbishop*, and archbishops were of a higher level than a regular bishop and were not under the same biblical mandates as the lesser-ranked bishops; thus she was "ministering" to his "needs." Throughout church history there has been sexual temptation. However, in this case it went beyond an extreme temptation to deception. In Matthew 24 Christ connects end-time deception to false prophets and false christs who use the name of Christ as an entry point for believers to hear their words but deceive the flock with their false teachings (Matt. 24:11, 24).

Christ warned, "Take heed that no one deceives you" (v. 4). Paul warned believers in the church to "let no one deceive you" (Eph. 5:6; 2 Thess. 2:3). The Bible warns that many false prophets and false christs will arise to deceive man (Matt. 24:11, 24). The Greek word *deceive* is *planao*, and it means, "to wander, to stagger, to be led off course by an outside influence." It is used in the New Testament of a false teacher who leads another person away from truth, causing that person to become enslaved in spiritual bondage.[5]

The ultimate purpose of God is to bring total deliverance to your body, soul, and spirit. The ultimate plan of the enemy is to prevent you from understanding and acting upon the truth that God is able and willing to use to release you from a spiritual, mental, and emotional prison. Herein lies an important truth: *the enemy never wants you to begin asking questions.*

In Christ's day some people would approach the Messiah and ask if He would cure them and make them whole (Matt. 8:2; Mark 1:40; Luke 5:12). After hearing the question, Christ's answer was YES; He was able and willing to heal each person who would believe! Once a sinner or a person in need begins to ask, "Can God help me?" or "Is it the will of the Lord to heal me?" or "Does God love me enough to answer my prayer?", then the question always leads to an answer, and the answer is always contrary to the lies and deception of the enemy! People will perish because of lack of knowledge (Hos. 4:6) and suffer needlessly due to a lack of understanding.

THE PATTERN FOR VICTORY

If I am praying for an individual who is without a redemptive covenant, and I perceive that person is being blinded to the truth and has dull spiritual understanding, there is a pattern for how I should pray for that person. First, I should pray that the "eyes of their understanding will be enlightened," a prayer that Paul prayed for the believers in Ephesus in Ephesians 1:18. The word *enlightened* is the Greek word *photizo*, which is used to indicate shedding rays of light on something to brighten it up. It is also translated as "illuminated" in Hebrews 10:32.

I like to use the illustration of the cameras we used before the digital age. Light-sensitive film was placed in the camera, surrounded by total darkness. However, when the shutter opened, the light-sensitive film produced an image called a negative, which was later developed into a photograph. If a photo came out too dark, it was due to a lack of the proper amount of light coming through the shutter or the opening. The film is your mind, the shutter is your eyes of understanding, and the light is the powerful revelation from the Bible. If you will open the shutter of your mind and allow the light of the Word of God in, your mind will become impressed with the right images and imaginations, which is the first process to your freedom!

After praying for the eyes of a person's understanding to be opened, we should then pray for the person to be filled with the knowledge of the Lord. Paul prayed for the Ephesians' understanding to be opened that "you may *know*" (Eph. 1:18, emphasis added)! Spiritual strongholds are established to exalt themselves against the knowledge of God (2 Cor. 10:5). I have traveled through Europe and toured castles and fortresses. These mighty stone structures were erected with much blood and sweat to defend what was on the inside and to prevent any entry from unwanted armies from the outside. The spiritual parallel is that mental strongholds are established to keep the victim in bondage on the inside and to prevent any outside knowledge from piercing the self-made or satanic-built barriers. The knowledge of God is light, and illumination takes a darkened mind and imagination and begins to expose the lies and deceptions that have kept the person bound.

Part of our prayer assignment includes praying against the many spirits of deception that freely roam in and out of a person's mind. Of course, when an individual "makes a pet" of his or her personal demons, it is difficult to cast out what has been welcomed into the house. Just as the prodigal son had to hit bottom to reach up, demons will never leave a person better off, but they will use and abuse that person, eventually dragging him or her into a pit of despair. That is when the light of God can flash into the hole of depression and bring a word that can bring the person out!

DEALING WITH PIGPEN SINS

The ultimate goal of Satanic deception is to separate believers from their relationship with their heavenly Father, strip them of their spiritual inheritance, and set them in a place of total despair—just like the prodigal son (Luke 15). This young Jewish man rebelled against the family, leaving the care of his loving dad, and demanding his future inheritance—which he eventually blew on harlots and riotous living (vv. 13, 30). Eventually his cash flow ceased, and he ended up in a pigpen, not just feeding swine but also eating husks, believed by some scholars to be the pod of a carob tree. Jews despise and refuse to eat pork of any type (Lev. 11:7). Thus feeding pigs would be the lowest form of work a Jew could ever perform.

This rebel was separated from the *presence* of his father but never from the *love* of his father! This is important to understand when you have a child or grandchild dealing with "pigpen sins." These are sins that are morally despicable and involve perverted passions. While some suggest all sin is morally despicable, there are sins of *natural affection* and sins of *unnatural affection*. It is natural for a man and woman to have physical attraction, and thus without restraint and discipline some couples have fallen into fornication (sex before marriage) and adultery (sex after marriage with someone not your legal companion). However, it is (despite some modern claims to the contrary) *unnatural* for a man and man or woman and woman to have the same type of attraction that would lead to sexual practices with the same sex. Paul wrote of this type of conduct being "without natural affection" (Rom. 1:31, KJV) and spoke of men "leaving the natural use of women, burned in their lust one toward another; men with men working that which is unseemly" (v. 27, KJV), causing them to be given over to "vile affections" (v. 26, KJV).

The stubborn son eventually fell as low as a man could go, yet his father never forgot about him, no doubt prayed for him, and always loved him. He was not in the father's *presence* but was always in his father's *heart*. When a former believer turns his back to the Word, to the path of the pigpen, he removes himself from the spiritual food at his heavenly Father's table, but he never removes himself from the heart of a caring God who hears the cries of a broken-hearted father and mother on earth.

When the young son ran out of money, he also ran out of friends. His friends were now a bunch of squealing swine living in the mud, and he was their source of provision. Eventually the son found himself looking up from the bottom, and something kicked in that stirred the desire to return home. It was his memories of a better time! At his dad's house he was served by servants instead of him serving pigs. He was fed the best instead of dried husks. He had a warm bedroom instead of looking up at the stars, shivering on cold nights. Concerning your own children, the enemy might take their bodies and abuse them, but as long as they can think, he cannot steal the memories you have made with them.

Who's Going to Bring Them Home?

Look at a modern parable using this story. A rich man had two sons. The youngest, a stiff-necked know-it-all, demanded his inheritance and moved out of the house to the city, free from the restraints of his parents. The father was grieved, concerned, and ceased not to pray day and night for his son's safety and eventual return home.

After months of prayer he heard a knock at the door. He opened it to see a bright-eyed man who said, "I heard you are praying for your son. My name is Faith, and you have to send me to where he is and believe with all your heart he is returning." The dad released Faith and began believing as never before for his son's break-through. Several months later Faith returned to inform the dad, "I tried, but he is so full of unbelief he wore me out." The father, however, continued to pray. Soon thereafter another knock was heard at the door. This time another man stood there whose name was Hope. He stated, "Sir, Faith sent me here to tell you not to give up on your son. You must not lose hope. Send me and hope for the best!" The father then sent Hope and filled his heart with anticipation of a good outcome. Months later Hope retuned with his report, saying, "I found your son, but he is so hard-hearted. I don't want to say it's hopeless, but I have no strength left for him."

The father of the lad broke down and began weeping. In a few moments a knock came, and there stood another man with beautiful eyes full of compassion. He said, "Sir, Faith and Hope sent me here to assist you. My name is Love, and you must love the lad unconditionally. Send love to him—as no one can resist unconditional love." The father was recharged with excitement, and Love went out to the son and reminded him of the love his mother and father had for him, reminding him of all the great times they had as a family. Yet the son was deceived in thinking that the harlots he was joining with were his true loves. He rejected the love of his own family. Love returned and told the dad, "I cannot tell you what to do, as I know of no one left that could solve this issue of your son's rebellion and departure from home!"

Just when the father was giving up, another knock came. He opened to door to discover a very aged man with a long white beard and long flowing hair, whose eyes were blue like the waters of the sea and whose skin was tanned and wrinkled with passing ages.

"Who are you?" the father asked.

"I am friends with Faith, Hope, and Love, and I believe I should now be released to get your son. I will bring him back—guaranteed!" The father was thrilled, until he heard the next statement. "Yes, I will bring him back, but I cannot promise you in what condition. I may bring him back healthy or sick, strong or weak, upright or broken—but I can bring him back."

The father said, "Please, sir, go find him and bring him home." As the old man turned, the father asked, "What is your name, sir?"

The old man said, "My name is Time—and in time I will bring him home!"

Time went out and found the son drinking at a bar. He whispered into his ear and said, "I think it's time you go home." The son laughed at the thoughts in his mind and kept on guzzling liquor until he passed out on the floor. He awoke in the bed of strange women. Time nudged him, "This is not good. You need to get back to your father." Months passed, and Time was there. After all, Time was there when he was born, and the steps of Time would only end at the graveyard, as death comes to all men.

It was at the lowest point of his life when he lost it all that the son came to himself. Yes, several years had passed, and the alcohol, drugs, and sexually transmitted diseases had taken their toll, but Time brought him home! Often a rebellious child must hit bottom before coming to his or her senses and realizing the goodness of both his or her earthly father and mother and his or her heavenly Father.

Never give up, even with *pigpen sins* or when the debauchery of evil has cloaked the soul and a veil of blindness binds their understanding. When the moment comes for their deliverance, just as with the man bound by spirits in Mark 5, Jesus knows how to send pigs running, cause chains to break, and put people in their right minds. Remember every promise, every word, and every dream God has given you, and fight the fight with the promises of God, such as the words of Jeremiah 29:11–13:

> For I know the thoughts that I think toward you, says the LORD, thoughts of peace and not of evil, to give you a future and a hope. Then you will call upon Me and go and pray to Me, and I will listen to you. And you will seek Me and find Me, when you search for Me with all your heart.

Our ultimate spiritual weapon of war is the written Word of God. Certain scriptures from the Bible are quickened to our spirit, giving us an immediate word from God to stand on for our conflicts and blessings. When a prophetic word is revealed to our spirit or through an accurate vocal gift, we, like Timothy, can fight a good warfare with the word that has been spoken to us (1 Tim. 1:18).

CHAPTER 2

WHAT I WOULD DO
IF I WERE SATAN

B EFORE WE DETAIL the mysterious past of our archenemy
Satan, let us get into his mind and discover three of his most
important "basic strategies" and ask, "If I were in his position, what would I do?"

I WOULD DENY THE IMPORTANCE
OF WORSHIPPING GOD IN SPIRIT

In Christ's time the Jews worshipped at the temple on Mount
Moriah in Jerusalem. The Samaritans were an ethnic group, a mix-
ture of Jews and Gentiles, whose worship center was located in
Samaria on Mount Gerizim. When Christ, a Jew, met a woman, a
Samaritan, at Jacob's well, the woman had been with five men—and

the one she was with now was not her husband—yet instead of talking about her moral weakness, she knew how to debate about religion! She demanded to know which mountain was the *real mountain* of blessing and was ready to argue the points for the hill above Jacob's well where Moses blessed Israel as the "true church" (John 4:4–29). Instead of debating the woman in a heated argument, Christ revealed the key to all worship:

> God is Spirit, and those who worship Him must worship in spirit and truth.
>
> —JOHN 4:24

If I were the enemy, I would undermine the idea that it is important to worship God at all. I would make the Christian faith "just another world religion" and convince the population it is just one of many ways to heaven. I would then make certain that the so-called worship experience became a very boring, dry ritual with no energy and power, filled with boring preaching, music that would fit in any funeral, and prayers that were prayed from paper instead of words from the heart. Thus a person could enter the stone cathedral and sixty minutes later exit the sanctuary totally unchallenged and unchanged. I would do this knowing that true worship in spirit welcomes the presence of God and in God's presence all needs can be met.

I would mock any group that expresses emotion in worship and call such people religious fanatics to intimidate others from attending the services, in the same manner that I had impressed the Pharisees to accuse the miracles of Christ as being from the power of Beelzebub, the prince of demons (Matt. 12:24–27). If I could make the people afraid to worship, then I could prevent them from experiencing God's life-changing presence!

I Would Deny
the Significance and Power
of the Anointing of the Spirit

Included in my denial of the need to worship would be the denial of the anointing of the Holy Spirit. Notice, it would not be a denial of the Holy Spirit Himself, but the denial of the *power* of the Holy Spirit. It was Christ who promised His disciples: "You shall receive power when the Holy Spirit has come upon you" (Acts 1:8). He also said they were to be "endued with power from on high" (Luke 24:49). The Greek word *endued* means, "to be *clothed with*"! Satan's covering was originally the glory and light of God, and the believer's covering is the power of the Holy Spirit.

Christ was anointed "with the Holy Spirit and with power, who went about doing good and healing all who were oppressed by the devil" (Acts 10:38). The power of the Holy Spirit, when it is released from a believer, is identified with the *anointing* of the Spirit. We know the anointing abides within a believer and assists in teaching us to understand God's mysteries (1 John 2:10, 27). The anointing also breaks the yoke (Isa. 10:27).

Many Full Gospel churches had believed in and accepted the anointing and power of the Holy Spirit in their services. The anointing is what creates the *electricity* and the special *charged* atmosphere a person can experience as the worship or preaching occurs. The enemy knows that the anointing is necessary to break yokes and bondages off individuals.

Satan has been effective in making some Christians deny the power of God. Paul warned that in the last days many would be "having a form of godliness but denying its power. And from such people turn away!" (2 Tim. 3:5). The Greek word *power* is the same word Christ used when He revealed that believers would receive power from the Holy Spirit. Over my many years of traveling I have heard some Christians deny that any of the nine gifts of the Spirit are active today, deny that a believer has authority over demonic powers, and deny the healing covenant of God through Christ to heal the sick today. If I were Satan, I would do all in my power to insure that as many Christians as possible denied the power and anointing of the Spirit. I would teach the congregation that it was a thing in the past and not a blessing in the present. Those believing this theory would have a "form of religion" but "deny the power." Paul wrote that you should "turn away" from rejecters of God's power!

I Would Deny the Importance of Being Under Spiritual Leadership

Satan's desire was to be "like the Most High" (Isa. 14:14) and to exalt his own throne (position) above all angels and above God Himself (v. 13). He desired to be in sole control of all the creation and felt he could do a better job than God was doing. Even when the tempter came into the Garden of Eden and tempted Eve, he told her if she ate of the tree of the knowledge of good and evil, she would be like the gods (Gen. 3:5). The fact is that Adam was already created in God's image and likeness (Gen. 1:26); the couple was already a part of God and His family!

It must be remembered that the root of Satan's sin was pride, as his "heart was lifted up" (Ezek. 28:17). The prophet Isaiah revealed the five statements Lucifer made in his attempt to rise above God:

1. "I will ascend into heaven" (Isa. 14:13).

2. "I will exalt my throne above the stars of God" (Isa. 14:13).

3. "I will also sit on the mount of the congregation" (Isa. 14:13).

4. "I will ascend above the heights of the clouds" (Isa. 14:14).

5. "I will be like the Most High" (Isa. 14:14).

Notice the words "I will." Not *we* will or *they* will (other angels), but *I* will. This angel was "lifted up" or self-exalted in his beauty (Ezek. 28:17). Have you ever met a person who continually spoke about himself or herself and his or her personal accomplishments, continually asserting, "I...I...I...mine...me..."? Discerning people say to themselves, "This person is really stuck on himself." Satan thought he could do what he could not do, and he failed at attempting *to be like God!*

If I were Satan, I would make people believe they needed no leadership in their lives—no pastor, no teachers, no spiritual covering—that they could do it all by themselves. In fact, I would continually plot to divide congregations over leadership issues. This is important for the enemy to be able to cause a division.

There are many reasons, but one stands out. Churches consist of families, and families are made up of children and youth. When moms and dads are in leadership positions, and there is disunity, they often bring the conversation of the church problems home to discuss without using wisdom, and their children overhear the conversations. When the parents depart the church in anger, they often speak ill of the former pastor or leadership, not knowing they are planting bad seeds in the hearts of their own children. As those children grow, they will lose confidence in the church and ministers.

When Moses was leading Israel out of Egypt, it was a *family affair.* Moses was the senior pastor, and his brother was the high priest. Moses's sister, Miriam, was a praise and worship leader, and Moses's father-in-law, Jethro, was a spiritual counselor! One of the leaders in the congregation, a man named Korah, complained that

Moses was taking on too much and that Moses should appoint him into a leading position. This rebel and his entire family soon discovered who was in charge—it was God—as the earth opened and swallowed them up, causing them to perish (Num. 16)!

Moses's leadership was challenged during his forty years, but the rebels always lost, and the prophet Moses always won.

I Would Exploit the Weaknesses of Christians

There are some believers who have a real struggle on the weekends. Friday and Saturday were normal, weekly party nights back in B.C.—*before* they found *Christ*! When the weekend arrives, they must keep themselves busy, or else when their minds are idle, the enemy will send thoughts to tempt them to return to their old lifestyles. We must remember that the game has never changed, but the plays in the book have.

As a believer matures in the Lord, immaturity is replaced with maturity, carnality is replaced with spirituality, and the desires for a lifestyle of sin are replaced with desires to encounter God's presence. As an infant believer, perhaps there were fleshly struggles that the adversary kept before you as bait to hook you back into a former lifestyle. As you overcame that sin, the bait changed. When trying to catch fish and nothing is biting, fishermen will change the lure or the bait, including the shape, the spinning motion, and the color, to catch the eye and curiosity of the fish. The same is true with the strategy of the enemy. The traps and snares that once tripped you up are exposed and useless in your walk as you mature and learn to avoid them. But watch out for the new trap and the new snare that you may not recognize! Satan changes his "bait" to attract new fish on his hook

As an example, during the growing-up years, illegal drugs were purchased from a drug dealer in a back alley. Then the dealers became high school and college kids. Now the youth can go into a normal pharmacy and obtain over-the-counter drugs that, in some cases, have caused death by overdosing. Drugs are still purchased, but the game plan has made it easier to obtain them.

The same is true with pornography. When I was growing up, porn magazines were kept under the counter at the drugstore. Later they were placed on a rack with a brown paper covering the intimate parts of the airbrushed photo on the cover. As years passed, the pornography became easily accessible through pay movie channels and cable networks that pipe the scenes directly into your home. The catch was that you had to pay for it, and many believers refused to have these types of pay movie networks in their homes on their television. Today the worst type of pornography is available with just the click of a button on the Internet. It is the same type of imagery that has been seen for years, but the method of distribution and availability has changed.

If I were Satan, I would find the weakest spot and strike. After all, no foreign army ever invades a nation with the intent of taking territory if they know they have no chance of winning the war. The adversary seldom attacks our strengths, but he always goes for our weak spot. When Satan tempted Jesus, we read that after forty days, Jesus was hungry. *Then* the tempter came (Matt. 4:2). Jesus was hungry, and the first mental dart thrown His way was, "If You are the Son of God, command that these stones become bread" (v. 3). Hunger is a normal appetite, and eating bread was a daily routine for most Israelites. However, the test was to move from what was normal and natural and to demonstrate the abnormal and the unnatural—making rocks become bread. Christ's weak spot was hunger, but Satan magnified the moment by making Him question His relationship as the Son of God. After all, God wouldn't want His Son to be hungry!

We all know our soft spots and weak seasons. If we will walk in the Spirit, we can dissect the pre-setup strategy of the prince of darkness. You can see his secret plans begin to unfold before the actual attack comes.

When the United States is about to go to war, there is always a massive transfer of money to military accounts and a movement of equipment in trains, planes, ships, and other means of transportation. It is a sign the battle is coming. If I know my weakness and understand the tools or resources the enemy uses to manipulate my weakness, then I must cut off the pipeline carrying the fuel. I know of men and women who contacted old boyfriends and girlfriends on social networking sites and eventually left their companions of many years to re-create a fantasy relationship with a former lover. I have also known of other couples who were headed in that same direction, but instead of falling into the trap, they simply removed their names and pages from the networking sites and thus stopped the possible setup that could have led to immorality occurring.

When planning major transitions, experiencing fast ministry growth, and reaching the masses through the gospel, I will often ask myself, "How would the enemy work to target this effort, and what doors can he get through?" We must continually evaluate the battlefield and observe the landmines on our side of the field, not just the ones in the far distance.

CHAPTER 3

LEARN HOW YOUR ENEMY THINKS

❧ ❧

O NE OF THE important keys for a team of soldiers to understand during a battle is how to *get into the mind of their enemies.* This process involves knowing *who* the enemy is, *how* the enemy thinks, the *places* where the soldiers are strong or weak, and the *types* of weapons they are armed with. As believers we should continually engage ourselves with discovering the mind of God through studying the sacred manual, the Bible, and learning spiritual, moral, and practical truths to live by. Often however, we are so consumed with desiring to know our destiny that we forget the battles in life that are geared to disrupt our destiny. Part of gaining spiritual understanding should be discovering the strategies of the adversary and using our information against him.

The first process is to know who your enemy is. If I were Satan, the first thing I would do is conceal the truth of who I actually am. Thus a person would never know it was me working, as my disguise would be so complete that I would not be considered the culprit. This process was seen in the Garden of Eden when the adversary used the body and voice of a serpent to deceive Eve (Gen 3:1–2). The serpent was a creature that the first couple was familiar with. Josephus wrote concerning the serpent:

> While all the living creatures had one language, at that time the serpent, which then lived together with Adam and his wife, shewed an envious disposition, at his supposal of their living happily…he persuaded the woman, out of a malicious intention, to taste of the tree of knowledge, telling them, that in that tree was the knowledge of good and evil.[1]

Scripture says, "The serpent deceived Eve by his craftiness" (2 Cor. 11:3). We know that the serpent is an image used for Satan (Rev. 12:9, 14–15). I suggest to you that if Satan had entered the garden as himself, as a fallen angel without using the body of the serpent, he would have been easily detected as a trespasser and identified as an unwanted guest. *But the enemy never shows up in his true identity.* Paul warned that Satan can transform himself as an angel of light (2 Cor. 11:14).

In the New Testament Paul was continually hindered in his ministry, and he compiled a list of those physical, spiritual, and satanic hindrances in 2 Corinthians 11:23–28. Yet he realized that the invisible and often undetected organizer of his opposition was a messenger (in Greek, an angel) of Satan (2 Cor. 12:7). Paul wrote to both the Roman church and the church at Thessalonica and indicated that although he had attempted to visit them both, Satan had "much hindered" him "time and again" (Rom. 15:22; 1 Thess. 2:18).

We should never blame all of our difficulties on Satan, as some things are a part of living. Satan did not give you the flat tire—a nail in the road did. Neither did he make you run out of gas—you forgot to fill up. He didn't make the tree fall in your driveway; the storm did. The devil didn't make you sick, but three plates of pork ribs sure did! Satan gets blamed for many simple daily hindrances. However, extreme opposition to the gospel and persecution can be a result of satanic interference.

JUST WHO IS SATAN?

To understand who Satan really is, we must look among the words of the Old Testament prophets. Many scholars believe Isaiah 14 is a reference detailing the events surrounding Satan's original fall and expulsion from heaven. Isaiah 14:12 begins by saying:

> How you are fallen from heaven, O Lucifer, son of the morning! How you are cut down to the ground, you who weakened the nations!

The word translated *Lucifer* is only found here in the entire Bible and is controversial among Hebrew scholars. The Hebrew word is *heylel* and actually refers to "brightness." Thus the word *Lucifer* has been understood to be a personal name, but in reality it is a word meaning, "a bright son of the morning or a bright morning star." This person of brightness called a "son of the morning" was among the first "heavenly lights."

There is also other prophetic insight found in Ezekiel 28. In chapters 26 and 27 the prophet gives a word to the king of Tyre, an earthly leader. Ezekiel continues his discourse in chapter 28 but then begins describing a creature that cannot be a human man. Ezekiel speaks of the "anointed cherub":

> You were the anointed cherub who covers; I established you; you were on the holy mountain of God.
>
> —EZEKIEL 28:14

Twice Ezekiel mentions this cherub (vv. 14, 16). A cherub is a created angel with many faces and was (is) assigned as a guardian of the presence and glory of God. After Adam's removal from the garden cherubim with flaming swords guarded the east entrance of Eden to prevent Adam from reentering the garden and eating from the tree of life in his sinful condition (Gen. 3:24). Two cherubim made from beaten gold were placed on the mercy seat (the golden lid) of the ark of the covenant, symbolically guarding the seat God descended upon yearly on the Day of Atonement (Exod. 25:19, 22; 37:8). Ezekiel revealed that this angel was the "anointed" cherub (Ezek. 28:14). This Hebrew word *anointed* is not the normal word for anointed or anointing, as in "anointing with oil" (James 5:14) or the anointing with the Holy Spirit (Acts 10:38). This word is *mimshach* and means a sense of expansion or stretching out the wings. Ezekiel further said this angel "covers," a word meaning, "to fence in and protect." Putting the two words together, it describes an important angel that protected by using its outstretched wings.

This particular angel appears to be a guardian of the light of God's presence and glory. A further study of this anointed cherub in Ezekiel 28:13–16 gives more insight into his activities in ages past. He was in Eden, the garden of God (v. 13). This could allude to the heavenly paradise or the earthly Eden. Either way, no earthly king of Tyre or anyone else was in the heavenly Eden, the garden of God, except this anointed cherub before his fall, or in the earthly Eden except the serpent and Adam and Eve (Gen. 3:1–2). Ezekiel said that "every precious stone was [his] covering" and lists nine semiprecious and precious gem stones that formed some type of breastplate or covering on the front of this angelic creature (Ezek. 28:13). These nine stones are the same stones fashioned among the twelve stones on the breastplate of the high priest in the Old Testament (Exod. 28).

We also read that he was formed with "tabrets" (KJV) and pipes. The word *tabrets* indicates timbrels for a tambourine: small objects that create a rhythmic sound used in this round percussion instrument. The *pipes* are not pipes such as a flute, but the Hebrew means a *bezel* or a *gemstone*. His outward design was prepared by God at his creation. He was "set" upon the holy mountain (Ezek. 28:14, KJV). The "holy mountain" is found in two locations—the mountain of God in heaven, called Mount Zion (Heb. 12:22), and later the earthly Jerusalem (Dan. 9:16). Certainly this refers to the temple of God in heaven on the sacred holy mountain of the Lord. This angelic being "walked back and forth in the midst of fiery stones," a special place somewhere in the heavenly temple (Ezek. 28:14). He was created perfect until iniquity was found in him, and he was cast out of the holy mountain (in heaven, v. 16). He corrupted his wisdom and became proud of his own brightness (v. 17), or his beauty. Ezekiel calls him a cherub.

THE FOUR FACES OF THE CHERUB

Herein is a mystery that is quite interesting. This anointed cherub is considered by many scholars to be Satan, or the bright "star" (Lucifer). When further researching the various places where a cherub is mentioned in Scriptures, we read of four "living creatures" encircling God's heavenly throne with the face of an ox, an eagle, a lion, and a man (Rev. 4:7). These unusual-appearing angels are called "beasts" (v. 6, KJV), which is translated as "living creatures." These angels are assigned to worship continually saying, "Holy, holy, holy, Lord God Almighty" (v. 8).

Ezekiel also observed these same forms of angels in his vision and gave a similar description of them to what is also recorded by John in Revelation 4:7. Ezekiel saw cherubim in chapters 1, 10, and 28; he also saw them in Ezekiel 41:18, where they are carved on the walls of the future temple in Jerusalem. Fifteen times in Ezekiel 10 (KJV) Ezekiel used the word *cherubims* describing the angels he saw in a vision. The reference in Ezekiel 10:14 reads:

> Each one had four faces: the first face was the face of a
> cherub, the second face was the face of a man, the third the
> face of a lion, and the fourth the face of an eagle.

Both John and Ezekiel describe four faces, but in Ezekiel the face of the "ox" in John's narrative is called the "face of a cherub" (Ezek. 10:14). Since these were the same heavenly creatures in both visions, the appearance of the face of a cherub would match the face of the ox in John's vision, as the other three are the same (eagle, lion, and man). In the Greek, "living creatures" in Revelation is actually a form of cherubim according to Ezekiel! These four living creatures minister before God continually. Scholars have noted a parallel between the four faces of the cherub and the symbolism of Christ in the four Gospels:

THE PARALLELS OF THE FOUR LIVING CREATURES		
The Cherub	**The Gospel**	**The Parallel of Christ**
Has a head of a Lion	Matthew's Gospel	Jesus is the Lion of Judah.
Has a head of an Ox	Mark's Gospel	Jesus is the servant.
Has a head of a Man	Luke's Gospel	Jesus is the Son of man.
Has a head of an Eagle	John's Gospel	Jesus is the eternal Word.

Satan also has four *faces*. Using the face of a man, he tempts mankind and uses men to lead other men into temptation and sin. The face of a lion identifies Satan as a "roaring lion" (1 Pet. 5:8), seeking "whom he may devour." The face of the eagle is unique, as the eagle is the prince of birds and can fly higher than most of the winged creatures. This is the image of Satan being the "prince of the power of the air" (Eph. 2:2). The ox is an earthly creature known for wearing a yoke and can become a picture of the face of Satan, whose goal is to bring people into captivity and bondage.

In summary, Satan was originally an anointed cherub, not a god as he desired to become. He is not equal with God but is continually in competition with God for the eternal souls of men.

The Division of the Angels

There are numerous Jewish and Christian traditions concerning the numbers and names of the angels. However, in the Bible there are only three specific angels named by name. The first is Michael the archangel (Dan. 10:13, 21; 12:1), Gabriel (Dan. 8:16; 9:21), and this anointed cherub, or Satan (Rev. 12:9). Revelation 12 uses the phrase "Michael and his angels" and "the dragon [Satan] and his angels" (v. 7), indicating that these chief ranking angels each have angels serving under their authority.

After studying angels and their ministry for many years, I believe they can be divided into three ministry categories. There are angels who are created as *warriors*, who are *workers*, and who are *worshippers*. Michael is the leader of the warring angels; when Michael is mentioned in Scripture, he is the angel of warfare and battle. He disputed with Satan over the body of Moses (Jude 9), engaged in war with the prince of the kingdom of Persia (Dan. 10:13, 21), and, in the future, will gather his angels to war against Satan and to cast him and his wicked forces out of the second heaven to the earth during the tribulation (Rev. 12). Michael and his angels are warring spirits doing battle against the kingdom of darkness.

The worker angels are "ministering spirits" and are sent to minister to believers (Heb. 1:14). When Gabriel appears, he is an angel on special assignment, bringing revelation directly from God to prophets. He was commissioned to bring revelation of children's birth to Zacharias, Elizabeth, and Mary (Luke 1). Gabriel is a worker engaged in linking the heavenly realm to the earthly. These could also be the same type of angels Jacob observed ascending and descending upon the ladder stretching from earth to heaven (Gen. 28:12).

This leaves the third category—the worshipping angels. Since this anointed cherub was upon the holy mountain on the stones of fire and had a covering of nine stones similar to the high priest's breastplate, it appears that the worshipping angels were under the authority of this special angel, whom we now understand became Satan after his expulsion.

It is uncertain exactly what Satan's original assignment was, but he certainly does not want to see men enter into the presence of God and experience the peace and joy of salvation. He attempts to stop true worship!

This fallen angel is our archenemy.

Having traveled the world since age eighteen, I have encountered many of the same questions from believers of all backgrounds that I believe need to be answered as we expose the strategies in Satan's playbook. The adversary continually plants the thoughts in our minds that he has much more access to our lives than we know and more freedom to move in and out of our situations than we can control. What are the facts? One of the most common questions deals with the adversary's ability to know our thoughts—or read our minds. Is this possible? The next chapter will explore this possibility.

CHAPTER 4

CAN SATAN READ MY MIND?

❧ ❧

I F INFORMATION ABOUT the future is released in advance, it comes from one or a combination of three sources.

SOURCES OF INFORMATION ABOUT THE FUTURE

Some future plans are set by men, and at times this information is released by men. This is especially true with advanced technology or military hardware that is being designed in underground facilities in top-secret labs. At times a leak occurs, and we are amazed at some new technical device or advanced weapon that is coming in the distant future.

Those who believe the Scriptures to be inspired, know that God Himself, using His Holy Spirit as the delivery agent, has provided mankind with a book with sixty-six internal books that reveal future events through the dreams, visions, and inspired words of the biblical prophets. Bible prophecy includes predictions where God pre-writes the headlines of papers thousands of years in advance! The Holy Spirit imparted the revelation necessary for human messengers to vocalize the message or, through inspiration, write on parchment the divine warnings, offering encouraging words of coming events as planned in the future kingdom of God.

The third method, used from the ancient times to divulge hidden information, is through the use of wise men, astrologers, mystical oracles, and familiar spirits. The ancient biblical empires, from Egypt to Rome and those in-between, were noted for their kings and leaders who staffed their administrations with occult-oriented individuals who often used bizarre methods to discover the future on behalf of their leaders.

In reviewing these three methods, the source of future information can be released by the spirit of men, the Spirit of God, or the spirits of the satanic kingdom. For those who desire to know the future, some would suggest they couldn't care less what the source of the information is and from whom it comes, just as long as it is accurate. Herein lies a major, serious problem. For those leaning on man-made methods or the use of familiar spirits, men can be and often are fallible in their predictions, and psychics operate through familiar spirits that are noted for being the leading spirits of deception. King Ahab discovered this truth too late when he relied on four hundred false prophets who predicted a victorious outcome in a coming battle. However, instead of returning to Samaria with a victory crown, the king returned wounded by an arrow, and bled to death in his chariot, dying near sundown. (See 2 Chronicles 18.) Not only does a psychic using a familiar spirit attempt to manipulate, intimidate, or dominate its victim, but also the same spirit will use deception to pull an innocent person into a web of mental confusion and false predictions that eventually lead to spiritual bondage, oppression, and depression.

THE REAL VS. THE COUNTERFEIT

In the spiritual realm there is the *real* and the *counterfeit*. No one has ever seen a counterfeit three-dollar bill because the Treasury department has never printed a real three-dollar bill. I have asked bank tellers how they separate real money from counterfeit paper currency. The answer is always the same. The reply is, "We spend so much time handling real money that we can feel something is wrong when we come across a counterfeit bill." In other words, something doesn't *feel right* about the counterfeit!

Some nominal church ministers occasionally attempt to frighten their members and warn them to stay far away from any and all supernatural manifestations, such as those seen in Full Gospel churches. The liberal theologians treat these manifestations as some form of an evil spirit deceiving fellow Christians. However, just as when there is something real, there will eventually be a copy; there can be no copy without the original!

The apostle Paul revealed nine gifts of the Spirit (1 Cor. 12:7–10). We will not take the time to expand on these individual gifts; however, the nine are divided into three categories: power gifts, vocal gifts, and mind gifts. The three mind gifts are word of wisdom, word of knowledge, and discerning of spirits (1 Cor. 12:8, 10). Solomon was endowed with extreme wisdom and used amazing insight to solve complicated problems. The second mind gift—the word of knowledge—is called, by some, *revelation knowledge*, which is the ability to search deep into the Scriptures and pull out the dynamic types, shadows, patterns, and biblical mysteries that reveal the "deep things of God" (1 Cor. 2:10). The third mind gift—discerning of spirits—not only includes a gift to detect evil and unclean spirits, but it can also discern the spirit of a person and look into the real motives and hidden attitudes of the heart. These gifts are designed to assist believers when dealing with difficult situations, difficult people, and the powers of the enemy at work through people and circumstances. They are also effective when ministering to individuals who need a supernatural breakthrough.

INFORMATION IN THE SPIRIT WORLD

We come to the question, "Can Satan read my mind?" At times it must certainly feel that he can, especially when you are engaged in a conflict that is waging war against the mind. We do know that God can certainly know the thoughts of the heart. In Christ's ministry we read where He "perceived" men had little faith (Matt. 16:8, KJV), perceived the wickedness of men (Matt. 22:18), and perceived their thoughts (Mark 2:8; Luke 5:22). The common Greek word used for *perceive* means, "to have knowledge about something, but from spiritual *perception* and not mentally known *information.*" If Christ lived on earth today, some would accuse Him of being a psychic or of reading the minds of His audience. However, this was a gift from the Holy Spirit, not from Satan, as Christ was anointed by the Holy Spirit for ministry (Acts 10:38).

The reason many Christians question if Satan can read a person's mind stems from the recent surge in television programs showing an alleged psychic telling someone in the audience (whom they say they have never met) information about their past that appears to be accurate. When we understand the Spirit world better, then we can see that this insight into a person's life can easily be revealed through the operation of certain types of spirits.

Information that is already known

With recent technology such as twenty-four hour cable news, the Internet, Facebook, Twitter, and other forms of communication, nothing is a secret any longer. The moment a scandal occurs and one person discovers it, within minutes the information can be known to millions of people. Information from the past is already history. Your personal family history may only be known to a few select people in your lineage, but the facts are already established.

Step into a room with America's most amazing mind reader. He begins to go into a minitrance—eyes closed, head slightly tilted, and he groans a few times. He looks toward a woman in the audience and suddenly begins to call her parents' names, her children's names, and the fact that there was a recent death to a loved one. The woman begins crying, gasps a few times, and the audience claps with amazement. How did this occur? One explanation is that this person has tapped into a familiar spirit; these spirits are acquainted with the person of the past and are simply giving out information that is already known.

The fellow was very convincing as he roamed across the rented auditorium, randomly calling people he did not know out of the audience, revealing the last four digits of their Social Security numbers, license plates, and other amazing information. He called a woman out revealing her last name. He was wrong. Then he told her the last four digits of her Social Security number. Wrong again. Then he told the license plate number of her car she drove. He missed that one too. Three strikes and he was out! He was exposed on the spot at that moment. This woman was a secretary and had driven her boss's car to the meeting, and the last name, last four digits of the Social Security number, and license plate were all her boss's—*not hers*. She recalled a man in a golf cart marked *Security*, when she was parking, and he had a laptop on the cart. He had a computer program that is used by repo companies, which reveals this type of information when you insert the license plate number. The "mind reader" had a small receiver in his ear and was being fed information from the man in a back room of the auditorium. So much for the drama and the powerful "gift" of this con artist![1]

Information about the future

We are told that only God knows the future. However, the spirit world, including angelic beings and Satan himself, know certain facts about the future, although Satan's information concerning God's ultimate redemptive plan through the crucifixion of Christ was unknown (1 Cor. 2:6–8). For example, demons know they are destined for the bottomless pit (Luke 8:31). They know that when Satan is expelled from heaven, he will have a short (limited) time remaining on earth (Rev. 12:12). King Ahab's death was being planned in heaven before the death ever occurred, and there were angels involved in setting him up for death—including a "lying spirit" (2 Chron. 18:18–22).

The point is that when any information is released from the spirit world, including actions planned by satanic agents and assignments of angelic messengers, that information is available for men to receive. If this information is unknown to men, then the two options of how the information can be delivered is through the Holy Spirit, such as warning of a satanic attack, or released through familiar spirits.

Information you speak out of your mouth

At times believers are unaware of how important it is to guard their mouths. When a person is arrested, he or she is read their Miranda Rights, which includes this statement: "You have the right to remain silent. Anything you say can be used against you in a court of law." If a person begins to reveal information that is damaging to him or her, then it can be presented in court.

In a spiritual sense, when you begin to speak out of your mouth of being afraid of being in a car wreck, of dying young with cancer, or of your children giving you trouble, don't think these words are just bouncing off the walls—*they are released into the spiritual atmosphere.* Both life and death are in the power of the tongue (Prov. 18:21). Thus the adversary has information concerning what weapon or fear tactic to use against you, and he can design a personalized assignment geared to fulfill your expectations!

Job had seven sons and three daughters (Job 1:2). According to Job 1:6, Job made animal sacrifices continually to cover for the possibility that while his children were feasting, they may have "cursed God in their hearts." Satan understood that Job's ultimate fear was to curse God, and Satan customized Job's attack around the belief that Job would curse God Himself if his wealth and health disappeared (Job 1:11; 2:5). Job's actions and words were used to plan a negative future for him by Satan.

When considering the parallels of Job's narrative with believers today, it is not necessary for Satan or anyone else to read your mind when you are giving out any and all information concerning your doubts, unbelief, fears, and the people who make you angry. Who needs to read what you are thinking when you are like a pipe with flowing water, always speaking and never refraining from negative talk?

I would never be afraid of Satan reading my mind—but I have discovered that I must be careful of him reading my lips and of the spirit world hearing my words and using them against me in the heavenly court. Satan is the accuser of the brethren before God day and night!

GUARD YOUR MOUTH AND YOUR MIND

Any believer can control visual and verbal information entering the mind by refusing to look at what is being seen or hear what is being spoken. However, we are weak when it comes to guarding our mouth, often not understanding that as Satan brings accusations about us before God, he can only use two things to prove his case— actions and words. There is an expression, "Loose lips sink ships," and I will add, "Loose lips stop spiritual breakthroughs."

Years ago I had been intently praying for someone very close to me who was struggling with personal problems. I had felt this person was making no effort to seek needed help and actually had no desire to be freed from a particular enduring bondage. I had prayed, believed, confessed, and at times would see a step of progress. Two days later it was three steps backward. I had witnessed this cycle, like watching a running back gain ten yards in two plays then being dropped in the backfield for a twenty-yard loss.

On this occasion we were seeing progress when suddenly I received a phone call that something had happened, setting the person back again. For some reason the stress of that season caused me to snap, and I began spewing out of my mouth words that were unlike me, such as, "I should just quit praying because nothing is happening," followed by "I'm getting tired of this, so if something bad happens, it will just happen." Other statements came forth, and within ten minutes I felt very depressed and totally defeated. That was when the Holy Spirit, in a small yet strong and firm manner, spoke to my spirit, saying, "Don't abort the breakthrough!" I was stunned and immediately convicted in my heart, as I knew from my own teaching what this meant.

DON'T ABORT YOUR ANSWERS TO PRAYER

I had taught that God dwells in the eternal realm and that He hears us pray the moment we speak words out of our mouths—or the same day (Dan. 10:12). However, heaven's accounting of time is different from earth time, as we operate on the basis that the sun cycle makes up a day, the moon cycle the month, and the earth's movement in its orbit a year. Time was made for earth and not for heaven, as one day with the Lord is as a thousand years and a thousand years is as one day (2 Pet. 3:8). Thus, if we pray today and confess publicly that we believe and know God has heard and will answer us, and one month later nothing has happened and we begin to confess with our mouths that, "Prayer doesn't work; God is not hearing me, so I quit," thirty days may have passed on earth's cycle of time, but in heaven it is as though that God hears you at the same time!

I knew that if I continued to open my mouth contrary to the faith words I had prayed, that the accuser of the brethren (Rev. 12:10) could *legally* use my own words against me before the heavenly court. You see, Christ's position in heaven is not that of a building contractor with a yardstick and gold nails who is building you a place to live. Jesus said, "In my father's house *are* many mansions" (John 14:2). *Are* is present tense—the mansions already existed in the time of Christ. Christ ascended to heaven to "prepare for us a place," meaning access to the Father and a place with Him in eternity! Presently, Christ is the High Priest of our faith, an advocate, ever making intercession for us at the throne of God (Heb. 7:1–28; 1 John 2:1).

This is why it's necessary for you to "ask in faith, nothing wavering" (James 1:6, KJV), "hold fast the profession of our faith without wavering" (Heb. 10:23, KJV), and "hold fast" to what you have received and heard (Rev. 3:3). Paul taught that because Christ is our heavenly priest, we must "hold fast our confession" (Heb. 4:14). To "hold fast" means to seize onto something, but also to hold an area down as if to prevent someone else from taking it from you. Today we would say to *stand your ground without moving*, or, as Paul would put it, "Having done all, to stand. Stand therefore" (Eph. 6:13).

While Satan may place thoughts and darts in your mind, if your mind if already filled with good or godly thoughts, he has no power or substance in his attempt to read your mind that will allow him to determine your direction. He will, however, read your lips and adjust his playbook according to your fears, unbelief, and verbal conversations. James wrote extensively about the power of the tongue and taught: "Let your 'Yes,' be 'Yes,' and your 'No,' 'No'" (James 5:12). The less we say, the less the adversary knows, and the less he knows, the better off we are.

CHAPTER 5

SATAN'S WARFARE BY DECEPTION

I N WARFARE IT is easier to fight a seen enemy with a known strategy and a clear plan of attack than an unseen enemy with an unknown strategy. It is quite different, however, when the assailant is a master of illusion.

Ehrich Weiss was born to Rabbi Mayer Samuel Weiss in 1874 in Budapest, Hungary; after spending some time in the Midwest in America, the family settled in New York in 1887. Ehrich eventually started a magic act, changing his name to Harry Houdini. In his day he was known as the master illusionist, often called a *magician* by his followers. However, there was nothing really magic about the many tricks he used to astound his audiences around the world. He was noted as the master escape artist who was able to escape from any type of handcuff or restraint placed on him, including his famous escape from the Washington DC jail that once housed the assassin of President James Garfield.[1]

One of his greatest feats was his underwater box escape in New York City's East River. *Scientific American* called it "one of the most remarkable tricks ever performed." Houdini's most remarkable feat was billed as the "Chinese Water Torture Cell," where he was stripped down to a pair of swim shorts, then bound with chains and large padlocks, locking the heavy chains around his body. Harry would be dropped in a water tank, upside down in the glass case filled with water with what appeared to be an impossible scenario for escape. He could hold his breath up to three minutes, but if he failed, he would drown. To the delight and the glee of the large cheering crowds, Harry came out of the tank dripping wet and alive.[2]

No one could ever figure out the illusion. However, on one occasion Harry attempted the trick in New York's East River in 1912, where he was chained into a box with two pounds of lead on top then lowered into the river. He escaped in fifty-seven seconds, leaving the manacles inside the box. No one ever caught the real key of the initial escape from the main padlock. Just prior to being lowered into the water, Houdini's wife would run to him and kiss him one more time in case his illusion failed. In reality, it was believed she inserted a master key in his mouth that helped him unlock the most important lock![3]

In reality, the *magician* was simply an *illusionist,* which means, "a deceptive impression or appearance." There was nothing mystical or magical about the escape, only in the eyes of the beholders and only in the skill and timing held in the hand or mind of the illusionist. I have discovered some interesting concepts from this story as related to the world's master illusionist, Satan. His most important strategy against believers is his age-old *experience and skill* and the ability to *time his attacks* according to the weakest moment in a person's spiritual, emotional, or physical life. As an example, during Christ's forty days of fasting in the wilderness, it was after Christ "hungered" that the tempter came (Luke 4:2–3, kjv).

DECEPTION CAN BE CAUSED BY SPIRITUAL BLINDNESS AND DEAFNESS

Christ spoke of having eyes and not seeing, having ears and not hearing (Matt. 13:14–15). This does not refer to natural deafness and blindness, but to those who see and hear in the natural but cannot spiritually discern and comprehend spiritual truth. Christ rebuked the Pharisees for their inability to recognize who He was and His purpose. They were "dull of hearing," and their "eyes they have closed" (Matt. 13:15, kjv). After Christ's resurrection, while walking to Emmaus, He engaged in a detailed conversation with two disciples who did not recognize who He was. The Bible says that their "eyes were restrained" (Luke 24:16). Later, when Christ prayed over the bread, breaking it and giving it to His disciples, "their eyes were opened and they knew Him" (vv. 30–31).

Deception blinds the spiritual eyes and dulls the hearing (or understanding). There is both *inward* and *outward* deception. Inward deception is *self-deception*; a person places his or her personal approval upon his or her own negative actions. Outward deception is *peer-deception*; other individuals pressure a person to follow their acts of disobedience. Peer pressure is the key that unlocks the door of peer-deception. With self-deception you convince yourself that what's bad is good and what's good is bad, what's light is dark and what's dark is actually light. For example, smoking is an unclean habit, yet people will smoke for years—while reading and ignoring the health warning on the side of every cigarette pack and often knowing someone who died with cancer from smoking. Deception says, "It can happen to others, but will not happen to you." The same is true for driving under the influence of alcohol. Thousands of accidents occur yearly from drunk drivers; however, self-deception causes a numbed brain signal that says you can drive drunk, never wreck, never get pulled over by the police, and get home safe. Self-deception caused David to get Bathsheba pregnant and to have her husband killed in battle. David married Bathsheba after her husband's death and thought no one would figure out what happened. Inward deception whispers to two teenagers that they can have sex and never need worry about a sexually transmitted disease.

Then there is *peer-pressure deception.* This is the *mass hysteria, party animal* gang that places verbal pressure upon a person to act in the same destructive, dangerous manner in which they are acting. Peer pressure places a mental weight and emotional burden upon the one being pressured and often forces a reaction that is out of line with the true will of the subject being forced to participate. One pastor has buried twenty-one youth in his community who have died of drug overdoses—and not from illegal drugs purchased in a back alley. But these kids had taken prescription drugs from their parents' cabinets and mixed them together. On the last party night of their lives, not one of these teens expected that before sunrise he or she would be hauled away in an ambulance to the morgue after experimenting with these *legal* narcotics. However, peer-deception convinced them it would be OK and nothing would happen. Deception shows you the *pleasure* but hides the *penalty.*

The Illusion Becomes the Deception

While in Israel my personal tour guide Gideon Shor related to me an amazing story that also has many parallels to the power of deception in the illusion. Prior to 1917 the Turks were in control of Palestine, and the British were making inroads to liberate Palestine from four hundred years of Turkish occupation. The Turkish soldiers were often poorly trained and very poorly fed and paid.

However, most seemed to have one weakness; they loved to smoke cigarettes.

As the British made secret plans to move troops from Egypt to Palestine and eventually take Jerusalem, these plans required them to take the area of Beersheba, which was a leading Arab city in the south. In a strange but effective strategy, the British began rolling cigarettes, mixing them with marijuana and opium. The British flew planes near the border, dropping packages of cigarettes. When the soldiers saw the cigarettes, they immediately began smoking them, noticing they had caused a rather *mellow* effect on them.

About this same time, a British general rode a horse in the area near Beersheba with a leather case carrying fake battle plans. He had smeared blood on the outside and was headed toward a group of Turkish soldiers. Seeing him, the Turks fired shots in the distance, causing the general to turn the horse, dropping the blood-coated leather case. When the Turks found the case, they thought they had wounded the Brit, causing him to drop the leather case. They turned the pile of papers over to one of their commanders. The papers appeared to be secret British plans of a set day to attack Gaza, which was south of Beersheba. Word spread among the Turkish military commanders. As the date of the "secret attack" arrived, the Turks thinned the battle lines near Beersheba, moving many troops toward Gaza. Oddly, along the way, they discovered more packages of "good cigarettes"—again laced with drugs, but unknown to the Turks. The Turks began smoking heavily before the battle to settle their nerves.

For those who are unaware of the effect of drugs, this combination of marijuana and opium slows the reflexes of the body and dulls the senses. The body reacts by feeling slow, lazy, and dazed. As a result, while the Turks were in Gaza, the British came to Beersheba and took the area—all because of the *warfare of deception*! The secret plans were false, the cigarettes were laced, and the general was never wounded! Beersheba was a needed prize for the Brits as it was a strategic town for the future movement of the British troops marching from Egypt to Jerusalem![4]

Boredom Is a Door for Deception to Enter

Many addicted individuals began abusing alcohol and narcotics in a group setting they joined at the encouragement of a fellow addict. The artificial high was a temporary replacement for their apathetic lifestyle and restless spirit. Boredom is a breeding ground for immoral and dangerous behavior. Take Sodom, for an example. When we think of the biblical city of Sodom, we think that the main sin was sodomy, which is true. (See Genesis 19.) However, the prophet Ezekiel lists one of Sodom's numerous sins as "abundance of idleness" (Ezek. 16:49). When two angels in the form of men (as the writer describes in Hebrews 13:2) went behind locked doors into Lot's house, "the men of Sodom, both old and young," rose up and desired to have relations with them (Gen. 19:4). Apparently the old men were influencing the young men. With an abundance of idle time, the mind is more open to the darts of the enemy. The old-timers used to say, "An idle mind is the devil's workshop."

I once asked several prisoners, "What is the most difficult thing about being incarcerated?" To my surprise they answered, "The boredom of the routine…we have nothing but time and not enough positive activities to stay really busy and productive with our minds." One of Satan's weapons is to make life so routine that it becomes dull like the monotone voice of a teacher in a class.

Boredom is often experienced as a result of not anticipating anything for your future. When you have an "I don't care" attitude, then every person you meet, every place you go, and everything you do will eventually become boring and dull. Your motivation for today and every day should be your thoughts of a good future.

Parents desire to help their children in life, yet one of the biggest mistakes is always providing money and resources for their children without them working for these resources. When I was growing up, my motivation for cutting grass, cleaning cars, and cleaning the church was my desire to have some personal income with which to purchase something or to have money for a girlfriend and me to go eat and have some fun. My mom and dad had four children and limited incomes; thus I worked for my own income and didn't just milk my parents for cash. It is the seeds of emptiness planted by the slack hands of motivation that lead people into drugs, with the deceptive intention of making them feel higher, picking them up, and causing them to "feel better." For a short season drugs may put a smile on your face, but in the long term they will weaken your brain, lungs, and heart, inviting into your life a premature death.

TAKING THE FIGHT
OUT OF THE FIGHTERS

When my Jewish friend Gideon shared the story I related earlier of the British victory over the occupying Turks while driving through Beersheba on a tour bus, I sensed these words: *the strategy of the enemy is to stop the fighters from fighting by taking the fight out of the fighters!* The *fight* of which I speak is the desire to *defend* yourself or to *resist* an oncoming assault. I immediately understood these words. If you as a believer cease from fighting the "good fight of faith" (1 Tim. 6:12), then the enemy wins by *default*—meaning you fail because you did not do what was required to defend your-self. All you must do to lose any spiritual battle is to simply *do nothing*. This is the way Satan is defeating many youth in this generation, by dulling and weakening their ability to fight the fight by medicating or making mellow the fighting nature and dulling it through addictions, just as the Turks were so "high" they couldn't fight the British.

One of the greatest battles of contemporary society is the battle of addictions, including addictions to alcohol, strong drink, and illegal drugs such as marijuana, heroin, crack cocaine, and other narcotics that raise you high then drop you low, eventually dulling the senses, numbing the mind and blurring reality. During many years of ministry I have personally met and ministered to thousands of all ages who have become chained, like Harry Houdini, to a bondage *that is not just an illusion*—but very real. However, just like with the master illusionists, things are not always what they seem to be. You and I see a person under a chain of bondage, an addiction, a spiritual or mental captivity. But what we see is only the *fruit* and not the *root* of the problem.

The root is often an emotional wound, a broken relationship, a wounded heart and spirit, and, in some instances, guilt, condemnation, and shame. For an addict, it is easier to escape the pain, the negative memories, and the reality of life by dulling the feelings and the senses. However, addictions will also leave the victim vulnerable to the swords and fiery darts of the adversary, as they are left without any defense against the battle assaults of an enemy who never plays by the rules.

Wounded Children

I cannot count the times in an altar service when a mother is standing behind a youngster, ages eight to thirteen, asking for prayer for a *rebellious spirit* that has come over the youth. At times I sensed the Holy Spirit requiring me to ask the mother, "So when did you divorce this child's father?"

Often the parent looks amazed and says, "How did you know?"

I replied, "I can see the pain in your youngster's eyes and face. He (or she) is not rebelling out of a desire for rebellion but out of emotional pain. The divorce placed an invisible but real wound in his heart, and he resents the person you married and is expressing it by resisting authority. You think rebellion is the root, but it is not; it is the fruit of rejection." It is those early wounds that, if unrepaired and left in secret, will become the back door for the dark spirit of deception to enter in later life, further frustrating the person and piling on more emotional baggage in a heart already packed with despair.

Many of today's youth who enter the "alternative lifestyle" can often recall a specific moment when they were verbally or physically abused by an adult of the same sex, or perhaps a girl saw abuse from her father or a son had no male authority to oversee his life. A spirit of rejection will always attract a similar spirit of rejection. This is often seen when a girl is raised in the home of an alcoholic father; she eventually marries a man who is also an alcoholic. Some young women fall in love with a young man who eventually physically, sexually, and verbally abuses them to the point that they hate all men. Looking for understanding, they turn toward another young woman with a similar experience. Both were hurt by men, both abused verbally, both rejected, so both understood one another.

Sounds good, right? But it's good only if their affections remain natural and pure; in this case they can be healed of the wounds. However, in many cases this situation leads to a same-sex relationship that continues for many years. This is how the master illusionist works. Watch the hurt in the right hand, but as you concentrate on the pain in the right hand, the real setup is in left hand. Thus, the root is not the fruit, and the fruit is not the root; what you see is often only on the surface.

We see the addictions and not the wounds, the rebellion and not the rejection, the drunkenness and not the depression, and the illusion but not the deception. Just as in the suggestion that Mrs. Houdini had a key in her mouth that was used to loose the chains on her husband, the key of a person's deliverance begins with faith in his or her heart that God is willing and able to help, followed by the confession of faith from the mouth:

> For with the heart a person believes (adheres to, trusts in, and relies on Christ) and so is justified (declared righteous, acceptable to God), and with the mouth he confesses (declares openly and speaks out freely his faith) and confirms [his] salvation.
>
> —ROMANS 10:10, AMP

A SPIRITUAL LIFE VISION CAN KEEP YOU ALIVE

The promises God has given you that are yet unfulfilled, and the dreams or visions in your mind that have not yet come to pass, can become incentives that help keep you living longer! For example, I have three assignments that I believe the Lord has placed upon my heart that will take time to complete.

The first is the construction of a major gathering place for reformation services, youth conferences, and mentoring of youth for ministry called Omega Center International (OCI). Following the completion of this facility, I was impressed to build a major youth camp for summer camps. The third project I have begun is a personal commentary on the entire Bible. These are three of the biggest and most expensive projects in the history of my ministry.

When I get up each morning, I continue with my normal routine of studying, praying, and writing books and magazine and Internet articles. But my main motivation is to follow and complete the three distinct dreams the Lord has placed in my spirit. I desire to be like Joshua, who the Bible says "left nothing undone of all that the LORD had commanded" (Josh. 11:15).

A spiritual vision will restrain deception. When the attractive wife of Potiphar threw herself at Joseph, he could have "gone with the flow" and committed adultery. But if he had, instead of being sent to prison for being *accused* of the act, he would have been killed for *performing* the act. Joseph remembered the two dreams he had as a youth of saving his entire household (Gen. 37:6–10), and he knew that being in Egypt was somehow connected to the fulfillment of those dreams. It is possible that because Joseph had hidden those dreams in his heart, a beautiful woman was unable to pull his dreams out and fill his heart with another purpose.

A dear friend, Walter Hallam, told me a great story about a general of the faith named Lester Sumrall. Lester was ministering in a church, and Walter was to serve as his personal assistant. After a service Lester went into the office and told Walter, "I am going to teach you how to run your race and finish your course." Walter was expecting a series of great revelations and nuggets that would transform his life. As Lester stood there, and Walter had his pen in his hand, Lester began to passionately cry out, "Don't sin!" That was the revelation and the conclusion of the lesson.

Sin threw the first couple out of the garden, brought on the universal flood, and caused the destruction of Sodom and Gomorrah. It brought Israel into captivity to their enemies and caused kings to lose their thrones. Defeating deception depends upon exposing and stopping the plot, which can also prevent private warfare.

The key to your deliverance lies in the Word of God penetrating your heart to the point that you are willing to agree with the promise of God and confess with your mouth the ability of God to bring redemption into your life. When you speak with your mouth, you are agreeing with what is in your heart, and the laws of the Holy Spirit can freely begin to operate in your life.

CHAPTER 6

CAN SATAN OR DEMONS *POSSESS* A CHRISTIAN?

᪥ ᪥

A S A TEENAGE evangelist in the late 1970s, I was invited to preach at a church in a northern state. After meeting the pastor, I was instructed by him not to preach any message teaching that a Christian could not be possessed by an evil spirit. That night I discovered why. After the altar service he stood up and instructed the ushers to hand out the brown paper bags. He then instructed anyone who "had a demon" to breathe hard and fast into the bag. Soon a few people passed out, and the pastor began rebuking demons. By this time I was looking for an exit and was about to make one through the drywall. About this time I was asked if I would like to go to the pastor's office and wait. Needless to say, I never returned to the "brown bag ministry" church where people hyperventilated in the name of deliverance.

During the 1970s and 1980s, both Pentecostal and charismatic churches were ministering to individuals who believed they were being manipulated or controlled by an evil spirit, often called by the general name a *demon*. However, the classical Pentecostal leaders and many charismatic leaders often differed on the theology of demonic *oppression* and demonic *possession*. Classical Pentecostals denied with no uncertain terms that any true Christian could ever be possessed by a demon. The charismatic community, however, would often have *deliverance services* in which they would invite Christians to have demons cast out of them. This question, Can a Christian be possessed by a demon?, has been one of the most controversial and at times divisive questions to answer. Let me begin by saying I have close friends who are theologically on opposite ends of the spectrum, and both love Christ deeply. However, I will do my utmost to be true to the Scriptures in this discourse on the subject.

WHAT IS A TRUE CHRISTIAN?

The first question we must ask does not address the issue of oppression and possession or a discourse on the body, soul, and spirit of a person. It defines a *true Christian*. The word *Christian* should be used to identify a true disciple of Christ (Acts 11:26)—one who has received a redemptive covenant and follows and obeys the instructions found in the New Testament. The word *Christian* is used twice—Acts 26:28 and 1 Peter 4:16—and it basically means, "a follower of Christ." However, the dedication and commitment levels of the early Christians in the New Testament era seem to be far different from people in today's Western culture who identify themselves as Christians.

Today a person can attend a Sunday morning service, go to the altar and pray a "sinner's prayer," walk out the door, and not return to church the remaining forty years of his or her life. However, if that person dies and the funeral is at the "home church," most of the time that person is preached into the eternal kingdom because they were a "Christian." In some Islamic nations, such as Egypt, if a person is not a Muslim by profession or was not born into an Islamic family, it is assumed that person is automatically a Christian, even though he or she may have never publicly confessed Christ or received water baptism and the sacraments. There are countless men and women who attend church on Sunday morning whose attendance identifies them as Christians to the casual observer. However, they never witness to a sinner, never attend church more than two hours a week, never give their tithes and offerings, and live weekly lives similar to the average sinner in town who has no understanding of the Scripture and is as lost as a shipwrecked man on an uncharted island.

Here is the issue. To identify a true *born-again, redeemed believer* who has been forgiven of his or her sins and cleansed through the redemptive blood of Christ (1 Pet. 1:18–19), there will be spiritual fruit on the vine of that person's life (John 15:8). Once a true follower of Christ becomes an active Christian after receiving initial redemption, then "old things have passed away; behold, all things have become new" (2 Cor. 5:17). Paul said we become a "new creation." Part of the act of redemption is to deliver us from Satan's power, as it is written:

> He has delivered us from the power of darkness and con-
> veyed us into the kingdom of the Son of His love, in whom
> we have redemption through His blood, the forgiveness of
> sins.
> —COLOSSIANS 1:13–14

This is where an important point must be made concerning Satan's ability to possess and control a believer. If a person is identified as a Christian simply because he or she prayed one prayer, attends church occasionally, or was raised in a Christian family, then this *name by association* does not prevent a Christian in name only from coming under control of various evil spirits. To be a Christian in name only is not living a life totally for Christ and free from sin. Such a person has no authority over the enemy. In much the same way, although demons "believe [that there is one God]—and tremble!" (James 2:19), this does not mean these *believing demons* have been converted and can enter a redemptive covenant. They know God exists, because Satan and the fallen angels under his control once worshipped God and have seen God. But their *belief* is not *saving faith* on their part. "Faith is the substance of things hoped for, *the evidence of things not seen*" (Heb. 11:1, emphasis added). Demonic spirits even identified Christ as the Son of God (Matt. 8:29; Mark 3:11), which is a requirement for a person to become a Christian (1 John 5:10–11), but these spirits who recognized Christ were also promised that their doom was set and sealed.

Christians Under Satanic Influence

The New Testament does teach that Christians can come under satanic influence, especially through temptations in the mind and the darts of the enemy. There are three New Testament examples indicating that Satan had placed thoughts in the minds of the individuals.

The first was Simon Peter, a chosen disciple of Christ (Matt. 4:18–19). In Matthew 16 Christ forewarned His disciples of a future time when He would be crucified. In his zeal Peter took Christ aside and reprimanded Him for this revelation, telling Christ, "Far be it from You, Lord; this shall not happen to You!" (v. 22). I'm sure Peter was stunned when Christ looked at him and said, "Get behind Me, Satan!" (v. 23). Because the name *Satan* is a proper name of the highest-ranking fallen angel, we assume that Satan himself was being rebuked for giving Peter the thoughts he spoke with his mouth.

The second example goes beyond Satan planting an ungodly thought. Satan's influence moved from a dart in the mind to a dart in the very heart of Judas Iscariot. Judas had already plotted to betray Christ, and at the Last Supper Satan "put it into the heart of Judas Iscariot...to betray Him" (John 13:2). Judas not only *thought of* betraying Christ, but he also *acted upon* his thoughts, because his thoughts were devilish (John 6:70). Satan eventually drove Judas to take his own life (Acts 1:18–19).

The third example is a married couple, Ananias and Sapphira. This couple owned a piece of land and made an agreement to sell it and give the proceeds to the ministry. When the moment arrived for them to present their offering before the apostle Peter, they withheld a portion for themselves. Peter confronted them separately, asking why they allowed Satan to fill their hearts to lie against the Holy Spirit (Acts 5:3, 9). Remember, Peter himself had once been subject to the sly whispers of Satan in his ear to rebuke Christ's comments predicting his suffering. I believe Peter had sharpened his discernment and sensed by the Holy Spirit a deceiving and lying spirit in the hearts of this couple.

Herein lies an important point. Both Judas and this couple were originally believers and active in the ministry. Judas was one of Christ's disciples, and Ananias and Sapphira were a prominent couple in the church. Because of the phrase "Satan filled your heart," it is assumed that Satan possessed these two individuals; thus believers can be possessed by spirits. True believers, however, will not lie and deceive as Ananias and Sapphira did. It was the lie and the deception that opened a door to the enemy to enter the lives of these individuals.

It is also important to see that Simon Peter was an active believer, but he had suddenly listened to the wrong voice. Judas was a backslidden disciple (he was a thief, John 12:6). Judas followed the wrong voice. Ananias and his wife were active members of the church, but they had conspired in secret to deceive the apostles and cheat God out of a vow they had made.

The point is that Christians can come under demonic influence without ever being *possessed* by a spirit. Paul warned the church not to allow Satan to get the advantage of them and not to be "ignorant of his devices" (2 Cor. 2:11). On one occasion Paul was informed of a young man who was committing fornication with his father's wife (his stepmother, 1 Cor. 5:1–5). Paul reprimanded the congregation for allowing this act to go unchecked among the congregation and demanded the congregation to "deliver such a one to Satan for the destruction of the flesh, that his spirit may be saved in the day of the Lord Jesus" (v. 5). This was a *sinning church member* whose sin was known to all. This fornicating man would, in all likelihood, have been called a Christian by the church. However, his unrepentant sin was opening a door to Satan to attack his flesh in some manner. Paul hoped that the effect of this satanic attack would bring the young man to repentance—that his soul would be saved in the day of Christ.

ATTACKS OF SATAN ON BELIEVERS

If as a believer you do not continually renew the spirit of your mind (Eph. 4:23) and do not cast down carnal imaginations (2 Cor. 10:5), you may find yourself under a mental oppression of the devil. The anointing of the Holy Spirit on Christ was the weapon used to heal "all who were oppressed by the devil" (Acts 10:38). The Greek word for "oppressed" in Acts 10:38 means, "to exercise dominion against a person." Oppression is normally considered an attack on the mind. However, there can also be a spiritual oppression. In addition, since Acts 10:38 deals with Christ healing men and women, then oppression is also a physical assault.

Oppression is different from possession. In the New Testament the word *possessed* is found fifteen times in the King James Version, and in each reference except two (Acts 4:32; 1 Cor. 7:30) it refers to a person or persons possessed by evil or unclean spirits. The word *possessed* in Greek is a long word, *diamonizomai*, which refers to being exercised or controlled by a demon. In the New Testament, when a person is possessed, there are strange and often violent manifestations that indicate possession. In Mark 5 one man controlled by literally thousands of evil spirits was crying night and day, cutting himself, and had supernatural strength (Mark 5:1–9). Below is a list of the signs from Mark 5 of possession by demons:

- He was crying loudly day and night—a sign of mental torment (v. 5).

- He was up all night and was not sleeping (v. 5).

- He was cutting himself—a sign he was attempting to harm himself or possibly commit suicide (v. 5).

- He was breaking chains and could not be restrained— supernatural strength (v. 4).

- He was living in tombs and not among the living (v. 3).

Another example is a young child whose father came to Christ for his boy's deliverance from spirits. The spirits had thrown the lad into water and into fire to destroy him (Mark 9:22). Possessed individuals are often violent, self-destructive, tormented in their minds, and making attempts to harm themselves or others around them. Oppression, however, is a pressure in the mind, body, and spirit, a mental heaviness that is unexplainable. The possessed are controlled *out of their spirits*, but the oppressed are *influenced in their minds*.

Believers Can Have an Infirmity

My father had great results in praying for the sick. His compassion toward the suffering was unmatched in any person I have ever met. He prayed for hours at a time for the healing of those suffering, and during the many years he traveled with me in ministry as a co-evangelist and conference speaker, he saw about sixteen people (that we knew of) healed of cancer. My dad's mentor as a young minister was his uncle Rufus Dunford, who had performed marvelous miracles through prayer. Before Rufus passed away, I met with him as a young eighteen-year-old, freshly-called-to-the-ministry, wet-behind-the-ears evangelist. I was conversing with Rufus at his home in West Virginia and began asking him about his many experiences in prayer and why so many people were healed during his ministry in the West Virginia mountains.

That day Rufus explained his belief that a vast majority of sickness and pain was the result of attacks from spirits against the physical bodies of individuals. He knew some difficulties were self-invited, such as clogged arteries from eating the wrong food, which can lead to a heart attack, high blood pressure caused by stress and other causes, and different types of illnesses. However, Rufus was convinced that serious diseases such as cancer, which destroy the body, were caused by a *spirit of infirmity* that agitated the cells in the human body. He often said that many ministers prayed and asked for a cancer patient to be healed of cancer, but he always rebuked a spirit of cancer that was attacking the cells. He commanded the good cells to be strong in the body. He did, by the way, have results when praying for individuals with cancer.

There are spirits called *spirits of infirmity* that can inflict suffering on a human body. The best biblical example comes from a physician's observation, a doctor named Luke. In Luke 13 Dr. Luke identified a woman in the synagogue who was bound by "a spirit of infirmity eighteen years" (v. 11). She is called a "daughter of

Abraham," a term used for a woman who believed in the Abrahamic covenant (v. 16). She was "bent over" and could not raise herself up (v. 11). Had she been examined by modern technology, her condition may have been a form of crippling arthritis or spinal disease or some form of a bone disease. However, Jesus identified it as a "spirit of infirmity" and revealed that "Satan has bound" her (v. 16). The Greek word for "infirmity" is *asthenia* and can be used to identify a weakness of the body or mind. The woman was afflicted with such weakness that she was unable to stand until the spirit was rebuked. Then she stood upright and was "made straight" (v. 13). Jesus "loosed" her from the spirit by saying, "Woman, you are loosed from your infirmity" (v. 12). By Jesus commanding her to be "loosed," He released this woman from the authority and control of the sickness itself.

I do acknowledge that sickness entered the world at the fall of Adam, but I do not believe all sickness is the result of a spirit. There are some diseases that are inherited and others that can come upon a believer or unbeliever by lack of exercise, not eating properly, or by stress, guilt, condemnation, and a host of other negative emotions. It is biblical that spirits can attack the physical bodies of a believer.

When Paul wrote to the church at Corinth concerning the Lord's Supper (the Communion of the bread and fruit of the vine), he warned that if the believers did not discern the Lord's body properly and partook of the Communion "in an unworthy manner," it would have a negative effect upon them. He wrote: "For this reason many are weak and sick among you, and many sleep [died prematurely]," because they did not discern the Lord's body. (See 1 Corinthians 11:27–30).

Can a Christian be Possessed?

When a professor from a major Christian college was asked, "Can a Christian have a demon?", he pondered a moment then replied: "A Christian can have whatever he or she wants!"

I understood this statement. The Bible says, "Whoever has been born of God does not sin, for His seed remains in him; and he cannot sin, because he has been born of God" (1 John 3:9). Then we read: "If we say that we have no sin, we deceive ourselves, and the truth is not in us" (1 John 1:8). This seems to be a contradiction. We *cannot* sin, and yet we *have sin*. This enigma can be answered when asking "Could Jesus have sinned?" Christ was tempted as we are, yet He did not sin (Heb. 4:15).

Physically, Christ had the ability to sin in His flesh, just as any human man can sin with his. However, Christ's desire to follow the will of His father and walk in complete obedience formed a restraint against the power of sin over Him. He had the potential of sin, but through resistance to evil He gained power over sin! We all have a potential of sinning, but when our *determination* for right is stronger than our *desire* for wrong, then we defeat the devil! Satan can only possess the willing. Believers are commanded, "Resist the devil and he will flee from you" (James 4:7).

What Does a Spirit Attack in a Christian?

Since man is a tripartite being consisting of a body, soul, and spirit, then there are three possible areas where the adversary can attack. The body of a believer is called the "temple of God," and the Spirit of God dwells in a believer (1 Cor. 3:16). Paul was using an analogy of the temple in Jerusalem with which all Jews were familiar, comparing it to a believer. Just as a believer has a body, soul, and spirit, the temple in Jerusalem had three separate areas that were constructed as one building called the *temple*. There was the outer court, the inner court, and the holy of holies. The outer court area would be the imagery of the body; the inner court area, the soul; and the holy of holies, the human spirit. The entire compound was God's house, but the divine presence of God dwelt in the holiest place, the chamber where the ark of the covenant rested.

In the law of God this area was so sensitive that when a Judean king entered the inner court (the holy place) and offered incense on the golden altar, he was smitten with leprosy (2 Chron. 26:16–21). The common Israelite was permitted in the outer court to offer sacrifices on the brass altar. However, the common Israelite was forbidden to enter the inner court or holy place, as these were reserved for the Levites (called priests). The Levites were then forbidden to enter the holy of holies except on one day out of each year—the Day of Atonement or Yom Kippur.

This imagery is important for the believer to comprehend. In the Old Testament we read where Satan stood at the right side of the altar resisting Joshua the high priest (Zech. 3:1–2). Satan was not and never would be permitted in the holy of holies where God came to commune with the priest. He was expelled from the heavenly temple because of his sin of defilement (Luke 10:18). God will not dwell in the same room with Satan!

When a person enters the redemptive covenant with Christ, his or her spirit becomes cleansed by the blood of Christ, and this cleansing forms a protective hedge in the same manner that the lamb's blood in Exodus 12 restrained the destroying angel from entering the Hebrew homes and slaying the firstborn child.

Notice the strong words of Paul as he warns believers not to be connected (yoked) with unbelievers:

> Do not be unequally yoked together with unbelievers. For what fellowship has righteousness with lawlessness? And what communion has light with darkness? And what

accord has Christ with Belial? Or what part has a believer with an unbeliever? And what agreement has the temple of God with idols? For you are the temple of the living God. As God has said: "I will dwell in them and walk among them. I will be their God, and they shall be My people."

—2 Corinthians 6:14–16

If God separates a true believer from the darkness of unbelievers, then how can we say that a true believer who is abiding in Christ is susceptible to being possessed by evil spirits? Only if a Christian ceases to follow Christ's instructions and willfully chooses to open the door to hidden or public sin can the forces of the enemy enter that person's life, including the mind.

In summary, the spirit of every true believer has been redeemed and is a picture of the holy of holies in the ancient Jewish temple, where the Lord Himself would dwell between the wings of the ark of the covenant, communing yearly with the high priest on the Day of Atonement. The believer's spirit is off limits to the intrusion of Satanic or demonic forces as long as the believer maintains covenant with God. The believer's mind is linked to the inner court, where the menorah illuminates the atmosphere, the smoke of prayers arise off the golden altar of incense, and the table of showbread feeds the soul (mind) from the Word of God. In this chamber there is a daily renewal of oil for the menorah, as the old wicks are replaced with new, and fresh oil is poured into the seven golden cups. There is incense on the golden altar in the morning and evening—a picture of the prayer life of a believer. The bread is replaced each Sabbath with fresh bread—just as believers must receive a fresh word from the Lord each Sabbath!

The mind must be renewed from the fiery darts (carnal and negative thoughts) of the enemy (Eph. 6:16). Satan does not possess the mind of any true believer but has access to send from the outside thoughts, ideas, and imaginations that must be cast down; thus the daily need to renew the mind. The outer court is the area of the body, and the brass altar and laver are the two main pieces of furniture in this area. This is also the area where the common Israelite can walk, and, in the Bible, the area where Satan stood at the altar to resist the high priest (Zech. 3:1–2). This court of the temple is parallel to the physical body. As stated, spirits of infirmity and sickness can attack the body of a believer, but they can also be expelled through the believer or an anointed minister exercising spiritual authority and rebuking the adversary. Christ gave His followers "authority…over all of the power of the enemy" (Luke 10:19). This legal authority over all of Satan's authority is another reason why the enemy cannot barge into the life or spirit of a covenant believer and exercise his free will in that person's life. Christ's authority serves as a restraining force!

CHAPTER 7

THE IMPORTANCE OF
FIGHTING PRIVATE DEMONS

※ ※

MANY YEARS AGO I received a call from a very dear pastor friend who was quite distraught. For several months he had been bombarded with attacks from outside his church that included investigations concerning taxes, betrayal of friends, a terrible sickness that had struck one of his children, financial stress in the church, and a local newspaper whose writers set out to humiliate him in the community. As this whirlwind of trouble was spinning into an uncontrollable storm, he was himself in a very dark depression, to the point that his primary care doctor told him he was burnt out and near a breakdown.

During this time he was hit with the strongest missile in the arsenal of the enemy. He was fighting a public war but also a *private demon*. The church and community knew what was being reported in the media, but the real struggle was taking place when he was alone and the darts of the enemy were flying against his mind. While these assaults were sudden, multiplied, and unexpected, these targeted strategies may have been planned years in advance.

We often assume that attacks of our adversary are sudden and perhaps were planned in what I call the *war room of hell* after Satan's secret agents reported, "Now is the time to attack." In reality, the enemy plans his plots for weeks, months, and even years in advance and then waits for the right time, placing the *right* people in the *right* circumstances for a person to fall into the snare. The adversary has his own list of your fleshly weaknesses, your previous habits, your spiritually dangerous former friends, and what sin magnet could pull you back into a spiritual prison. The enemy capitalizes on weakness.

THE *AKAIROS* MOMENTS

Consider the example of Christ, who was tempted during forty days by Satan himself. After the temptation was ended, the Bible says that Satan "departed from him for a season" (Luke 4:13, KJV). This word *season* in Greek is *kairos,* and it means a "set time" or an "opportune time." You see, not all time is an *opportune time*—the surroundings, people, and places may not at that moment fit the adversary's plan. In the Greek, if a certain prefix is added to the word *kairos*, it changes the meaning. If you add *eu* in the front, it becomes the Greek word *eukairos* and means to be "happy, pleasing or a pleasurable time." If, however, you add the prefix *a* before the word, it becomes *akairos* and has a negative meaning, "bad times or a bad season."[1]

God has an *eukairos* (happy) season for you, but the plan of the adversary is to design as many *akairos* (bad) times and seasons for you as possible. In our example from Luke 4, Satan had thrown his dart at Christ by questioning if Christ was the son of God (Luke 4:1–11). It would be about three and a half years later when, at the cross, men would yell at Christ, also demanding: "If You are the Son of God, come down from the cross" (Matt. 27:40; see also Mark 15:30; Luke 23:39). Thus, about three and a half years passed from the first temptation (Luke 4) to the crucifixion, which became the more *appropriate or opportune season* to attack Christ again. Satan was observing the movements of Christ throughout His ministry and was setting up an *akairos* moment!

Notice that during the first temptation in the wilderness, the enemy initiated the question, "If You are the Son of God…," after Christ had fasted for days and *was hungry* (Luke 4:2). Forty-two months later, at the cross, Christ had been beaten and was bleeding from His hands, feet, back, and head as weakness and pain smote His flesh. At this *akairos* moment the enemy again returned, using people as his megaphone to blast the same question: "If You are the Son of God…then prove it!" This was the more opportune time to bring back a counterattack against Christ (Matt. 27:40–43). Being hungry after forty days of fasting is the best time to tempt a man with food. After being humiliated, beaten, and abused, the physical weakness of Christ was the set season to bring up the first temptation again and see if it would work this time. Christ never submitted to the voice of Satan or people; thus He conquered death and hell!

The enemy takes advantage of bad circumstances, personal and family conflicts, rebellion in children, and other forms of disruptions, distractions, and discouragement to strike a blow. Lot was "oppressed by the filthy conduct of the wicked" (2 Pet. 2:7). David confessed he was "weak…though anointed king" (2 Sam. 3:39). Christ was hungry, and then the enemy commanded Him to prove His Sonship by turning rocks into loaves of bread (Matt. 4:3).

Another example is Samson. His private demon was his

attraction to Philistine women. This strong man of Israel would sneak across the Israeli border to the land of his enemies, spending the night in the house of a Philistine beauty queen named Delilah. She continually "vexed" Samson with her words, attempting to pull from him the secret of his physical strength. Scripture says: "And it came to pass, when she pestered him daily with her words and pressed him, so that his soul was vexed to death, that he told her all his heart..." (Judg. 16:16–17). Literally this woman wore Samson down emotionally with her continual demand for his greatest secret. She may have used that old ploy, "If you *really* love me, you will tell me!" A person will often submit to temptation in an area of personal weakness easier than to one that person has the strength to resist. A door must be opened for the entrance of a private demon, which is a personal and private battle that no one sees in public, but you wrestle with it in private. The demon does not necessarily need be a literal spirit, but it can be a bondage or addiction that is as strong as a literal spirit that can control your mind and emotions.

WHY MEN OFTEN FIGHT IN PRIVATE

Both men and women fight personal and private battles, but men seem to struggle more with revealing their weakness than women. Men are hunters by nature and are designed by their Creator to take dominion and authority over God's creation (Gen. 1:26–28). This desire to dominate can be seen when a fellow will sit in a boat in the hot sun for hours attempting to catch that eight-pound bass in the lake. Or when the man stands for hours in twenty-degree weather in a deer stand, hoping to come home with that buck's rack to mount above his fireplace mantel. When it comes to hunting, fishing, sports, and even trying to chase the perfect woman down the aisle of the church as his wife, men are by nature hunters and dominion takers. Then they can become content when they catch their *deer* or their *dear*!

One of my wife's close friends observed that before she was married, her future husband sent flowers and cards, opened the door of the car, called her "sweetheart," and checked with her on the phone. This continued until after the honeymoon. She was perplexed that since that time there had been no cards, flowers, phone calls at work, or tender "sweetheart" words being said. I told Pam to tell her that her fellow loved the *chase* to get her, but now that he had his *catch*, the chase was over and he was no longer inspired. It's like a deer hunter once deer seasons ends. He just waits until the next season. This self-made perception that men have of their ability to conquer can actually become a snare when it comes to their own private battle.

Most men have an inner perception of themselves that they can take charge and handle any stress, temptation, additional pressure, and negative circumstances. When they are lost driving in a city, they often keep driving in circles, knowing that "just around the next corner" is that road they've missed for the past twenty minutes! When playing a game in front of their children at the carnival, it's, "Let me try one more time," then, "Just once more," followed by, "OK, this is my last attempt." The one-dollar game becomes an eight-dollar challenge—a chase—to prove he can win the prize. By nature men want to conquer by using their own reasoning and strength.

In the battle against a private demon, this is a significant difference between a man and a woman. A woman often seeks out another person, usually a woman or counselor, to open up to and detail her feelings and her struggle. On the other hand, men will say nothing but will fight for days, weeks, and months, saying to themselves, "This will go away if I just hang on long enough," or "I can handle this; all I have to do is just quit this...stop that...not go there any more...," and on the mental reasoning goes. This is a part of that *hunt-and-conquer* mind-set that convinces a fellow that he can do all things through his own efforts as he strengthens himself!

The Preacher Had "No One to Tell"

Many years ago a world-recognized minister was caught in a very serious allegation that proved true. Pictures and stories filled the television, newspapers, and tabloids, blasting the sin of this minister for the entire world to see. Later this same minister was speaking privately to several close friends, and they asked him why he did not go to someone he trusted and tell them he was struggling with thoughts that eventually led to his actions. His reply was that in his position, "Who was there that I could trust?" He felt anything he said in private would be repeated in public and bring harm to him, his family, and the ministry. In reality, it would have been better to expose it to friends and gain freedom than to be exposed to the world. After the news broke, I recall many people saying, "He is a liar, deceiver, and a hypocrite. He preached one thing and lived something else."

What most people do not know is that this same man prayed intently after he sinned and begged God for cleansing and forgiveness. He fought a private demon, but he was also seeking forgiveness. By definition he is not a "hypocrite." A true hypocrite would indeed preach one thing, live another, and never ask for cleansing, never weep hot tears of repentance, and never seek God's help for freedom. A hypocrite lives in and enjoys the struggle. Judas was a hypocrite; by position he was appointed an apostle, but he was a devil in his thoughts. A struggling believer seeking help is not a hypocrite but is a person who needs total freedom.

Behind the bright eyes are sleepless nights and behind the smile is a frown of pain. Some people identify a believer who struggles between spiritual and carnal, faith and doubt, addictions and freedom a *hypocrite*, but the *struggling believer who is reaching out for God's help is not a hypocrite.* In reality, there are many individuals who believe in God, have a love for Christ, have a knowledge of the Bible, and yet are battling private demons—personal and private conflicts including "fleshly lusts which war against the soul" (1 Pet. 2:11). Struggling believers could be identified as "weak in faith" (Rom. 14:1), or someone struggling with "infirmities of the weak" (Rom. 15:1, KJV), or as a person who has a "weak conscience" (1 Cor. 8:7–12).

However, the last thing a minister of the gospel should do is simply comfort the weak and aid them in their weaknesses by covering them in what I call *sloppy agape*, or a sloppy form of Christian love that comments, "God understand your situation, so don't worry; it will all work out." Try telling a drug addict or a person bound in the chains of alcohol that God loves them and it will all work out; when they are in torment and despair, such a statement does not *comfort*. It takes more than comforting words; *it takes deliverance and freedom.* It takes more than a pat on the back, a big smile, and charm to bring deliverance to the captives. *You can't pet your pet sin, and you must not accommodate private demons* that are robbing you of freedom.

One of the areas where we have lacked teaching in the body of Christ is to explain to people why believers struggle after they are converted. When growing up, I heard ministers proclaim that we were "saved" and "on your way to heaven." There was much teaching about the wrongs of sin and the glories of heaven, but not enough teaching on why we struggle on earth.

I have discovered that some spirits may not be direct demonic spirits but are *soulish*—meaning an emotional tie to a person. These soulish ties, often called *soul ties*, tie a person emotionally to another until the struggler becomes codependent upon another person. This is fine if that other confidant is your companion who is standing with you spiritually through your struggle. However, far too many times to even comprehend, what has happened is that a man becomes codependent upon another woman or a women upon a man who is not his or her companion. That inner voice tells you that this other person "really understands you," "is more compassionate for you," and "really cares about you." Thus begins the private battle in your mind, and you desire to see or speak with this person every day.

It may begin as a soulish relationship, but if it persists, then a spirit can enter the crack in the door, and it becomes an obsession leading to control. No Christian man or woman ever intended to enter a friendship that led to an emotional relationship and an eventual physical affair. When revealing your secret struggles, you must speak to the *right persons*—not the wrong ones.

Years ago one of my mistakes was when I fought a terrible mental struggle and never told my wife until after the struggle ended. That conquering mentality seized me as I thought, "I'll fight this by myself."

Turn On the Light

As I have related before, as a minister of the gospel, at times I have experienced various forms of attack from the spirit realm. Many years ago I recall taking an overseas trip to a former Communist nation. While staying in a hotel with a fellow missionary, late one night I literally saw a demonic spirit manifest at the foot of my bed. It appeared to be very old, with long hair that looked as brittle and hard as steel wool. The eyes glared, and the facial expression was wrinkled and a cross between hate and anger. The image lasted only a few seconds, but within days a mental battle had been initiated that continued for several months. Upon returning home, I encountered the most severe form of mental oppression and depression in my life. For several days I blamed it on tiredness, then as days turned to weeks, I placed the blame on being overworked, but as weeks turned to months, my desire to study, pray, fast, and preach became void, and I increasingly wanted to run away from it all and said I was *burned out*. Notice my excuses: tiredness, overwork, and burnout. That was the common rational explanation. In reality, I was under a serious attack of some spiritual power that was oppressing, harassing, and attempting to control my thinking.

It finally became so intense that while preaching one hot July in a white tent in Alabama, I stopped preaching and told the seven hundred to seven hundred fifty attendees that I was fighting a terrible battle and needed God to deliver me from it. After giving an altar invitation, I was headed to the church on the hill to change out of my wet clothes when a group of about sixteen of my closest friends said, "You are not going anywhere until we pray for you!" They grabbed the bottle of anointing oil and drenched my hair, laid hands upon me, and prayed with such energy and force that I began laughing—not out of disrespect, but out of what this scene must look like to the Lord. As I arrived minutes later in the pastor's office, I looked into the mirror and laughed so hard when I saw my greasy hair, disheveled shirt, and the sawdust from the tent floor covering my pants legs.

When departing that night, a precious friend said to me, "You did the right thing. Now the enemy has nowhere to hide because you exposed him to the light!" I have had many years since my freedom from depression to think about what it means to *expose it to the light*. This spiritual principle is the first in the foundation of your personal freedom—exposing what is hidden to the light.

Our adversary is connected to darkness. Spiritual ignorance is a form of darkness. The common Greek word for "darkness" in the New Testament is *skot'os*, from a word that literally and figuratively means to be "shady or obscure." Darkness is a result of a lack of or the omission of light. Satan's kingdom is called the "power of darkness" (Col. 1:13). There are demonic entities that are identified as "the rulers of the darkness of this age" (Eph. 6:12). Those who work in cooperation with evil are called the "works of darkness" (Rom. 13:12). The night is the time when sinners and sin are released at a greater measure than the day, because "men loved darkness rather than light" (John 3:19).

On the other hand, light is linked to God and His kingdom. Beginning with Creation, a supernatural light first appeared in the darkness, even before the sun, moon, and stars were created (Gen. 1:3, 16). Christ was present in the beginning with God and was that first light of creation in Genesis 1:3. John spoke of this light when he wrote, "The light shines in the darkness, and the darkness did not comprehend it" (John 1:5). The Greek word for "comprehend" is *katalambano*, which is from two words—*kata*, meaning "a dominating force," and *lambano*, meaning "to grab hold of or to seize control of." Combined, these two words mean, "to grab hold of something and to suppress it." The enemy would attempt to seize the light and suppress it from entering your mind and spirit, but when any light shines in any dark place, the light always, and I do mean always, overpowers the darkness, and the darkness cannot control the light. As children of light (Eph. 5:8) we can overpower darkness through Christ

Your very first process—or first step—to receiving physical, emotional, and spiritual help from any bondage, including private wars, is to understand that the bondage, emotional prison, and spiritual struggles that entangle you in your private life must be exposed to the light before you can receive help. This *light* begins by first acknowledging that you have a problem, an addiction, and sin nature that is out of control. You will never be free until you admit you are in need. For example, there were two thieves on the cross— one on either side of Christ. One man was rebuking and the other was repenting. The latter admitted he was guilty and asked Christ to remember him (Luke 23:42). When something is dismembered, it is taken apart or torn apart. In a sense, to be remembered could imply to put something together. By confessing he needed redemption through Christ, the thief was asking to be put back together again—made whole—even in his death!

Darkness cannot hide in the light. You will be relieved when you finally say, "I have a bondage, and I need God's help." The noose is loosed, the chain is weakened, and the prison door is shaking. Then there is the moment of confessing your sin and asking the blood of Christ to cleanse you (Eph. 1:7). The removal of sin purges the conscience and through faith releases guilt and condemnation (Rom. 8:1). Following this action, we are then to, "Lay aside every weight, and the sin which so easily ensnares us" (Heb. 12:1), which includes also separating from individuals and people who are breeders of disobedience, holders of chains, and bondage makers.

SET FREE—INDEED

Christ came to set men free. We read: "Therefore if the Son makes you free, you shall be free indeed" (John 8:36). The Greek word for "free" here is *eleutheroo*, which means "to liberate" and figuratively means to "exempt a person from any type of liability." Prior to making this statement, Christ said, "You shall know the truth, and the truth shall make you free" (v. 32). This word *know* has a variety of meanings, but it can also refer to knowing a person in an intimate manner. Since Christ Himself is "truth" (John 14:6), then to "know the truth" is more than having a head knowledge of Christ; it is to have a relationship with Christ. Through your relationship with Christ, you are released and made free from sin. Through the discipline of the Word you are free *indeed*. Deliverance gets the bondage out of you, and discipline keeps it out of you.

Discipline means to guard your eyes, ears, mind, spirit, and any entry point from an invasion of unwanted people, pictures, and information. The ability to sin has always been in the earth since Adam's fall, but the availability to sin has become more accessible. With cable, satellite, the Internet, iPads, iPhones, and instant pictures and technology, the ease in which one can step from imagination to image is with the touch of a screen. When Delilah tricked Samson, we read where she fastened his hair "with the pin." When he awoke and fled, he "went away with the pin of the beam, and with the web" (Judg. 16:14, KJV).

In our technology-driven world today, with a *pin number* and access to the World Wide Web, our minds have become the battleground. It was David who said, "The LORD my Rock, who trains my hands for war, and my fingers for battle" (Ps. 144:1), referring to the sword and the bow. In our generation we should make this verse our prayer, as it is our hands and fingers on computers, e-mailing and using remotes that can click us with one touch into an image or words that will pave a path for a private demon. It is the blood of Christ and the Holy Spirit who help discipline the believer and help in our weaknesses (Rom. 8:26–27).

CHAPTER 8

CAN SATAN KILL ME
OR MY FAMILY?

❧ ❧

I HAVE A MINISTER friend (whom I will leave nameless) who related an interesting story to me. At the time she had an international ministry that was seen globally on television, with as many as eight thousand attending events and conferences. One morning while walking through the house, a voice spoke in the ears of my friend and said, "I am going to kill you." Turning to see if someone was in the house, she realized it was the voice of the enemy, and it brought a chill and caused a weakness in her body. For several days following, a terrible foreboding of death filled the air. However, to counter the voice and the darts of death, she began to pray, fast, and take the Lord's Supper (Communion) daily.

The events of the following weeks were things that would make a good script for a Hollywood thriller. Part of it involved the plane she used to fly from meeting to meeting. On several occasions the plane began experiencing difficulty, including one occasion in which the fuel lines quit delivering fuel to the engines. Another time the pilot announced engine failure and could not land at a close airport as ice was in the air, and ice can easily bring a plane down. Only her continual prayer brought a miracle in the air, and the plane landed safely. There were several incidents that I will not share that occurred over the next six months—all of them presenting a possible physical threat to the life of the minister.

Can Satan take the life of a believer or of members of that believer's family? There is no doubt that there are seasons in which *death assignments* are set for a family or a family member. For example, King Saul was the father-in-law to David, who had been anointed to be the future king of Israel. Saul's jealousy of David opened a door for an "evil spirit" to torment Saul's mind, and this translated into Saul attempting to kill David on numerous occasions. The old king became obsessed with the idea of removing David, because in Saul's mind, his sons were assigned to replace him after his death. Only when the evil spirit controlled Saul did Saul throw javelins and attempt to take David's life. (See 1 Samuel 16:14–19:9.) Notice that Satan used a person—Saul—to plan the assassination strategy against David. Any evil spirit without a human body to dwell in is completely limited to what it can do.

After Christ's birth Herod sent soldiers to slay all children under the age of two, hoping to kill the future king of the Jews (Matt. 2:16). When Christ returned from His forty days of being tempted of the devil, He preached His first message in His hometown of Nazareth. It stirred the hometown folks to the point of attempting to push Christ off a cliff (Luke 4:29). On another occasion, while He was ministering in Jerusalem, the religious opposers of Christ considered stoning Him, but Christ escaped from their hands (John 10:31–39). The New Testament reveals several secret plots to remove Christ from public ministry—all planned by the religious hierarchy—but each time they failed (Matt. 21:46; Mark 12:12; John 7:30; 10:39). When the time came for Christ's redemptive assignment to be fulfilled by His death on the cross, He informed His disciples that the prince of the world was coming, but he had "no hold" on Him (John 14:30, NIV). The Amplified sums up the meaning of this statement this way:

> I will not talk with you much more, for the prince (evil genius, ruler) of the world is coming. And he has no claim on Me. [He has nothing in common with Me; there is nothing in Me that belongs to him, and he has no power over Me.]
>
> —JOHN 14:30, AMP

Christ was enlightening His followers concerning the events that would follow within a few hours. Christ would pray until His sweat became as drops of blood as He agonized in the Garden of Gethsemane (Luke 22:44). He was arrested, stood trial, was beaten with a Roman whip, and was later crucified. Christ wanted His closest disciples not to think that Satan had finally gained the upper hand, because His death was in the plan of God and not in the plan of Satan. Christ would "lay down His life and take it back up again" by the will of the Father, not by the design of Satan! (See John 10:18.) Only when Christ was willing to die was death able to gain a final blow. However, even death was not prepared for the resurrection, because Christ kicked the bottom out of the grave and came out swinging the keys of death and hell, announcing that all power was given Him in heaven and earth (Matt. 28:18; Rev. 1:17–18).

WHO HAS AUTHORITY OVER DEATH?

Prior to the crucifixion Satan appears to have had some form of limited authority over death. This is seen in the events surrounding

Job. This righteous man was surrounded by a supernatural hedge that prevented any form of satanic assault on Job's possessions, family, or his health. When the hedge was removed, Satan seized or destroyed all the livestock, slew Job's ten children in a windstorm, and later came back requesting to attack Job physically. (See Job chapters 1 and 2.) In Satan's request to mount the second wave of attacks, we read:

> So Satan answered the LORD and said, "Skin for skin! Yes, all that a man has he will give for his life. But stretch out Your hand now, and touch his bone and his flesh, and he will surely curse You to Your face!" And the LORD said to Satan, "Behold, he is in your hand, but spare his life."
>
> —JOB 2:4–6

Notice that the Lord instructed Satan to "spare his life." Without the supernatural hedge of protection, it appears the adversary would have been able to strike Job to the point of death. However, Satan was put under restrictions by God Himself. Even through Job was smitten with a flesh-rotting disease (Job 2:7–8; 7:5), he survived this terrible test and lived a total of one hundred forty years after the attacks, seeing his children, their children, and even four generations of descendants (Job 42:16).

With the death and resurrection of Christ, the Lord seized Satan's authority over death. One of my favorite passages dealing with Christ defeating death is found in Hebrews 2:14–15:

> Inasmuch then as the children have partaken of flesh and blood, He Himself likewise shared in the same, that through death He might destroy him who had the power of death, that is, the devil, and release those who through fear of death were all their lifetime subject to bondage.

Let's consider the question, "Can Satan take my life or the lives of my family members?" There is no question that the adversary will attempt to create circumstances in which a believer's life can be taken prematurely. When Peter drew his sword and cut off the ear of Malchus while the soldiers were arresting Jesus, Peter could have been arrested at that moment and could have been crucified alongside Christ, as Malchus was a servant of the high priest (John 18:10). However, Jesus destroyed the *evidence* that would have been used to accuse Peter when He placed the ear back on the head of the man who was assaulted. Satan had desired Peter to sift him as wheat, and this was no doubt a part of the strategy (Luke 22:31).

Notice the number of times when Paul was close to death. The apostle was stoned in the city of Lystra and left for dead (Acts 14:19) but was raised up when the disciples gathered around him in prayer (v. 20). He was severely beaten and chained in prison, but God sent a midnight earthquake and initiated the first "jailhouse rock," setting the prisoners free (Acts 16:23–37). Paul later faced the possibility of the ship he was on crashing into rocks and drowning the crew (Acts 27), and after escaping to an island with the entire crew of survivors, Paul was bitten by a deadly viper. He shook it off into the fire and felt no harm (Acts 28:3). On numerous occasions the life of Paul was in danger to the point of death—but in every instance he escaped.

Toward the conclusion of Paul's ministry in Rome he was arrested, placed in prison, and died by beheading. Did Satan finally succeed in killing this faithful apostle? Not according to Paul. In his final letter to Timothy Paul wrote:

> For I am already being poured out as a drink offering, and the time of my departure is at hand. I have fought the good fight, I have finished the race, I have kept the faith.
>
> —2 TIMOTHY 4:6–7

Paul had escaped numerous life-threatening circumstances, yet in this moment of his life he was "ready to be offered," a term that is similar to the Old Testament sacrifices that were placed on the altar. He was laying down his life as the ultimate sacrifice and offering for the cause of Christ. Could not the Lord have sent an angel to release Paul, as had occurred when the angel of the Lord released Peter from prison (Acts 12:6–11)? The answer may be found in that Christ predicted Peter would live to be an old man (John 21:18), and at the time of Peter's arrest and death threat he was still young and had many years remaining in ministry. This prophetic word of Christ outweighed any form of death threat against Peter, and the angel released Peter to continue fulfilling God's purpose. In Paul's case he was an older man and felt his assignment was complete. Therefore he asked for no intercession from God for his release, but he was ready to depart this life and enter the eternal, heavenly kingdom. Christ could not be arrested and slain without His willingness to submit, and Paul was spared until the time he said his departure was at hand and he was ready for the journey.

When Saints Want to Go Home

This is perhaps difficult for family members to understand, but a believer can *will to live* or *will to die*. I know of several occasions when the church family would join in prayer for a fellow member and believer to be raised up from a bed of sickness, yet that person passed. In some instances it was learned late that in private the believer had told close friends that he or she was *tired of the battle* and desired to go home to be with the Lord.

My own father lived a healthy strong life until he entered his seventies, when he battled diabetes. Despite the fact he had prayed for thousands of people who received a definite healing touch, he himself suffered in the latter years of his life, requiring dialysis three times a week. His doctor was going to place a feeding tube in his body to assist in receiving nourishment for his body. He told the doctor and Mom, "Don't let them put that tube in me to keep me alive. I'm weary, my body is worn out, and I am ready and excited about going home to be with the Lord!" At that point we all knew Dad had *willed* his destiny from earth to heaven. All of the prayers and intercession that could fill up a sanctuary are void once the will of a person being prayed for changes from *keep me on earth* to *I'm ready for heaven.*

Never view the departure of a believer to heaven as some defeat. I have always said, "You cannot threaten a believer with the idea of going to heaven!" Years ago a woman who was married to an alcoholic was continually harassed for her Christian faith. One Sunday morning the husband demanded her to stay home or he would shoot her and kill her. In arrogance he demanded a response from her concerning his death threat. She replied, "If you shoot me, I'm going to heaven, and if you don't, I am going to church!" She went to church. She wasn't threatened with the thought of going to heaven, which is the ultimate *high*.

WHO HAS THE KEYS OF DEATH?

If Satan still retained the keys of "death and hell," then he could possibly control the angel of death and kill whomever he wished whenever he wished. Herein is an important point. Don't you think that if he had this authority, he would have killed you a long time ago, long before you discovered your destiny, before you entered the ministry, before you made a difference as a soulwinner, impacting lives around you? Most ministers who have a global ministry can look back to one event in which their lives were almost taken before the time of their calling to God's work. The day my father, Fred Stone, was born on a cold snowy day in West Virginia, the midwife who assisted in delivering him carried him outside in a blanket in the snow. When my grandfather arrived with the coalfield doctor,

Dr. Hatfield, the midwife was screaming, "This is my baby…the Lord has given me this baby!" Dad's mom was holding onto the door frame, yelling to her husband, William, "Get her! She has the baby." If Granddad Stone had been ten minutes later, Dad would have died in the snow and cold.

Many years later in 1962, my mother and dad were in a serious car accident outside of Elkins, West Virginia. Dad was traveling about fifty-five miles an hour and topped a hill where he slammed into a car that was in the road without any brake lights. Dad bent the steering wheel across the drive shaft, and Mom's head broke the windshield and her kneecap was crushed by impact with the dashboard. At their feet lay their two-year-old son in a pile of broken glass. Mom thought the lad was dead, and a great sorrow swept over her. When the fellow began crying for his shoe that had come off his foot by the impact of the crash, Mom knew he was OK. I was the little fellow that survived an impact into the dashboard. Dad and I discussed this accident many times, and prior to his journey to heaven he reminded me, "Son, when we had that car accident, I was starting a new church in West Virginia, and I thought the enemy was trying to hinder my ministry as the accident set me back awhile. However, I now believe you were the ultimate target, because your ministry has gone around the world, and my work centered just in small local churches."

When my sister Diana was young, the doctor gave her penicillin, not knowing she was allergic to the drug. The reaction was so severe that Mom and Dad were uncertain if she would survive. Prayer became the weapon of war to defeat this physical battle between life and possible premature death.

Many of the early healing revivalists of the late 1940s and 1950s had stories of their own miraculous deliverance, which became a motivation for the compassion they felt toward the sick and suffering. This was before the days of advanced medicine and surgical procedures used by today's medical professionals, and faith in God was, at times, your only possible solution for a miracle! Numerous stories could be recounted demonstrating how close a person came to death—yet survived through prayer and intercession.

It is important for a believer to understand that the keys (or authority) of death are no longer in the control of the kingdom of darkness. The door of heaven does not open on this side of heaven, but from the inside, where Christ has the key to open the door of eternity and welcome His children into the kingdom of heaven! With Christ controlling the key of hell, He can shut the door to this underworld of the departed when you receive Him in a redemptive covenant. He will keep you out of the land of eternal damnation. Holding the keys of death, He alone determines when and how you will depart this life. Death, however, is an appointment. You may live a short life or a long life, but at some point your life will end: "It is appointed for men to die once, but after this the judgment" (Heb. 9:27). The word *appointed* refers to a moment that is reserved and laid up for a particular time. If Christ should delay His return, we will all die in the future. Yet we must never be concerned about Satan's authority over death, as he has been stripped of his authority by the resurrection of Christ.

THE MAIN THING

We must remember that Satan comes to "steal, and to kill, and to destroy" (John 10:10). He will certainly do what is necessary to disrupt your life and your assignment. Christ taught us to pray that God's will would be done on earth as it is in heaven (Matt. 6:10). Being in God's will does not prevent trouble, trials, and, at times, even suffering, as biblical prophets and apostles can testify to, but being in God's will gives the Father the opportunity to intervene on your behalf. I am not blessed because I am exempt from trouble, but I am blessed because I keep surviving the attacks of the enemy!

Being in God's will is to walk in His assignment for you and for you to follow the written Word of God for your daily life, using the spiritual principles established by Christ and the apostles. Believers can fight any spiritual battle with confidence when they know they have followed the will of God for their lives. The will of God is discovered through prayer and study of the Word and by following the doors God opens in your life. Christ was never intimidated by Satan or the forces of darkness, as He knew He was doing the will of His Father in heaven.

The next chapter will answer questions concerning the will of God

CHAPTER 9

DOES SATAN KNOW THE
WILL OF GOD FOR ME?

I AM ASKING THIS question in a broad manner, because Satan can only be in one place at one time. When a believer uses the name *Satan*, it refers to the entire members of his dark kingdom, not just to Satan himself. This is why I often speak of the *enemy* or the *adversary*. Your spiritual enemy and adversary could be demonic spirits or people motivated by evil. One common question I have been asked during years of evangelistic ministry is, "Does Satan know the will of God for me?" Before answering this question, let us establish some important facts.

He Knows What Has Been Written and Spoken

The first biblical prophecy is about six thousand years old and was given by God Himself after Adam and Eve sinned in the Garden of Eden. God said that the seed of the woman would bruise the head of the serpent (Gen. 3:15). After this prophecy was made known, the adversary immediately went after the sons of mankind, especially the oldest sons. Eve conceived two sons, Cain was the oldest, and Abel was the youngest. In a fit of jealousy over an offering, Cain slew his brother and became the first murderer. With Abel dead and Cain marked by God, Satan thought he secured a defeat. However, Seth replaced Abel as the third son of Adam and carried on a righteous lineage through his descendants (Gen. 4:25). Generations later Isaac had twin sons—Esau, the eldest, and Jacob, the youngest. The oldest sold his birthright and lost his blessing to the youngest (Gen. 25; 27:36). Jacob would enlarge the family with twelve sons. Reuben, being the firstborn, would normally be given the rights of the family blessings and birthrights. However, Reuben lost his birthright after he defiled his father's bed by sleeping with his father's concubine (Gen. 49:3–4). From Eden to the time when the enemy sought to slay Christ after His birth, the devil knew the prophetic scriptures and knew a future person was assigned to bruise his head!

He Knows the Revealed Prophetic Scriptures About Himself

The first predicted defeat of the old serpent, the devil, is found in Genesis 3:15. The second major prediction came through Isaiah the prophet in Isaiah 14, where the doom of Lucifer is revealed. Isaiah predicted that he would be: "Brought down to…the lowest depths of the Pit" (Isa. 14:15). This information was passed down for hundreds of years and was known in the demonic realm. Luke 8:31 reveals that the demons in the man of Gadera prayed that Jesus would not "command them to go out into the abyss." The Greek word for *abyss* is translated as the "bottomless pit" in Revelation 9:1–2. Thus these spirits knew their final doom hundreds of years before Christ began His public ministry. Certain types of odd-looking creatures are bound in the bottomless pit and will be released for a season during the Tribulation. (See Revelation 9.) The obituary of Satan was written more than nineteen hundred years ago by John in Revelation 20, who predicted Satan's final destiny would be the "lake of fire" (v. 10).

GOD REVEALS HIS WILL SUDDENLY

I was studying the lives of the ancient patriarchs when I noticed something that I had never observed before. At times the will of God was made known before a person's birth or early in that person's life, and a battle often ensued after God's will was publicly discussed or announced. However, when the time for the will of God to be fulfilled arrives, it always arrives suddenly and, at times, unexpectedly. I believe the reason for this swift fulfillment was to prevent the enemy from having time to plot disruption of the assignment.

Joseph was given a prophetic dream as a teenager concerning his destiny. At age seventeen he was sold as a slave, landed in Egypt working in a rich man's house, was falsely accused of adultery, and subsequently spent years in the king's prison. In one day he was brought out of the jailhouse to interpret Pharaoh's dream, and within one hour he was moved from the prison to the palace as Pharaoh's second in command. His exaltation from a prisoner to a prince occurred so fast that the enemy had no opportunity to set another trap and snare Joseph from his destiny!

Moses slew an Egyptian at age forty and became a fugitive

from the Egyptian law enforcement, which sought to kill him. His journey landed him in the heart of the Midian desert, where he became a shepherd for a man named Jethro. After forty years in the wilderness Moses received a sudden visitation and suddenly returned to Egypt to withstand the stubborn Pharaoh. When the Egyptian magicians began pulling tricks out of their bags and imitating the miracles of Yahweh, Moses's God wore these fakers out. They could not compete with this sun-tanned desert shepherd, who said that a burning bush told him to, "Let My people go!"

David spent much of his early life, from age seventeen to thirty, being chased through the desolate Judean desert like a deer by a hungry hunter. In this case he was the deer, and his father-in-law was the hunter. This chase continued off and on for thirteen years, until finally Saul was slain in battle. In one day Judah set David up as their king. He went from the desert to the throne within twenty-four hours.

Prior to David's death a coup occurred in the kingdom. One of David's rebellious sons declared himself as his father's replacement when David died. Another of David's sons, Solomon, was only a lad and was not considered in the contest for king, but after Bathsheba interceded to David, Solomon was placed on the king's mule, anointed with holy oil by the true high priest, and was proclaimed as king. David was king for forty years, and this transfer to Solomon occurred within twenty-four hours. The kingdom's leadership shifted without giving the enemies of David any time to prevent the process.

As another example, God knew that in the future, the Jews in the 127 provinces of Persia would come under a death sentence from a Hitler-like personality named Haman. The Lord set up a Jewish orphan girl in a beauty contest and gave her favor with the king. On a chosen day Queen Esther broke Persian protocol and entered the king's chamber to expose the death plot of Haman. This deceiver and his ten sons were hung on the gallows Haman had prepared for Mordecai. The execution was so swift that the adversaries of the Jews were stunned and backed away from the decree to annihilate the Jewish race in the Persian Empire.

Look at other major prophetic events that unfolded in just one day. The church was born in one day on the feast of Pentecost (Acts 2:1–4). The nation of Israel was reestablished by a United Nations declaration. However, the announcement was proclaimed by Ben Gurion in Israel, and the nation was reborn between May 4 and 15, 1948. The city of Jerusalem was divided between Jordan and Israel until the 1967 Six-Day War, when, on the third day of the war at ten o'clock in the morning, Jerusalem fell into the hands of Jewish soldiers; today it is the biblical capital of Israel.

We receive bits and pieces of God's will for our lives often like pieces of a puzzle that must fit together to form the picture. Paul said, "We see through a glass, darkly" (1 Cor. 13:12, KJV). It is possible that God reveals His purpose—some call it *your destiny*—in bits and pieces because if He were to reveal the whole picture, you would be overwhelmed with the scene. You might be too afraid to flow in the path or so excited that you start running through stop signs and jumping roadblocks and end up missing His will due to your unrestrained zeal. When I was a teenage minister, the Holy Spirit revealed to me a seven-point outreach plan that I began to print on the back of a small thirty-two page book I had printed. Part of the outreach included media outreaches, which began as radio and later developed into a prophetic video series, and in time became a weekly telecast aired around the world.

As a young traveling evangelist at age eighteen or nineteen with an income ranging between six thousand to fifteen thousand dollars a year, if the Lord had told me that by age fifty-two my yearly television airtime budget would be close to four million dollars, I would have passed out and said, "What television airtime? I don't own a camera, studio, or a VCR!" Yet today we have built two ministry facilities and are constructing a gathering place and a future youth camp. I have discovered that God will not overwhelm you with cares of life, so He reveals His will gradually. When you complete one assignment, He will inspire you toward a second assignment, and then another. He will not lead you past your last assignment. If you have not completed the first assignment, don't expect the second one to drop out of the sky.

IF WE DON'T KNOW, THEN SATAN DOESN'T KNOW

Read these verses carefully:

> Likewise the Spirit also helps in our weaknesses. For we do not know what we should pray for as we ought, but the Spirit Himself makes intercession for us with groanings which cannot be uttered. Now He who searches the hearts knows what the mind of the Spirit is, because He makes intercession for the saints according to the will of God.
>
> —ROMANS 8:26–27

One of the believer's greatest weaknesses is not knowing *what* to pray for. We know *how* to pray—to the Father in Jesus's name (John 15:16; 16:23). We know who to pray to and where we target the prayer, but it is the *what* that restrains us. If we are uncertain of what to pray for, then certainly Satan is uncertain of what God's plans are for our lives! The reason the Spirit "makes intercession through groanings" is that there is a prayer language of the Holy Spirit that bypasses the human intellect (1 Cor. 14:14–15), and if the human intellect is unfruitful, then there is a strong possibility that the intercession of the Holy Spirit through your prayer life hinders the adversary from discovering the will of God for you. Another verse penned by Paul further expounds on this thought:

> For what man knows the things of a man except the spirit of the man which is in him? Even so no one knows the things of God except the Spirit of God. Now we have received, not the spirit of the world, but the Spirit who is from God, that we might know the things that have been freely given to us by God.
>
> —1 Corinthians 2:11–12

Praying in the Holy Spirit is a wonderful way to discover the will of God. Remember that the plan of the enemy is to pull you away from the path of truth into your own carnal desires and thus disrupt the ultimate purpose of God in your life. If we as believers don't always know what to pray for as we should, then the adversary certainly has no insight on something that only the Holy Spirit can reveal!

SATAN'S GREATEST TOOL— WRONG RELATIONSHIPS

While the adversary may not know God's will for your life, he is master at one strategy from his playbook that is effective to both distract you or to pull you away from God's perfect will. There is always a back door in your life that, if left unlocked, can be the opening for wrong relationships that can draw you like a magnet away from the center of God's will.

When you think of a *wrong person* in your life, you are possibly imagining a person who is very carnal or fleshly, sneaking in and slowly pulling you into the net as a spider web does a fly. However, I have learned that for dedicated believers, usually a wrong relationship is not some heathen cloaked in light who comes like a knight in shining armor. Most believers are on guard for such obvious, dysfunctional agents of deception and would never fall for such a monster. Don't be surprised if the wrong relationship is actually sitting in the same church with you and may be in the choir or the local youth group!

This is especially true with single youth. I preached my first message at my dad's church in Salem, Virginia, at age sixteen. By age eighteen I was traveling in three states conducting local revivals in churches, staying two to three weeks in some congregations. It didn't take long for me to discern that there were mothers and grandmothers who felt the highest *call* for their daughter or grand-daughter was to marry a *preacher*. Usually, when a mom invited this single fellow over for lunch or dinner, I knew the game—there was a single daughter or granddaughter who was also present for the occasion. Don't get me wrong—I was no model in looks (in fact, I looked like a bleached-out skeleton with baggy rags), but it wasn't about looks—it was about the ministry and getting that girl married to a minister as soon as possible!

From the time I was sixteen to about twenty, there were several young women whom I thought I would marry. However, after prayer and judging things from my spirit and not my flesh, something did not *click* with the idea of marrying them. I was in a four-week revival in Northport, Alabama, when I felt the real *click*, the inner knowing that I had met my life's soul mate—beautiful little Pam Taylor with her inspiring Southern accent. She has been literally everything I needed in a wife, mother, and ministry leader.

I have learned that if the enemy can't stop your vision, he will impart another vision in an attempt to create division, because anything with two visions will split the main vision. This is the purpose of wrong relationships, to pull you from the true dream and vision God has planted within your spirit. Any relationship (outside of your personal family) that continually drains you instead of pouring into you is a distraction to you. A true companion will always impart instead of tear apart, and will bless you and never curse you. Remember that *lust is blind* and *love is kind*. Fleshy soul ties will leave your tank on empty, feeling used and abused, broke, busted, disgusted, and not trusted.

Your entire destiny is tied to the will of God, and in order to defeat it, distract it, or delay it, the enemy will plant a tare in your field (Matt. 13:38), a goat in your flock (Matt. 25:32–33), a bad fish in your net (Matt. 13:47–48), or a Judas in the leadership! However, the Holy Spirit provides a gift of "discerning of spirits" (1 Cor. 12:10), enabling you to detect the inner motives of individuals. In this manner you can hedge in those God has assigned with you and hedge out the wolves in sheep's clothing (Matt. 10:16) and the distracters to God's purpose. A wolf may look and act like a sheep, but it cannot hide its wolf footprints as it walks. Believers should continually pray for the will of God to be revealed and are given that gift of prayer through the Holy Spirit (Rom. 8:26–28).

CHAPTER 10

WHAT IS THE GREATEST WEAPON
SATAN USES AGAINST A BELIEVER?

THERE IS A secret that the adversary hopes you never find out—the greatest single weapon he uses against a believer. To discover this weapon, we go back in time to the trial of Christ and His conversation with His disciple Peter. Christ chose twelve disciples, and perhaps the boldest and most outspoken was Simon Peter. Christ revealed that Peter would deny Him, and Peter replied, "Even if I have to die with You, I will not deny You!" (Matt. 26:35). The other disciples never denied Christ—they simply ran for their lives and went into hiding during the crucifixion! Peter, however, attempted to prove his loyalty when he took his sword and sliced off the ear of the high priest's servant (v. 51). Then he secretly entered the area where Christ's trial was being held. While warming himself by the night's fire, he was confronted and told that he was a disciple of the Nazarene. Peter denied this to the point of cursing in order to prove he was not a follower of Christ. Peter feared for his life. After Peter heard the rooster crow, he came to himself, left the area, and wept bitterly (vv. 69–75). Peter was guilt ridden and knew he had been unfaithful to his promise of never denying Christ.

At the resurrection, when Mary saw Christ alive, the angel of the Lord that had removed the grave stone enabling the women to look inside gave instructions for Mary to: "Go, tell His disciples— and Peter—that He is going before you into Galilee; there you will see Him" (Mark 16:7). Why was it important to specifically invite Peter to meet with the risen Messiah? When we read the narrative of events following, Peter was back in Galilee fishing when Christ showed up on the shore telling them to come and dine. While the text is unclear, it appears that Peter may have gone back to his family fishing business after making a *fool of himself* by saying he would never deny Christ and then denying Him. I have seen this fleeing occur when a good church member has a moral failure. That person often quits coming to church—not because he or she is living in the sin, but because that person is simply too humiliated and embarrassed by the failure to return to church.

After dining with the disciples, Christ asked Peter three times, "Do you love me more than these?" All three times Peter replied, "You know I love You." Each time Christ instructed Peter to "Feed My sheep" (John 21:15–17). It is significant that Peter denied the Lord three times (Matt. 26:34; Luke 22:34) and Christ required Peter to confess he loved Him three times. This was done in the sight of the ten other disciples, and I believe it was done to remove all doubt from the others that Peter truly loved Christ and was called to be an apostle. Certainly this was proven when Peter stood up on the Feast of Pentecost after the Spirit was poured out and preached a brief message, which converted three thousand Jews to the Messiah, adding the first three thousand Jewish converts to the Christian church.

What one weapon would be effective to cause an on-fire minister to quit the ministry and go back to working at a secular fishing business? What weapon would cause a good member to quit church and never return? What weapon is the greatest block to your worship, prayer life, and walk with God? The answer is one word that many believers have never explored but have experienced—the weapon of *condemnation*.

A POWERFUL WEAPON

Early in the ministry I discovered the difference between *conviction* and *condemnation*. The Holy Spirit "reproves" the world of sin (John 16:8, KJV). This word *reproves* is a word for *convict* or *convince* a person; it even carries the idea of rebuking a person for his or her error. When a person is convicted in a court of law, that person is declared guilty of the crime. We can only be delivered from our sins when we first acknowledge we are guilty we are a sinner. But the amazing aspect of God's heavenly court is that if you say you are innocent when you are guilty, you lie—but if you will admit you are guilty and confess your sin, you will be released and forgiven! Conviction *of sin* is different from condemnation *for your* sin. Condemnation as a spiritual meaning is the sense of guilt that follows a person after sinning. If a person is a believer and sins, there will be a *sense of remorse*, just as there was with Peter when he wept bitterly for his failure. This sense of sorrow is not a bad thing, as it indicates that the Holy Spirit is dealing with you and bringing your sin to light for the purpose of confession to Christ and cleansing (1 John 2:1). Once a believer has been forgiven of sin, a tool that Satan uses is *condemnation*, or holding the action over the believer in an attempt to prevent him from having confidence in himself and in God.

The *power of condemnation* is seen when feelings of condemnation accompany a believer who is attempting to offer prayer:

> My little children, let us not love in word or in tongue, but
> in deed and in truth. And by this we know that we are of
> the truth, and shall assure our hearts before Him. For if
> our heart condemns us, God is greater than our heart, and
> knows all things. Beloved, if our heart does not condemn
> us, we have confidence toward God. And whatever we ask
> we receive from Him, because we keep His commandments
> and do those things that are pleasing in His sight.
>
> —1 John 3:18–22

Spiritual condemnation impacts our confidence. Confidence produces a feeling of assurance. It is easy to spot a person who lacks confidence, especially in conversation. A person lacking confidence often points out his distresses, failures, and lack of friends, and he focuses in on the negatives surrounding his life and seldom accepts a challenge for fear he might not succeed. A confident person will take on any challenge, and if he fails, he will try again until he succeeds.

The power of condemnation is such a strong weapon in the arsenal of the enemy. The adversary certainly does not want you to understand how it works and how to defeat his mental darts.

Examples of Condemnation

The Holy Spirit convicts of sin, but once you are forgiven, He does not bring additional guilt or condemnation. Condemnation after being forgiven is evidence of the enemy playing on the minds of believers, hoping to make them feel a lack of God's love for them. They will say, "There is no way that God can still love me after I have fallen so low in the mire of sin." This will be followed by comments such as, "There is no way God would hear me pray, because I have failed Him." The third level concludes with, "I may as well give up and quit, because I have ruined my life and the lives of my family members." All of this is caused by the weapon of condemnation.

This occurs especially when a noted minister falls into a moral or spiritual assault such as adultery, drunkenness, or financial scandal. I know of one man, whom I consider a long-term friend, who encountered so many attacks of the enemy at one time that I wondered how one man could stand under the pressure. While under the pressure, he turned to fleshly ways to handle the stress and found himself divorced and bound by alcohol. Being a noted minister, the negative press releases only added to the guilt and condemnation. One day I was speaking to a close friend of his, who said, "He is so ridden with the guilt and condemnation of his past that he is unable to forgive himself." That is the result of condemnation. Condemnation does not always tell you that God cannot hear your prayer, but it makes you feel that you are not worthy to pray. One of the greatest battles for a woman who has had an abortion or a man who has had an extramarital affair is being able to forgive herself or himself for the failure.

John indicated that if we have condemnation in our heart, we have no confidence in our prayer, and we doubt that God is hearing us. This doubt transmits into unbelief. Any prayer prayed in unbelief cannot be answered, because the road to answered prayer is paved from heaven to earth by faith.

Condemnation is possible because we are unable to forget in the manner God forgets. Once we have been forgiven, the Almighty remembers our sins no more. Humans, however, not only can remember what was done, but they also can recall the details of the actions and words. This inability to erase the memories from the computer mainframe of the human intellect becomes a snare of entrapment for your own thoughts.

Mental recall is certainly a gift from the Creator. Without this unique ability you would never learn to speak, write, solve mathematical equations, or remember your children's names. Recall is priceless when remembering scriptures and using the divine Word of God for encouragement, instruction, and practical Christian living. Recall, however, is a stumbling block when a person has failed spiritually or morally. The images are printed on the mind like pictures on the pages of a book, and the reminder of the failure and sin is like a haunting voice from the past, whispering from deep within a person and retelling the events in slow motion. It is like a black-and-white motion picture without sound, replaying forgiven images for the purpose of condemnation.

How does a believer deal with condemnation once forgiven of sins?

DEALING WITH PET SINS

The writer to the Hebrew believers reminded them that great men and women of God had proceeded them and had become "a great cloud of witnesses" watching them (Heb. 12:1). He compared the present believers to those running a race and looking to win the prize at the finish line. His instruction was twofold. First, he said to, "Lay aside every *weight*, and *the sin* which so easily ensnares us" (v. 1, emphasis added). The Greek word for "weight" is *ongkon*, and it means what is *crooked* or *hooked*, meaning anything that is attached or suspended by a hook and hanging by its whole weight. It is used only here in the New Testament. In classical Greek it was used in the sense of swelling, tumor, or even pride. Its usual meaning was a heavy weight. In the context of this passage where the writer of Hebrews was referring to running a race, he was instructing believers to lay aside the weights and burdens that would weigh them down in their attempt to run and gain the prize.[1] Weights could be pride, unforgiveness, doubt, worldliness, and other carnal hindrances that weigh a believer down in his or her race to the finish line.

The writer then mentioned the "sin" that easily besets the believer. The King James Version reads, "...which doth so easily beset us." The phrase "easily beset" is also found only here in the New Testament. It means, "standing well around," or, more clearly, something that is near at hand and readily available. *Barnes' Notes* has a great series of commentaries on the meaning of this phrase:

> Passow defines it as meaning "easy to encircle." Tyndale renders it "the sin that hangeth on us." Theodoret and others explain the word as if derived from [peristasis]—a word which sometimes means affliction, peril—and hence, regard it as denoting what is full of peril, or the sin which so easily subjects one to calamity. Bloomfield supposes, in accordance with the opinion of Grotius, Crellius, Kype, Kuinoel, and others, that it means "the sin which especially winds around us, and hinders our course," with allusion to the long Oriental garments. According to this, the meaning would be, that as a runner would be careful not to encumber himself with a garment which would be apt to wind around his legs in running, and hinder him, so it should be with the Christian, who especially ought to lay aside everything which resembles this; that is, all sin, which must impede his course.[2]

For a runner to effectively run a race and have any opportunity to finish in first place, it would require removing any excessive baggage, loose clothing that could cause him to trip, and freedom in body, mind, and spirit to focus on the racetrack and how to set a pace in the race and finish strong. Notice that the writer of Hebrews did not use the term to lay aside the "sins" (plural) but the "sin" (singular)—a certain besetting sin. It refers to one single sin that a believer struggles with. For some it may be pride; for others, their tempers; and for others, an area of lust of the flesh or of the eyes. I have called this a *pet sin*, as it is a sin that is easily available and near a person, yet it becomes a distraction and a terrible weight when a believer is trying to stay focused on spiritual things. He knew that unless a person dealt with the weight and sin that bogs him down, he may never successfully complete the race.

In my library I have a collection of old books, some dating back to the sixteenth century and many from the days of the early "healing revival," a well-known revival that came to America from about 1948 to 1956. Among the books is a collection from one of the early revivalists called *My Besetting Sin!* It seemed to be an odd title for a well-known minister, but he used the Hebrew 12 passage as the main text. Without explaining what his besetting sin was, he gave a miniature discourse on the subject of laying aside the sin.

Years later after writing the book, his besetting sin became public knowledge when, prior to preaching under his big tent, he was arrested in a major city for driving under the influence of alcohol. He was bailed out and was told to confess before the congregation, but when he arrived, the people believed he had been set up by the police. Instead of confessing and asking for prayer for his own deliverance, he preached over top of his besetting sin, and a short time later, he suddenly passed away while in a hotel room in California. Some who personally knew him and traveled with him said they never knew he had this problem and were surprised when it surfaced. However, despite his love for God, which was genuine, and his gift to preach, which was powerful, his weight and sin defeated him toward the end of his life, costing him a powerful legacy.

A similar story was related to me by a fellow minster concerning a minister whom I knew of from childhood. My father said this man could quote hundreds of scriptures and had an amazing faith to pray for the sick. In a tent crusade in the early 1950s, with his own eyes my father saw this man pray for a man with a large goiter, and it instantly disappeared. This was accompanied by several people who were healed of eye trouble, including Dad's younger brother, William. In the late 1950s this man pastored a ten-thousand-member church in Pennsylvania. At one time it was the largest church in America, and his voice was heard over the radio on the East Coast.

Through a series of tragic events he divorced his wife and left his children to be raised by their mother in another state. He continued to pastor and eventually ended up living like a hermit in a small apartment in the back of the church. Because he suffered from depression, he turned to alcohol and only refrained from the substance when he knew he was going to preach. It was his confession before his death that struck my heart.

An evangelist friend visited him and asked him questions about his life. In response he made this comment: "For many years I have had a struggle in my flesh. However, I have never denied the Word of God, never denied the name of Jesus, never denied God's power, never denied Christ's saving blood, never denied the faith, and never turned my back upon God. May God remember this when I stand before Him." This was such a sad confession; he did many things right, but one thing wrong—he never got victory over his besetting sin. While I know of his sin, I will not be his judge—God alone is the Judge of all men, and only God knows the man's true spiritual condition at the moment of death and whether he made confession or repentance to God.

There are weights and sins that only God's power can deliver a person from, and there are other weaknesses that we are to "cleanse ourselves from all filthiness of the flesh and spirit" (2 Cor. 7:1). The word *filthiness* is used four times in the New Testament (2 Cor. 7:1; Eph. 5:4; James 1:21; Rev. 17:4). Oddly enough, four different Greek words are translated as *filthiness* in these four passages. The word used by Paul alludes to a stain, like a stain on a garment. He is referring to *sins of the flesh and spirit*. The fleshly sins are found in Galatians 5:19–21; they are self-explanatory and can be visibly witnessed in a person's words or actions.

Filthiness of the spirit, however, refers to those things on the inside that are not necessarily visibly seen by others. A person can hold bitterness, fear, anger, and unforgiveness, which defile and stain the human spirit, yet put on a smiley face and no one know the turmoil occurring inwardly.

All cleansing and forgiveness comes through Christ's blood. However, as believers we have the divine right to exercise authority over all of the powers of the enemy and to close doors that have been opened by our own choices. In no way is the writer to the Hebrews teaching that we can bring our own deliverance without Christ, but through Christ we can exercise the power to lay aside the weights and sins. One fact is clear. We will never remove what we enjoy and never cleanse what we permit. Willingness to be free must be mingled with the desire for freedom. When desire and willingness collide, then freedom is knocking at the door.

When Preachers Preach to Themselves

There have been noted ministers who preached powerful messages against sin and gave altar invitations with hundreds pouring to the front of a large auditorium and weeping with conviction. Years passed, and these same ministers were exposed in the very sins they were denouncing in others. Of course the cry of, "Hypocrite, hypocrite," filled the airwaves and was used to describe these men's ministries. Even the body of Christ questioned if the men ever really believed what they were preaching.

Being a fourth-generation minister and personally knowing hundreds of ministers, I can tell you a small secret about such men as mentioned above. Many times they are preaching to themselves. This may seem an odd enigma; however, when standing in the pulpit and preaching with unction from the Lord, they are actually providing temporary relief to their own spirits and minds. Often they leave the pulpit with a determination never to participate in that failure again. At times the minister may go for weeks or months without falling into the *pet sin*, and when the feelings begin to arise, they will reproach themselves by preaching the same convicting message to others to bring that conviction of the Spirit upon themselves. However, if the mental battle and the avenues of temptation are not removed, they can eventually succumb to the previous temptations.

When men experience a sudden failure, they are not necessarily *hypocrites*. They may have spent much of their lives serving Christ. A hypocrite would be a person who continually condemns others but is privately practicing the same sin they are condemning others for.

Remember that the same powerful word from God that set you free can also set free the very person preaching the message to you, as the Word of God is "quick [alive], and powerful [energized], and sharper than any twoedged sword" (Heb. 4:12, KJV). The Word of God divides the soul from the spirit, or separates the carnal man from the spirit man! This is why a believer can experience a refreshing in his or her mind after sitting under an anointed word from the Lord. The sword of the Spirit begins to cut away the clutter and the weights that are attached to the soul or mind of the listeners.

THE PROCESS OF TOTAL FREEDOM

For a believer to have total confidence in his approach to God, he must have a sense of the righteousness of God and confidence in his relationship with Him. All condemnation must be removed, and a believer must see himself or herself as a son or daughter of the Most High, someone who is loved by the heavenly Father and who has a covenantal relationship with Him. As believers we do not need to be taught the basic elements of repentance and forgiveness, because it was repentance that introduced us to the new covenant of redemption.

There are no words to express the feelings a sinner experiences when Christ forgives him of sin. The phrase coined by Christ—"born again" (John 3:3)—best describes the sense of a new lease on life, a new beginning. "Born again" can mean to *procreate a new person*. The Holy Spirit re-creates a new being from the inside out. This is the initial step of freedom. From experience we all know that a babe in Christ, or what we term a new convert, will often fail in some manner in his or her early walk with God, either through the works of the flesh or by not making the break from wrong influences.

Just as we would never expect from a newborn baby what we would expect from a teenager who has lived in our home for eighteen years, so too believers need to exercise patience with a newborn Christian. But as the believer grows, spiritual maturity must take place.

Christ initiates a freedom in our lives, but it is up to us to mature in our walk from a babe who drinks milk to an adult who eats spiritual meat (1 Cor. 3:2). As our growth continues, so does our level of freedom, in the same manner that an infant matures into a child, a child into a teenager, and a teenager into an adult with responsibilities. The longer you serve Christ, the more you will discover that there are *weights and besetting sins* that you will "lay aside" (Heb. 12:1). When looking back, you will be amazed at how much you grew in the "grace [favor] and knowledge of our Lord and Savior Jesus Christ" (2 Pet. 3:18).

Freedom can only be extended based upon the knowledge you have of your deliverer. When a teenager does something wrong or harmful, you will often say, "What were you thinking? You knew better." The fact is, all believers who know the Word and act contrary to it can be asked, "What were you thinking? You knew better."

TIRED OF ASKING GOD
FOR FORGIVENESS?

There are some in the Christian faith who believe that all sins—past, present, and future—are forgiven with one repentance, and thus a believer should never ask for the forgiveness of any sin in the future. This is actually contrary to the entire New Testament. Christ predicted that Peter would deny Him and informed Peter: "Simon, Simon, behold, Satan hath desired to have you, that he may sift you as wheat: But I have prayed for thee, that thy faith fail not: and when thou art converted, strengthen thy brethren" (Luke 22:31–32, KJV). The Greek word used here by Christ for *converted* means, "to revert or to go again; to return again." The same word is used by Peter when he gave instruction for the religious Jews to, "Repent therefore and be converted" (Acts 3:19). Christ interceded for Peter that his "faith should not fail" (Luke 22:32). If Peter lost his faith following his failure, he could turn so far away that he would never return.

The strongest messages of Christ's commandment to His own people to repent are found in the messages to the seven churches in the Book of Revelation. Seven times Christ demanded the church to repent, or else they would experience severe separation and judgment from Christ Himself (Rev. 2:5, 21–22; 3:3, 19). John wrote that we should not practice sin, but "if anyone sins, we have an Advocate with the Father" (1 John 2:1). When a believer falls into a sin as a true child of God, the conviction of the Spirit will follow the actions of that person, and a true child will return to the Father and seek cleansing to prevent his or her spirit from being stained by the sin.

The power of asking for forgiveness cannot be underestimated. A story I shall never forget came to me from a minister I knew who fell into the sexual sin of adultery with a married woman from his church. He said that each time he sinned, he would return to his office and pray for hours, vowing he would never do it again. But the seductive power of the woman would overwhelm him. For six months he would repeatedly sin, then beg for mercy, sin, and ask for forgiveness. He said, "One day I got up and said to myself, 'I am so tired of asking for forgiveness that I'm not asking anymore.'" That day he was caught with the woman, and in a few days he lost his church. Months later his wife separated from him.

He told me something profound: "As long as I was sincerely seeking God's help and wanted deliverance, God extended His mercy in my struggle. However, when I was overcome by my actions and chose not to turn to God, then God turned me over to being exposed." This should not give a false confidence to anyone who is secretly sinning and repenting, thinking that as long as you repent, you will never be exposed, for some individuals are exposed the first time they fall. I do believe, however, that God is merciful when a person is sincerely seeking His help on a consistent basis, because God is moved by humility and submission to His Spirit.

I have often wondered if God ever becomes weary of the same child asking for forgiveness from a struggle he is engaged in. Then I began to think about my own son and daughter when they come to me asking for forgiveness. I cannot refuse them, and I am proud they saw their error and are striving to do better. When Peter asked Christ how often he should forgive a brother who transgresses against him, he suggested, "Seven times?" Jesus answered to forgive seventy times seven, which totals four hundred ninety times. In actuality, Christ was emphasizing to Peter and all others that they should be willing to forgive an offending brother as often as necessary. To be released from conviction requires repentance, and to be released from condemnation requires knowledge. Paul wrote:

> There is therefore now no condemnation to those who are in Christ Jesus, who do not walk according to the flesh, but according to the Spirit.
>
> —ROMANS 8:1

In Romans chapter 8 Paul dealt with the struggle between the flesh and the Spirit. The flesh cannot understand the things of the Spirit, and the Spirit cannot abide with the things of the flesh. It is like mixing oil and water—they separate and never join. Condemnation will cease when we walk to please the Spirit of the Lord and not the flesh. The flesh is weird, because it begs to be fed, but once you feed it, then it begins to make your spirit man feel sick. Once you begin to feed the spirit man using the Word of God, prayer, worship, and fellowship with other believers, the flesh nature is brought under control to the will of the Spirit.

I have said for years that when the enemy comes to torment you of your past, remind him of his future. He is an unemployed cherub that was removed from his position as a worship leader in heaven, and he hangs with other losers called *fallen angels*. Remind him that his obituary is already written and his final destination is the lake of fire! When your sins are brought up, speak up and confess: "I am forgiven by the blood of Christ, and the accuser has no evidence against me in Christ's name!" Do not practice sin and pray for victory in every area of your life. But should you fall into a trap, immediately confess to God and ask Him to give you power not to succumb to the same repetitive sins.

THE BLANK PAGES

Since condemnation is Satan's greatest weapon against a believer, then forgiveness is the greatest counter weapon. The following story demonstrates this truth. Year ago I was ministering in Africa and met the sound man for one of the world's greatest missionary evangelists. He related this story to me:

> Years ago there was a great pastor and preacher who had served God for many years but fell into immorality and lost his ministry. For a period of time he lived in sin and

rebellion against God. Eventually he made his way to Christ, and his relationship with the Lord was completely restored. He was filled with remorse and shame for his failure and questioned how God would ever use him again.

One night he had a marvelous dream. He was standing in heaven where an angel had a book of his life, recording the detailed acts and events from the moment he received Christ until the moment of this dream. As the angel opened the book, there was a record written of each specific good event or act and the date on which it occurred. The angel would point to the page, read a good deed, and say, "This you did for the Lord." This was repeated numerous times. The fellow was becoming distressed, as he saw the time line in the book moving toward the day when he sinned and totally failed the Lord. He was fearful of what the angel would reveal and say.

When the angel turned the page where the date would have recorded his sin, it was blank. As the pages were turned, each page held no written record of the sin. When he asked, "Sir, why are these pages blank?", the angel replied, "This is what the Lord did for you!" Then the actual date in which he repented and was restored was recorded in the book, and the angel continued to read, "This you have done for the Lord."

Perhaps this is the literal meaning of Isaiah 43:25: "I, even I, am He who blots out your transgressions for My own sake; and I will not remember your sins." You can defeat the weapon of condemnation, knowing that true repentance leads to true forgiveness and the blotting out of your transgression!

CHAPTER 11

WHAT IS THE GREATEST WEAPON SATAN USES AGAINST A SINNER?

✧ ✧

I F WE SUBMITTED to a survey among Christians as to what they believed was the greatest weapon the adversary used against a sinner, we would receive numerous possible answers, often based upon what they perceive to be the main obstruction preventing their own unconverted family members from receiving Christ's redemptive covenant. Some would specify a particular sin or habit, or perhaps an addiction to drugs or alcohol. One word describes the spiritual condition of a sinner—*sin*. However, *sin* is more than the root word for the word *sinner*. Sin is described as any action contrary to man's and God's laws. Men call this a *transgression of the law*, while God identified disobedience to His commandments as *a sin*. When Cain slew his brother Abel, becoming the world's first murderer, God Himself used the word *sin* to describe

Cain's action (Gen. 4:7). The Hebrew word for *sin* means, "a transgression with a penalty associated with it." It is easy to say that the adversary's greatest weapon is sin. However, there is one aspect of sin that is actually his greatest tool.

The writer of Hebrews wrote concerning the hall of the heroes of the faith and mentioned Moses. He said, "By faith Moses, when he became of age, refused to be called the son of Pharaoh's daughter, choosing rather to suffer affliction with the people of God than to enjoy the passing pleasures of sin" (Heb. 11:24–25). The adversary has such success in retaining his control on the unsaved because of the *pleasure of sin*. The word *pleasure* commonly used in the New Testament can refer to a person living in extreme luxury for personal pleasure (James 5:5) or to using the flesh to gratify desires (Rom. 1:32, KJV).

Christ warned that the "pleasures of life" would choke out the growth of God's Word in a person's life (Luke 8:14). Paul also warned that in the last days men would be "lovers of pleasure rather than lovers of God" (2 Tim. 3:4). Paul wrote to Titus and told him that some believers in the past were "serving various lusts and pleasures" (Titus 3:3). In one of Paul's strongest discourses against sins of the flesh, he informed believers that not only do unrepentant sinners know that God will judge them for sin, but they take pleasure in their sins (Rom. 1:32, KJV). James spoke of rich men who used their wealth to live "in pleasure and luxury" while ignoring the needs of the poor (James 5:1–5).

Herein is an important fact to understand concerning sin. If the act of sinning had no pleasurable feelings connected with it, then the adversary would go out of business within a few weeks. The drug dealers would be penniless, and the nightclubs with bars would close their doors. The prostitutes would need to find another occupation, and the porn industry would cease from the Internet. The growers of cannabis would turn to farming fruits and vegetables for their incomes, and, in general, the sin industry would suffer a deadly blow. All of the above vices are generating billions of dollars in sin money globally because of one phrase: "the pleasure of sin."

If a Christian attempts to tell an average sinner that there is no pleasure in sin, that person was either converted in childhood or has been free from bondage for so long that he or she has forgotten that sin "feels good." If sin did not have that "feel-good feeling," it would not attract the flesh and would not lead men and women into its clutches and ensnare them. You can never convince a sinner that sin does not have a pleasurable feeling; you must remind that person in the firmest manner that its pleasures only last "for a season" (Heb. 11:25, KJV).

It Pays to Serve the Devil

The youth of this generation are being bombarded and reminded of the pleasure of sin without being reminded that "It pays to serve the devil"! Here is how it works.

The youth of today are being offered the latest drug that is being marketed by "pimps of pleasure" south of the border, but they are not being told that in six months they will be rushed to the ICU in a coma. At age eighteen they are excited to join the gang at college, free from the restraint of their parents, and party on weekends, drinking alcohol and getting that *buzz* effect. They cannot see that the following year they will be paralyzed in a car accident because they were drunk and visually impaired while driving back to the dorm from a local bar.

Then there is the issue of premarital sex. Since the pressure is on, a girl loses her virginity to a fellow she has known for only a few weeks, only to discover months later that she now carries one of several sexually transmitted diseases. In fact, public schools will not make the stats known, but in some states more than half the youth in the high schools already carry some form of sexually transmitted disease, which will cause great problems for them and their companions when they marry.

There have been great ministers of the gospel who entered chat rooms on the Internet and became acquainted with secular women, eventually meeting them in secret locations for a brief tryst. The final outcome was that the action was discovered and exposed, and the minister lost his ministry and family. So it is very evident that it does pay to serve the devil. The short-term payment is pleasure to the flesh, but the long-term payday comes when the party is over.

It is difficult for sinners to understand the end of the story when they fall spiritually and have only begun to "live." I have actually heard people say that one day down the road they want to serve the Lord—after they are married with children and are ready to settle down in a home and raise their kids in church. But right now they want to live a wild life of parties and pleasure and to experience freedom from any restraining ideologies that would limit their personal preferences for indulgences. What they cannot see through the dark blinders covering their understanding is that *the wild seeds they plant today will become the weeds in the garden of their life tomorrow.*

Satan Wants to Keep You From the Truth

The enemy does his best to keep a sinner from discovering one important simple truth about God. It sounds simple, but this truth is powerful, especially when dealing with a person whose bondage was an addiction to drugs and alcohol. Satan does not want you to know that you *can literally experience God's presence by feeling it!* I realize there are entire denominations that minimize the significance of having an *emotional spiritual experience.* In fact, in some of these churches any form of emotion being expressed in their worship services is banned or forbidden. Only an academic-type message is presented in the formal Sunday morning setting, which is presented to a group of rather stiff Christians who are anticipating dismissal by noon to beat the church across town to the restaurant. One of the possible reasons these types of nominal churches often have members who still participate in certain "acceptable Christian vices and habits" is because the feeling for sensual pleasure has never been replaced with the tangible feeling of the presence of the Holy Spirit. If I were the adversary, I would certainly hide the fact that God's presence can and should be felt not only from the sinner but also from these churchy types who give God a *weak* two-hour visit during seven days of their *week*.

I have known of individuals who were alcoholics and went to an altar to confess their sins, yet for years they remained alcoholics even though they were also an active member of a church. Their attendance was based upon a feeling of relief they acquired by removing the guilt of six days of sin by honoring God one day out of the seven. In such cases there is not a release of God's presence, rather just a rigid religious performance of classical type singing accompanied by a brief sermonette.

A boring, emotionless church service full of no-feeling religious rituals will never replace the feeling of the false high obtained from alcohol. The same is true of those bound by other addictions. How can a redeemed addict who is accustomed to tingling nerves from the feeling of drugs in the bloodstream sit for years in a power-less form of so-called Christianity and not expect to be drawn back into the desires of the flesh?

I know what some are thinking at this point, as I have heard the same repeated thought over the years—"We do not serve God by feelings, but we follow Christ by faith." Certainly this is true, as we "walk by faith, not by sight" (2 Cor. 5:7). However, neither should we avoid expressing our faith by using our God-given emotions. We cry at funerals, smile and hug our children, kiss our companion with an accompanying "I love you," and attend our favorite sports event and yell until we are hoarse. We become angry when receiving an unexpected bill in the mail and rejoice when an unexpected check arrives. Then we walk into a sanctuary and in the name of *reverence* sit silently like a group of adults would sit at a funeral. I remind people that *reverence is not deadness*, and in heaven God is not frightened by verbal praise, because His created angelic beings worship Him day and night (Rev. 4:8).

Check out this following series of comments. A minister was once rebuked by a person who criticized the music and worship of the youth in a church, asserting that, "God is not deaf!"

The minister reminded this person, "Neither is God nervous. Based on the Psalms, He seemed to enjoy hearing His people praise Him on musical instruments." The complaining person countered by saying, "Those who praised Him with music verses can only be found in the Old Testament."

The minister rebutted by saying, "The last time I read the Psalms, it was still a part of the Bible, and we are told in the New Testament that 'ALL Scripture is given by inspiration of God, and is profitable'" (2 Tim. 3:16).

The final argument was, "I've read the entire Bible, and nowhere in the Bible did Jesus ever shout, cry aloud, and jump up and down."

The minister replied, "You are right," to which a smile of delight broke across a face that had not smiled the entire time. He said, "You agree?", and the response was, "Certainly. But everyone whom Jesus touched and healed *did act that way*, so because He is touching these youth today, they are only reacting the same way the people reacted in the Bible."

There are many older individuals who are quite content with a two-hour Sunday morning program, preplanned on paper and acted out according to the set time. These church members must understand that of all the youth raised in the Christian faith, 66 percent will no longer be attending church by age thirty. Only 33 percent of teens attending church report that God and church will play a role in their lives once they are on their own. This loss equates to about eight hundred thousand youth leaving the church between their junior year in high school and their sophomore year in college.[1] There are thousands of churches in America whose pews are filled with a faithful remnant, and when these believers depart, there are few youth and couples filling the pews. Eventually these churches will either be closed or sold.

I want to make this clear: The Holy Spirit can be experienced and literally felt, and He should be felt in the life of a believer. We are told that the kingdom of God is not "eating and drinking, but righteousness and peace and joy in the Holy Spirit" (Rom. 14:17). Joy and peace are considered feelings; they are emotions and are manifestations of the kingdom of God within us.

DRUGS ARE THE COUNTERFEIT FOR THE SPIRIT OF GOD

Years ago, on two different occasions in two different states, I was speaking with businessmen who were former cocaine addicts. Both had a serious habit that had cost them thousands of dollars each week. I am thankful to say I never took any form of drugs and can serve as an example to demonstrate that a teenager can serve God and never fall prey to alcohol or drug addictions. I asked these men what it was like on cocaine and why it was so addictive. I then asked them what the key was to remaining free from such a powerful, addictive substance. I was stunned that they both gave me the identical same response, and I have heard the same answer given by former addicts on numerous occasions.

They both said that the drug ignited the pleasure part of the brain, and this was why it was so addictive. Then here was the part that stunned me. They both said that when they were converted to Christ, the moment they were baptized in the Holy Spirit and received the prayer language of the Spirit, they felt the exact same energy and force in their body that they experienced when they were high on the drug! In fact, both said that the feeling brought upon them upon receiving the power of the Holy Spirit was actually greater in measure than any high they experienced on any form of drug. Both men said the following: "I believe that this type of drug is a counterfeit to the power of the Holy Spirit. Satan came up with something to keep people high so they would never know the freedom in Christ and the power that is in the Holy Spirit!"

I don't expect the average Christian to understand their comparison, yet former drug addicts who are now under the control of the Holy Spirit certainly understand the need of a divine replacement feeling for the false feeling offered by man-made chemicals and drugs. What if somehow every person in America who was addicted to drugs or alcohol and living their lives for a dangerous pleasure could fully comprehend that their deliverance was possible through Christ and that the emotional highs could be replaced with true righteousness, peace, and joy? How would the knowledge that their Creator was more than a steeple on a church and a robed choir, but a powerful deity whose presence could be experienced change their perception of Christianity?

As long as the adversary can bind a sinner to the desire of pleasure for a season, he has maintained a most powerful spiritual weapon to keep that sinner in a personal prison. The lust for another high, another buzz, another mellowed-out feeling will keep the victim under the dominion of darkness. Once, however, the eyes of understanding are opened and the same person is permitted to taste of the power of the world to come, there is a flame of hope that will ignite in the heart and eventually burn the fetters off his soul and bring him into not just a mental agreement with Scripture, but also into an experience of freedom that can be felt.

The process begins by simply believing the promises and determining to turn from your captivity and ask God for His delivering power for your life.

Any unconverted individual should be reminded that the pleasure of sin is only for a season and that Satan has a payday coming, as the "wages of sin is death" (Rom. 6:23). I am reminded of the number of famous Hollywood celebrities and world-renowned singers and musicians who all died young during my own lifetime; some under fifty and others under forty years of age. Payday came when their hearts could no longer take the stress of the highs and lows of narcotics flowing in their bloodstream. They departed this life before they should when the adversary knocked on the door—John's pale rider called *Death* (Rev. 6:8) galloped into their homes and hotel rooms calling their names and shooting the arrows of death in their direction, ending their time on earth.

God Himself ensures that His followers experience pleasure in His presence—and not just for a season but for eternity! Job may give the best summary of the difference between serving the Lord and rejecting His love, when he wrote: "If they obey and serve Him, they shall spend their days in prosperity, and their years in pleasures. But if they do not obey, they shall perish by the sword, and they shall die without knowledge" (Job 36:11–12). David understood this truth when he penned, "You will show me the path of life; in Your presence is fullness of joy; at Your right hand are pleasures forevermore" (Ps. 16:11). As a former drug addict once said, "There is no high like the Most High!"

CHAPTER 12

THE TRUTH BEHIND SO-CALLED HAUNTED HOUSES

❦ ❦

W ITH THE TELEVISION remote in my hand, I was slumping in my brown easy chair in front of the television, switching satellite channels when my slumber was interrupted by a program in which an alleged psychic was introducing himself with a unique gift: the ability to communicate with the spirit of a departed loved one. Normally I never waste good "chilling-out time" on such a ludicrous claim until I heard the self-proclaimed link between the dead and the living announce that the spirit of Adolf Hitler was in his presence. This spiritual con man had amassed all sorts of electronic devices, including an infrared camera, high-speed digital video, and special gadgets that measured the room temperature and even some equipment he claimed could register the actual energy in a room or space.

In my opinion, his serious claim to consult the dead became a comic act, as every time the floor creaked or the wind blew through an old window pane, the people with him screamed out in fear, "Did you hear that?" Moments later a frightened fellow yelled, "I saw a dark shadow in the window!" The music accompanying their commentary only added to the spooky atmosphere emitting from the television, and the grainy, almost 1930s-looking film with the slightly green tint helped create a more sinister appeal for the curious viewer. While most devout Christians and especially biblically astute believers ignore these so-called reality programs, millions of youth and occult curiosity seekers are lured into these alleged documentaries, remaining glued to their chairs for every noise and possible ghostly image presented. Eventually some viewers make their own efforts through mediums and psychics to consult the dead in an attempt to imitate their psychic star and hear from the "other side." Often this contact is attempted in a setting with what is identified as an alleged *haunted house*.[1]

What Is a Haunted House?

A *haunted house* by definition is allegedly a home that is inhabited either permanently or occasionally by the disembodied spirits of a departed person. The *spirit* is often believed to have been a former inhabitant or a person who was familiar with the house or the property. What identifies a house as *haunted* is the strange and often unexplainable supernatural activity that allegedly occurs in or around the house. Some may believe only a small number of people believe in haunted houses. However, in a Gallup Poll conducted in 2005, it was revealed that 37 percent of Americans, 28 percent of Canadians, and 40 percent of the British citizens believe in the paranormal activity that occurs at a haunted house.[2]

There have been numerous reports of individuals who have lived in a house where paranormal activity occurred. Dwellers said they have heard bells ringing or voices in the night when no one was present. Others describe the clear sound of footsteps going up and down stairs, doors slamming and furniture moving by itself, breaking glass, and foggy-looking apparitions that suddenly appear in mirror reflections at times. What has enforced this belief is evidence from some cameras that have captured apparent apparitions on film, which have been described as a departed person's spirit that appears for some unknown reason. For many years, after closer examination, many of these so-called "spirit pictures" have turned out to be frauds and fakes, captured by an experienced photographer or a film developer manipulating negatives. However, there have been several occasions when the image was unexplainable and quite dramatic. These pictures and the stories of seeing these "ghosts" as retold by educated and respectable men and women only increase the interest in the supernatural, causing Hollywood to ride the wave of popularity, producing money-making movies on the paranormal, the supernatural, demons, and ghosts.

There is one thread that seems to tie together most of the so-called "haunting" research across the country and even in other nations. When detailed research is conducted concerning who lived in the house and the events surrounding their lives, there was often an unusual death, a violent murder, or some form of shedding of blood that occurred at or near the location. In other words, each location can be linked in some way to *death* and is often linked to some form of the *shedding of blood*. This is important, as you will discover in this section of the book.

A DEPARTED LOVED ONE— OR A FAMILIAR SPIRIT?

If these old houses are "possessed" by some type of a spirit, then the real question become this: Is this the spirit of a departed person, or is it actually a *familiar spirit,* which the Bible warns against seeking? Scripture is clear as to what happens when a human being passes away. We are all a tripartite being of a body, soul, and a spirit (1 Thess. 5:23). At death the spirit and soul depart the body, and the body returns to the dust of the earth (Gen. 3:19; Eccles. 12:1–7).

When the early patriarchs died, the Bible teaches that at death they "gave up the ghost" and were "gathered unto their fathers" (Gen. 25:8, 17, kjv; 35:29, kjv). The old English word *ghost* used in the 1611 King James translation referred to the inner spirit of each individual—the part that is eternal. When the human spirit departs from the physical body, it retains a similar appearance and feature of the physical body that it indwelt (1 Cor. 13:12). "Giving up the ghost" is a phrase used to describe the *departing of the soul and spirit from the physical body.* After the spirit departed, the early patriarchs were said to have been "gathered to his people," which is a term used concerning Abraham, Isaac, Jacob, and Aaron (Gen. 25:8; 35:29; 49:33; Deut. 32:50). This indicated that their spirits were all gathering in one place, which in the Old Testament time was a chamber called *Sheol,* the world of departed spirits, somewhere under the earth (Luke 16:19–26). This same concept of giving up the ghost is recorded by three Gospel writers the moment Christ breathed His last breath and cried, "It is finished." At that moment He "gave up the ghost" (Mark 15:37, kjv; Luke 23:46, kjv; John 19:30, kjv). Some suggest that this phrase simply means the people simply ceased to be or quit breathing. However, let's examine what occurred with Christ after He died.

First, one of the two dying thieves beside Christ prayed that Christ would remember him when Christ entered His kingdom. Christ replied, "Today you will be with Me in Paradise" (Luke 23:43). Both Christ and the thief died before the sun set that day. Christ had previously informed His disciples that, "As Jonah was three days and three nights in the belly of the great fish, so will the Son of Man be three days and three nights in the heart of the earth"

(Matt. 12:40). Some who do not believe the soul and spirit leave the body at death say this phrase, "heart of the earth," means Christ would be in the grave for three days and nights. However, other scriptures tell you what Christ actually did when His "ghost" (soul and spirit) departed from His body. He actually descended to the paradise chamber (Abraham's bosom) to preach to those spirits imprisoned under the earth!

> Now this, "He ascended"—what does it mean but that He also first descended into the lower parts of the earth? He who descended is also the One who ascended far above all the heavens, that He might fill all things.
>
> —Ephesians 4:9–10

What was the purpose of Christ's descent into the lower chambers of the earth? Peter wrote:

> For Christ also suffered once for sins, the just for the unjust, that He might bring us to God, being put to death in the flesh but made alive by the Spirit, by whom also He went and preached to the spirits in prison.
>
> —1 Peter 3:18–19

After Christ cried, "It is finished!", from the cross (John 19:30), His spirit descended into the chamber for the righteous as He preached to the spirits of the righteous dead. We must remember that these spirits in a place called "Abraham's bosom" (Luke 16:22) would have included Abraham, Isaac, Jacob and his sons, David, the prophets, and all Hebrew people who had died in a covenant relationship with God under the Law of Moses. Many of these individuals would have lived under the Law of Moses for fifteen hundred years. Thus, Christ would have preached a three-day message of God's plan of redemption and revealed what He had accomplished on the earth. One man, a repentant thief, was with him in Paradise, confirming the plan was true. After all, this unnamed former thief was the first to be crucified under the Law but to die under grace!

The proof that Christ was ministering in this subterranean prison was what would occur the morning He arose. At His own resurrection Christ brought these righteous souls out of this chamber! This is recorded by Matthew:

> Then, behold, the veil of the temple was torn in two from top to bottom; and the earth quaked, and the rocks were split, and the graves were opened; and many bodies of the saints who had fallen asleep were raised; and coming out of the graves after His resurrection, they went into the holy city and appeared to many.
>
> —MATTHEW 27:51–53

These "saints" were Old Testament saints whose souls and spirits joined their bodies as they were resurrected and seen alive in Jerusalem. The biblical evidence reveals that once a person departs through death, a righteous person's soul and spirit will be brought into Paradise in the third heaven (2 Cor. 12:1–7), but a sinner or unbeliever who dies without a redemptive covenant is separated into the compartment under the earth called hell (Luke 16:22–23). The most important point to bring out is that once the human spirit is placed in one of these two chambers, *there is no indication that the spirits are permitted to freely roam the earth or to return to the locations of the former homes and "haunt" the places where they once lived.*

CONSULTING THE DEAD

Some use a story of King Saul consulting a witch to place approval upon searching out the spirits of the dead through what is called a séance. In 1 Samuel 28:7–14 the biblical writer relates a very bizarre story about a witch who was asked by King Saul to make contact with the departed soul of a righteous man named Samuel.

> Then Saul said to his servants, "Find me a woman who is a medium, that I may go to her and inquire of her." And his servants said to him, "In fact, there is a woman who is a medium at En Dor." So Saul disguised himself and put on other clothes, and he went, and two men with him; and they came to the woman by night. And he said, "Please conduct a séance for me, and bring up for me the one I shall name to you."
>
> Then the woman said to him, "Look, you know what Saul has done, how he has cut off the mediums and the spiritists from the land. Why then do you lay a snare for my life, to cause me to die?" And Saul swore to her by the LORD, saying, "As the LORD lives, no punishment shall come upon you for this thing." Then the woman said, "Whom shall I bring up for you?" And he said, "Bring up Samuel for me."
>
> When the woman saw Samuel, she cried out with a loud voice. And the woman spoke to Saul, saying, "Why have you deceived me? For you are Saul!" And the king said to her, "Do not be afraid. What did you see?" And the woman said to Saul, "I saw a spirit ascending out of the earth." So he said to her, "What is his form?" And she said, "An old man is coming up, and he is covered with a mantle." And Saul perceived that it was Samuel, and he stooped with his face to the ground and bowed down.

There is a controversy concerning this passage among some scholars. Some suggest that the departed spirit of Samuel the prophet was brought forth from an inner chamber that held the departed souls of the righteous under the earth to speak to Saul. Others believe this was a familiar spirit that was imitating Samuel.

Let's look at the textual evidence to find clues as to which interpretation is more in line when comparing scripture with scripture.

First, the Spirit of the Lord had departed from Saul, and the tormented king sought a witch for information about his future. The first argument that this apparition was a familiar spirit is that the Holy Spirit always follows the Word and will of God (John 16:13). As the text indicates, God refused to answer Saul by the required scriptural method; therefore He would not choose a witch to bring a message from a righteous man. Second, consulting with the dead is forbidden in the law of God. God would not go against His own law to please a backslidden king and give him a message from another world. There is no other biblical record of a person asking for a message from a departed person. Third, a witch was used to gain the information. Saul had already made a threat to put all witches to death (1 Sam. 28:9). The Old Testament law required that witches, wizards, and familiar spirits were to be cut off from among the people (Exod. 22:18; Deut. 18:10). Just as Elijah destroyed the false prophets of Baal and refused to join their allegiance (1 Kings 18), the Almighty was jealous for His people and for their righteousness.

The witch was operating through a familiar spirit, which is a demonic power that can imitate the dead. Again, it was forbidden to consult or to listen to a familiar spirit, as this type of spirit uses *known information* of persons, places, or things and can deceive the living with such knowledge (Lev. 19:31; 20:6; Deut. 18:11). Those in the occult world that conduct actual séances often deceive grieving families by tapping into a familiar spirit that imitates the departed loved one. The same can be true concerning this witch and the spirit she conjured up. Notice the witch saw "gods" going up and down in the earth. I would suggest these were either the spirits of departed souls that were dying and being carried into the underworld (such as occurred when the rich man in Luke 16 died), or these alleged "gods" were a manifestation of evil spirits that have access to the earth and the underworld. In the Book of Job, when God asked Satan where he had been, the adversary replied, "To and fro on the earth, and from walking back and forth on it" (Job 1:7; 2:2). Angels have access to heaven, and evil spirits have access to the regions under the crust of the earth.

When this spirit emerged, King Saul never personally *saw* the person with his eyes, but he asked the witch for a description. She described the spirit as an "old man...covered with a mantle," and Saul *perceived* it was Samuel (1 Sam. 28:14). Remember, Saul never saw this spirit, and the information came from the mouth of the witch with a familiar spirit—it was not the voice of what was allegedly Samuel. In this process the witch is acting as a medium, or a go-between between Saul and the spirit. This was how (as it is today) a person who allegedly consults the dead brings information to the living. The alleged departed never speaks through the air in an audible voice, only through the voice of the medium, or in this case the witch.

All of the above evidence indicates that this spirit was a familiar spirit that had specific knowledge. The main argument that this was literally Samuel comes from the precise accuracy by which this being from the underworld predicts would happen to Saul and his sons:

> Then Samuel said: "So why do you ask me, seeing the LORD has departed from you and has become your enemy? And the LORD has done for Himself as He spoke by me. For the LORD has torn the kingdom out of your hand and given it to your neighbor, David. Because you did not obey the voice of the LORD nor execute His fierce wrath upon Amalek, therefore the LORD has done this thing to you this day. Moreover the LORD will also deliver Israel with you into the hand of the Philistines. And tomorrow you and

> your sons will be with me. The LORD will also deliver the
> army of Israel into the hand of the Philistines."
>
> —1 SAMUEL 28:16–19

The details of this prediction are:

- The Lord has departed from Saul.

- The kingdom of Saul had been stripped from him and
  given to another (David).

- The reason for Saul's rejection—he did not destroy
  Amalek earlier in his rule as king.

- Saul would lose the battle, and he and his sons would
  die the next day.

- Saul and his sons would be brought to the sheol compartment under the earth.

If this were Samuel, how would he know these details? If this
were not Samuel, but a spirit, how would it know these details?
First, much of the information was already known throughout the
kingdom of Israel.

- The Lord had departed from Saul (1 Sam. 16:14).

- Saul's kingdom had been stripped from him and
  given to David (1 Sam. 15:28; 16:1–13).

- Saul was rejected for not obeying God and destroying
  the Amalekites (1 Sam. 15:1–28).

A familiar spirit is a demonic spirit that has become familiar
with the people, places, and events that have occurred in a specific location. These types of demonic spirits desire to remain in
the area of the country where they originated or where they have
controlled individuals throughout the history in that region. For

example, when Christ expelled the demons from the man in the tombs, the spirits requested that Christ not send them out of the country (Mark 5:10). Spirits become comfortable with their familiar surroundings. Christ told of an unclean spirit going out of a man, seeking rest, and finding none. The spirit then attempts to return to the person or the original location. If he can, he then invites seven other spirits, more wicked than himself, to join him in an attempt to live in and control his former house (Matt. 12:43–45).

Alleged contact with the dead is called *necromancy*. This was practiced among the heathen nations and empires of antiquity, but it was forbidden by the Lord in the Law:

> Give no regard to mediums and familiar spirits; do not seek after them, to be defiled by them: I am the LORD your God.
> —LEVITICUS 19:31

> There shall not be found among you any one that maketh his son or his daughter to pass through the fire, or that useth divination, or an observer of times, or an enchanter, or a witch, or a charmer, or a consulter with familiar spirits, or a wizard, or a necromancer.
> —DEUTERONOMY 18:10–11, KJV

The English word *necromancer* is supposed to be a practice of consulting the dead for the reason of predicting the future. The pagan tribes were very much into worshipping the dead, as was indicated in God's warnings to the Hebrew people. The Almighty told His chosen not to put any "cuttings in your flesh for the dead" (Lev. 19:28), neither should they "shave the front of your head for the dead" (Deut. 14:1). This information undergirds my point: the familiar spirits are familiar with information from the past and are able to relate it through the voice of a person who opens himself or herself up to being controlled or possessed by these spirits. In what is called the New Age movement, individuals connect to strange spirits by *channeling* them through their own physical bodies. Some claim these are "ascended masters" from the past whose spirits roam through the cosmos bringing supernatural or divine insight into numerous cosmic mysteries linked with life. I read occasional stories of some who claim ancient Indians had given them insights from the past, and the information revealed later proved accurate through detailed historical research. This allegedly *proves* that these spirits are the spirits of ancient men and women. In reality, it *proves* nothing when you understand the operation of a familiar spirit.

These incidents prove that the spirit world is real, and second that these are not the spirits of the departed but of demonic entities that have existed since the fall of Satan. Any past information can be revealed to a medium who channels evil spirit. The deception reaches its climax when family members have lost a loved one through death, and they consult a medium who claims he or she can make contact with the departed soul. Once the process begins, the spirit begins to inform the medium about an event in the person's life or accurately names several family members. The family is overwhelmed with joy to know they have contacted their loved one, and at times they are told certain things to do to make this spirit happy or at peace. For several years a famed psychic hosted a popular television program in which he claimed to make contact with the dead. I watched how at times he would manipulate a question to get a certain response or would hit and miss until he could finally put together a story line that the family agreed was a message from the nether world.

In the Bible we do read where Moses (who had died) and Elijah (who was translated) appeared to Christ and began sharing details about Christ's future suffering in Jerusalem (Matt. 17:1–4). This was a rare instance and was directed under the supervision of God Himself. Christ did not conjure up these men for information, as

Christ was already familiar with God's plan and purpose for His suffering. God sent these former famous prophets to reveal additional information to Christ. However, the law of God in Scripture would totally forbid the use of mediums, soothsayers, fortune-tellers, and witchcraft in any and all forms. This practice is nothing to play with and is a very dangerous spiritual bridge over dark waters that a believer should never cross.

A believer must rely upon biblical methods to receive spiritual insight, direction, and the path for the future. We can all be assured that Christ will return (1 Thess. 4:16–17), that the righteous dead will be raised at the resurrection (1 Cor. 15:52), that heaven exists, and we will abide for eternity in the New Jerusalem (Rev. 22). We will rule and reign with Christ for a thousand years if we are faithful (Rev. 20:1–4).

As stated earlier, many of these alleged houses are places where blood was shed through murder, suicide, or a violent death. In the world of the occult it is common for spirits to be attracted to shed blood. Almost all religions that are linked to idolatry have some form of blood connected to the worship of the idol. When Cain slew Abel, the voice of Abel's blood cried out to God from the ground (Gen. 4:10). We are uncertain how blood released from a human body can have a voice that can be heard in the spirit world, but there are numerous illustrations that the violent shedding of blood can mark a spot that spirits can be familiar with.

EXPELLING SPIRITS FROM A HOUSE

On several occasions strong believers have moved into a new house (previously inhabited but new to them) in a new neighborhood, only to experience strange noises, shadowy figures, and objects moving in the night. How can a family of believers remove such an unwanted presence from their dwelling?

One of the most bizarre and unusual stories was related to me by my friend Evangelist Randy Caldwell. Years ago his brother pastored a church in Arkansas and had a man who had attended the church for some time but never made a strong commitment to Christ. One night the pastor received a call from the man, who bluntly announced, "Preacher, I am going to end it all tonight. I can't take it anymore." This fellow planned on committing suicide and said he already had the gun in his hand. The pastor asked him not to do such a terrible thing and said he would come to see him and talk with him if he would allow him to. The man replied, "When you pull into the driveway, if you see my shadow in the window, then knock on the door." The pastor rushed to the home late that night, and upon arriving saw the shadow of the man walking in the living room window.

Once the pastor came into the house, he closed the door, and the man pointed the gun to the pastor's head and stated, "You are a fool for coming. Tonight I am going to kill myself, and I am going to take you with me." The man was so controlled by spirits and so delusional that nothing the pastor said brought relief. In fact, the pastor began quoting scriptures. As the man continued pointing the gun, threatening to pull the trigger, the pastor reminded him that this was not something he really wanted to do, but it was the enemy working on his mind. Randy said, "There wasn't a moment when my brother was not praying or quoting a scripture." It was after about an hour that a most frightening thing occurred.

A door in the living room suddenly opened by itself and slammed. The pastor heard what sounded like a woman in high heels walking across the floor. Suddenly the sound stopped at a rocking chair in the living room. The pastor watched as the cushion in the chair pressed down as though someone were sitting in it. Then the chair began rocking on its own. Needless to say, great fear came over the minister as he was in the middle of the greatest demonic manifestation he had ever encountered. The man then said, "You want to know who this is? Her name is Maude. Do you want to see Maude?"

The pastor replied, "I didn't come to see Maude; I came to see you," and began quoting scriptures while the chair continued to rock. The man then said, "You want some coffee?" He then snapped his fingers, and the coffeepot began to percolate on its own.

Suddenly a boldness from the Holy Spirit came upon the pastor. As this man said, "Maude has told me to kill you tonight," the pastor began rebuking this demon entity and commanding the man to be delivered. He quoted Scripture out loud and maintained his authority in Christ. After about one and a half hours of this warfare, the chair quit rocking, the footsteps came across the room, and the door shut. The man then dropped the gun and began praying with the pastor.

It would be many years after that when, according to Randy, it was discovered that a Gypsy woman who lived in the area was under a strong occult demon and was believed to be responsible for sending the familiar spirit to the house of this man who was weak in faith and had allowed a spirit of death into his home.

THE DECEPTION IS THIS

If these haunted house hunters were to admit the truth and confess the haunting is nothing more than a roaming demonic entity, then they would be confessing accurate information to the viewer. However, they call these places "haunted by the spirits of the dead," as through when a person dies, his or her spirit simply departs the body and roams from place to place and can only find rest when whatever has prevented a peaceful rest is dealt with. I have heard them call these the "restless spirits of the dead," but these alleged experts on the departed souls of men never give the viewer the understanding of how you comfort a "restless spirit." The deception is to call these demonic powers the "spirits of the dead," as this would imply that the dead go neither to heaven or to hell but simply float from place to place, haunting houses and buildings at their own will.

This generation is obsessed with the paranormal, but it must be taught the supernatural from a biblical perspective. Often pastors must spend their time ministering words of encouragement to their members from Sunday to Sunday and are not always aware of the paranormal culture brewing in and around them and of the desire for this generation to understand the world of angels and spirits. This hunger must be met with biblical warnings related to occult practices and biblical knowledge of the spirit world and its operation.

Once a person dies, that person's soul and spirit immediately depart and will abide in one of two places until the resurrection of the dead—either Paradise in the third heaven (2 Cor. 12:1–4) or a chamber in the underworld identified through both Testaments as hell (Luke 16). Any spirit that haunts a house, building, or property is not a spirit of a human but a spirit familiar with that particular region.

THE AUTHORITY OF CHRIST'S NAME

On of the greatest proofs that such manifestations are the operation of unclean or familiar spirits is the fact then when a believer begins to exercise spiritual authority over the atmosphere in the home, these manifestations will totally cease.

As a young teenage minister I became very interested in the subject of demons and evil spirits. I would spend hours and at times days researching everything I could find related to spiritual warfare and demonic encounters. To my amazement I began to experience odd manifestations from the spirit realm, especially at night. There was a six-month period when I was literally awakened by my bed shaking or sounds of furniture moving and eventually voices cursing. On several occasions there were visible manifestations of spirits cloaked in dark garments and hoods and hiding their faces. This was not my imagination, but it was literal and very mentally tormenting and frightening.

At that time my mother was secretary at a state office where a powerful man of God, Floyd Lawhon, served as evangelism director for a major Full Gospel denomination. She went to him privately and said, "Could you talk to Perry? He is obsessed with the subject of demons and is having all types of strange things beginning to happen to him." Floyd called me in his office, and I will never forget what he said as he looked at me: "Perry, as long as you concentrate on demons, they will show up. If you preach and concentrate on Jesus, then He will show up!" I realized I was giving the adversary too much attention, and he was accommodating my interest. I began to preach faith, Jesus and His authority, and as Floyd Lahon said, the presence of Christ began to manifest and deliver individuals from the oppression of the enemy.

Herein is the point. Those who focus their attention on activity in the spirit world, including searching for "ghosts" in a "haunted house," will eventually have a spirit encounter of some type. However, this ghost is not a former member of the community whose spirit is in limbo traveling the sphere of time and light attempting to discover a place of rest. It is a spirit, but not one to be encountered or entertained. The fact that the authority of God's Word, Christ's blood, and a believer's resistance to these forces can expel them from the premises indicates the sole rule of God's kingdom over the kingdom of darkness and exposes the deception of the alleged haunted house as seen on television each week.

CHAPTER 13

CAN SATAN PUT A GENERATIONAL CURSE ON A BELIEVER?

꽃 꽃

THIS QUESTION NEVER seems to come up when personal circumstances are going great and there is money in the bank, food on the table, and a nice easy chair to relax in at that new home you just built on the lake! In good times a believer will confess, "God is good all the time," or "I'm blessed to be a blessing," or may even be overheard saying, "God is better to me than anyone else."

However, when a deadly sickness, accident, or sudden severe trial strikes, some believers tend to believe that God has turned on them. They see the Almighty lifting His hand of blessing and permitting Satan to unleash a curse, perhaps for some past sin or some generational iniquity long forgotten that is arising from the grave of the past to haunt them and to wreak havoc upon all of God's blessings! The theory is that since the ancestors never *paid* for the sin, someone must pay, and it must be me! I can't tell you how many times I have heard believers say, "Things seem to be falling apart. I don't know what I have done wrong," as though God is punishing them for an act of disobedience that they themselves are unaware of.

This *curse fever* seems to creep into a believer's mind following a terrible trial or tragedy. In recent years there has been a strong teaching in the body of Christ concerning *generational curses*. Varied explanations have been given for different types of sickness, difficulties, financial stress, and other anxieties believers encounter—the results of a *curse* they must break. Before answering the question, "Can a Christian be under a generational curse?", we must understand that trouble and negative circumstances are simply a part of life. As it is written, "Man who is born of woman is of few days and full of trouble" (Job 14:1). Another verse states:

> For affliction does not come from the dust,
> Nor does trouble spring from the ground;
> Yet man is born to trouble,
> As the sparks fly upward.
> —JOB 5:6–7

The Book of Job is an entire narrative dealing with the suffering of a righteous man. Had some ministers of today been living in Job's day, they would have declared that Job was under some form of a generational curse instead of acknowledging that he was targeted by a satanic assignment. The Book of Job begins identifying Job as "the greatest of all the people of the East" (Job 1:3). He was blessed with seven sons and three daughters (v. 2), all of whom owned houses. Job 1:3 lists the portfolio of his estate:

- Seven thousand sheep
- Three thousand camels

- Five hundred yoke of oxen

- Five hundred female donkeys

- A very large household

Like a flash of lightning suddenly striking a home and burning it to the ground, Job experienced a series of multiple events that brought destruction, loss, and grief to him. A group of wild nomads, Chaldeans and Sabeans, invaded his estate, rounding up his camels, oxen, and donkeys for themselves and forcing the livestock to stampede away from Job to their own lands (Job 1:14–15, 17). Fire from heaven (perhaps a storm of lightning) struck the farm and burned seven thousand sheep (v. 16). As this thievery and natural disaster were occurring, a wind from the wilderness struck the home where his ten children were celebrating with their oldest brother, crashing the dwelling down upon the entire clan and claiming the lives of Job's three daughters and seven sons (vv. 18–19). In a matter of hours the wealthiest man in the East had become the poorest man in the East. As if this were not enough, he was later stricken with boils that covered his skin (Job 2:7).

As soon as Job's three friends—Eliphaz the Temanite, Bildad the Shuhite, and Zophar the Naamathite—heard of his tragedies, the men came to "comfort" him (v. 11). Job's physical condition with the boils was so severe that they did not recognize him, and they ripped their garments and sat in the dust with Job for seven days without saying anything (vv. 12–13). This was an ancient custom for collective grieving. The Hebrew name *Eliphaz* means, "the endeavor of God." The name *Bildad* means, "confusing or a person of contention." The third name, *Zophar*, in Hebrew can mean "rising early."

In chapter 32 a fourth man showed up, Elihu the Buzite, and continued the dialogue. The name *Elihu* means, "My God is He." These men began a series of discourses that the Book of Job divides into three main cycles. The first cycle is chapters 4 through 11. The second cycle is chapters 12 through 20, and the third is chapters 21 through 31.

The main speeches given to Job from his friends attempt to explain to Job *why God allowed or sent the severe trouble to Job's life*. The main theories are that Job must have some type of hidden sin in his life or was perhaps too self-righteous, and therefore God was attempting to humble him. Job defends himself, and his friends are unable to identify any sin he has committed that would have opened the door to such trouble. The basic theology of Job's friends seems to be that if you are a good moral person, you will automatically live a life of favor and blessing, but if you commit any form of sin or evil, you are marked for God's judgment. Thus the assumption was that for Job to have experienced total loss, he must have committed some known or secret acts of sin to anger God and was deserving of his sufferings.

After weeks and perhaps months of these friends debating, discussing, and attempting to explain what they really did not know or understand, God eventually came on the scene in a whirlwind and revealed the following:

> And so it was, after the LORD had spoken these words to Job, that the LORD said to Eliphaz the Temanite, "My wrath is aroused against you and your two friends, for you have not spoken of Me what is right, as My servant Job has."
>
> —JOB 42:7

While these friends were sincere in their *observations*, they were sincerely incorrect in their *opinions*.

Just as Job's friends did, when a terrible tragedy happens to a believer, other believers attempt to comfort the person by trying to explain *why* it happened. A child passes, and a friend will suggest, "Heaven needed an angel, so the Lord took the child." A minister dies young, and someone explains that: "God needed him in heaven to prepare for the return of Christ." These statements have been used and may be sincere, but they do nothing to comfort for the loss. In reality, there are seasons of difficulty and trials that cannot be explained, and we must simply trust God's will and wisdom. Some things we will only understand when we join God in heaven.

JOB—LIVING ON THE LEFT HAND OF GOD

There are numerous Scriptures that mention the "right hand," including the "right hand of God" (Acts 2:33–34; 5:31; 7:55–56; Rom. 8:34; Eph 1:20). In Scripture the phrase "the right hand of God" alludes to authority, dominion, and power. For example, when Jacob was blessing his grandsons Manasseh and Ephraim, he crossed his hands and placed his right hand upon the younger son instead of the older (Gen. 48:13–18). Normally the right hand was placed upon the older son, who was the heir to the blessing and birthright of the family. The right hand of the patriarch was considered the hand of special approval and blessing, especially in times of prayer and of transferring spiritual blessing to the next generation. However, Job mentioned the "left hand of God," a term found only in Job.

> Look, I go forward, but He is not there,
> And backward, but I cannot perceive Him;
> When He works on the left hand, I cannot behold Him.
>
> —JOB 23:8–9

From a rabbinical perspective the left hand of God alludes to the side of darkness, trial, and difficulty—the opposite of favor and blessings found on the right hand. The concept originates at Creation when God created the two opposites of light and darkness.

From a rabbinical concept light was formed with God's right hand, and darkness was separated with His left hand (Gen. 1:18). On God's right hand a person encounters God's favor, blessings, and increase. However, on the left hand there is darkness, trial, and anguish.

In Job 23 this suffering saint confessed he was searching for God by moving forward and looking backward, but he could not find Him. Job then admitted that he was living on God's left hand—where He works. Job acknowledged that despite the terrible affliction and anguish to his flesh, his soul, and his emotions, God had a left hand or a left side that He was still working through. God is with us, even in the most severe crisis, dark trial, and suffering.

The facts are that we live on a planet experiencing the travail of famines, earthquakes, storms, floods, and natural disasters that can impact the food supply, drinking water, our homes, and businesses. A natural disaster does not necessarily indicate some form of judgment on an area, as weather phenomena have been occurring for centuries and often run in cycles. Christ said it this way: "He makes His sun rise on the evil and on the good, and sends rain on the just and on the unjust" (Matt. 5:45). I have said, "In life bad things happen to good people, and good things can happen to bad people."

What the generational curse doctrine seems to miss is that God is *always working* in the life of any believer who has a covenant with Him and is truly serving the Lord with all of his or her heart. The steps of a good man are ordered of the Lord (Ps. 37:23). If believers experiencing difficulty was some sign of a curse, then the apostle Paul would have been the most cursed man in the New Testament! Here is what he encountered during his missionary journey:

> I am more: in labors more abundant, in stripes above measure, in prisons more frequently, in deaths often. From the Jews five times I received forty stripes minus one. Three times I was beaten with rods; once I was stoned; three

times I was shipwrecked; a night and a day I have been in the deep; in journeys often, in perils of waters, in perils of robbers, in perils of my own countrymen, in perils of the Gentiles, in perils in the city, in perils in the wilderness, in perils in the sea, in perils among false brethren; in weariness and toil, in sleeplessness often, in hunger and thirst, in fastings often, in cold and nakedness—besides the other things, what comes upon me daily: my deep concern for all the churches. Who is weak, and I am not weak?

—2 Corinthians 11:23–29

Imagine believers in the first century telling Paul, "You are under a curse for your past sins because you consented to Stephen's death (Acts 7:58–60; 8:1), persecuted believers, threw some people in prison, and caused many to blaspheme (Acts 22:4; 26:11)." Before his conversion Paul did all of the above. However, Paul's difficulties were not based upon his past actions, as he said he forgot the things that were behind and was reaching for the things that were before (Phil. 3:14). Paul dealt with a "messenger of Satan," which he called a "thorn in the flesh," that harassed him on a continual basis (2 Cor. 12:7). Paul's sufferings were often initiated by Jewish religious leaders who resented his conversion to Christ and sought to restrain his message by using persecution, arrest, and pressure to stop him. It was impossible for Paul to be suffering from some curse of disobeying the law when he wrote that "Christ has redeemed us from the curse of the law" (Gal. 3:13).

Practical Reasons for Difficulty

Some believers will say, "I am in this mess because of being raised in such a dysfunctional family." I remind them that most of the great families in the Bible had slight dysfunctions or dysfunctional members in them; yet they succeeded in doing the will of God!

Noah spend one hundred years building an ark, rode out a global flood for one hundred fifty days, came out of the ark, planted a vineyard, and got drunk and laid around naked in his tent (Gen. 9). Lot was righteous enough to escape the burning destruction of Sodom, but later he lay drunk in a cave and unknowingly committed incest with his two daughters (Gen. 19:30–36). Abraham was a man of great obedience and the father of the faith, yet in fear he lied about Sarah being his wife (Gen. 12:11–13). Isaac was also fearful for his wife, and to protect himself he fibbed, saying Rebekah was his sister (Gen. 26:7). As a young man Jacob was willing to deceive his father in an attempt to steal his brother's blessing and birthright (Gen. 27). After hearing their sister was raped, Simeon and Levi went after the men and slew an entire tribal family. Jacob was so upset at one point that he told his sons, "You…make me to stink among the inhabitants of the land" (Gen. 34:30, kjv). Gideon led three hundred men into a battle to defeat the huge Midianite army, yet following the victory he used a golden offering to make an ephod, causing Israel to worship the golden image (Judg. 8:27). Other failures fill the Bible, such as Samson's weakness with Philistine women (Judg. 14–16); of David being a "Peeping Tom," which led to an affair in the palace (2 Sam. 11), and of Solomon's lust for women, which led him to assemble seven hundred wives and three hundred concubines (1 Kings 11:3), with the result that these strange women turned his heart away from God (vv. 1–4).

The many moral and spiritual challenges of these early patriarchs and kings were not the result of *generational curses* causing the difficulty and failure, but they were simply the works of the flesh (Gal. 5:19–21) and the struggle with the carnal nature (1 Cor. 3:1–4). It is easy for a fallen believer to blame his trouble on the devil, but many times *it's not a devil that's on them but the flesh that is in them.* Individuals who are deep into the teaching about generational curses often believe that everything negative is caused by a curse. I have met individuals who deal with anger issues in their family, and they remind people, "It's just a generational curse." Others struggle with adultery and use the excuse: "It's part of the curse in my family lineage." It is possible for people to become so entrenched in this *curse* concept that they cease to take personal responsibility for their actions. The idea of being cursed becomes more of a *cop-out* for permitting your own actions, thereby never taking personal responsibility for dealing with your flesh.

REDEMPTION CHANGES YOUR CARNAL NATURE

One of the supernatural blessings of those who have received a redemptive covenant through Christ is that the act of redemption is not just a mental process, but it's a literal transformation that occurs within the human heart and spirit. Those who have entered into a new covenant of redemption through faith in the blood of Christ and the forgiveness of sins are new creations! The Bible says that if any man is in Christ, he is a new creature (*creation*), and the old things pass away and all things become new (2 Cor. 5:17). This covenant is initiated when a person repents of his or her sins and turns from wickedness. It is written: "If we confess our sins, He is faithful and just to forgive us our sins and to cleanse us from all unrighteousness" (1 John 1:9). Once we have been sealed in the covenant through the shed blood of Christ, then "old things have passed away; behold, all things have become new" (2 Cor. 5:17). From God's perspective He takes the sins of the past, forgives them, and never recalls them again. Isaiah wrote, "I, even I, am He who blots out your transgressions for My own sake; and I will not remember your sins" (Isa. 43:25).

Biblical References to a Generational Curse

The two most often quoted passages that deal with generational curses are taken from the Torah:

> For I, the Lord your God, am a jealous God, visiting the iniquity of the fathers on the children to the third and fourth generations of those who hate Me, but showing mercy to thousands, to those who love Me and keep My commandments.
>
> —Exodus 20:5–6

> The Lord, the Lord God, merciful and gracious, longsuffering, and abounding in goodness and truth, keeping mercy for thousands, forgiving iniquity and transgression and sin, by no means clearing the guilty, visiting the iniquity of the fathers upon the children and the children's children to the third and the fourth generation.
>
> —Exodus 34:6–7

These two verses say nothing concerning a "curse" but indicate a *visitation* from God for iniquity. In these passages the Hebrew word for "visiting" is *paqad*, and it can mean, "to visit (with friendly or hostile intent)."[1] In these passages the intent is to bring judgment for the iniquity of the fathers who are *passing the lifestyle of sin to their children and children's children*. A good example is when Christ wept over Jerusalem, recalling how God sent the city many prophets whom they slew and rejected. Christ said judgment would come upon His generation because they "did not know the time of [their] visitation" (Luke 19:44). The Greek word for "visitation" is the word *episkope* and can mean, "an inspection (for relief)."[2] God intended to bless and bring relief to His holy city, but the people's actions instead brought destruction to the temple and to Jerusalem about forty years later in A.D. 70. Christ said that Jerusalem's destruction was a result of shedding the innocent blood of the righteous from Abel to Zechariah the son of Berechiah, who was slain between the porch and the altar (Matt. 23:35). Notice that God paid a visit of judgment because the iniquity of shedding innocent blood had been passed down.

When placing the Exodus 20:5–6 passage in the context of the subject matter, the Almighty was instructing Israel to have no other gods except Him. Israel was to serve the one and only true God. In verses 3–4 the Almighty was forbidding His people from worshipping the likeness of any living creature. Thus, if they did commit idolatry, God would visit their iniquity, or allow judgment for their sin. This literally occurred when Israel later worshipped the golden calf while Moses was on Mount Sinai receiving the Ten Commandments. After forty days Moses returned to the camp and saw the Hebrew idolaters dancing before the golden idol. Moses instructed the Levites to slay the sinners, and three thousand of the covenant breakers were slain for their actions (Exod. 32:28).

The Exodus 34 narrative, the second passage used to identify generational curses, is the account of Moses returning to the mountain the second time to receive a new set of the Ten Commandments on stone tablets, after he broke the first set in anger over the Israelites worshipping a golden calf (Exod. 32:19). This generation of cow worshippers and individuals who left Egypt were not permitted to inherit the Promised Land due to their sin of idolatry (Num. 14:22–23). Thus God "visited their iniquity" by removing their inheritance from them. The Lord knew that if idolatry were permitted among the fathers, the sin would continue through the sons and the children of the third and fourth generations. This was a warning of judgment on the iniquity of idolatry. The same warning of visiting the iniquity on the fathers is also found in a third reference in Deuteronomy 5:9, which reads similarly to the two Exodus passages. However, there is an important addition to the warning found at the conclusion of the Deuteronomy passage:

> ...visiting the iniquity of the fathers upon the children to the third and fourth generations of those who hate Me, but showing mercy to thousands, to those who love Me and keep My commandments.
>
> —Deuteronomy 5:9–10

There are two very important points seldom emphasized when teaching that a Christian can be under a generational curse. The first point is the visitation of iniquity, which comes to those who "hate" the Lord—not to those who "love" Him and "keep His commandments." This is stated in both Exodus 20:6 and Deuteronomy 5:10. Second, mercy is given to thousands who love and keep God's commandments. Thus there is a separation given between the *obedient* and the *disobedient*, those who *love* the Lord and those who *hate* the Lord.

It is clear in both Testaments that those practicing evil and passing the practices of all forms of sin on to their children are certainly subject to experiencing the disfavor of God at some point after He has dealt with them and they have rejected His love and mercy. However, there is also ample evidence that a true believer cannot be cursed with any form of judgment from a past sin—either their own sins or those of their ancestors—if they are actively loving God and keeping His commandments! If the adversary could *legally* bring up our sins and accuse us of iniquity that has long been forgiven, then the blood of Christ and God's ability to forgive are both weak and void of power. However, the Bible teaches that if we sin, Christ the High Priest of heaven is faithful and just to forgive us our sins and to cleanse us from all unrighteousness (1 John 1:9). We are informed that Satan is "the accuser of our brethren, who accused them before our God day and night"

(Rev. 12:10). The word *accuser* is a Greek word, *kategoros*, and it refers to a person who is against a person in the assembly or, as we would say, a prosecutor who accuses a person of injustice. Satan's accusations are completely ineffective when a believer has been forgiven of his or her sins, as the *sin evidence* has been erased and there is no *legal* action that can impact the believer's life.

Because the three main passages used to identify a generational curse are in the portion of the Scripture known as the Law of Moses, Paul's words in Galatians hold a powerful truth. He wrote: "Christ has redeemed us from the curse of the law, having become a curse for us" (Gal. 3:13).

The "curses" mentioned in the Law of Moses that come as the result of God's judgment upon His people's disobedience and rebellion included many specific things, including curses...

- In the city and in the country
- On the production of crops, the increase of livestock
- On the fruit of the body
- That cause cursing, confusion, and rebuke against whatever you try to do
- Of physical attack of disease and physical problems, bringing death
- Of natural disasters of drought, famine, and pestilence
- Of financial disasters and thievery, economic loss, bankruptcy and foreclosure
- Of failures in relationships, loss of family
- Of defeat in war, capture by the enemy, captivity in foreign lands
- Of loss of reputation

Since believers are redeemed by Christ's blood and in covenant with God and following the Word of God, no curse of the Law or curse outside of the Law can *stick to* an active believer.

Curses by Witches and Occult Groups

The question has been asked, "Is it possible for a verbal or ritualistic curse from a witch, Satanist, or occult group to actually affect a true believer?" My first response is to recall when the king of Moab asked the seer Balaam to stand on the mountains of Moab, look into the valley, and curse the children of Israel (Num. 22:6). As Balaam attempted to speak, only blessings poured from his words. In anger the king rebuked the prophet, moved him to another peak on the mountain, and demanded him to curse the Hebrews, yet each time, only blessings came forth (Num. 23). Finally Balaam confessed that he was unable to curse those whom the Lord had blessed—and Israel was under the blessing of God (Num. 23:8). God's covenant with Israel was stronger than the curse of a king.

The same is true with individuals who have received Christ's redemptive covenant. Christ's blood forms an invisible yet active hedge of protection against spirits sent from the occult. In the early 1980s I preached a four-week revival in Northport, Alabama, which was known throughout the entire community. I returned a year later, and one afternoon a call came to the church office from a young woman who was involved with a group of witches. She said she wanted to know my *secret* of power to resist curses. She related that their group had sent death spirits on assignment in the past, but in my case, the spirits returned to them without any results. I invited her to the service; she came that night and during an altar invitation was set free from numerous unclean spirits.

I later told her that the spirits of the occult were unable to penetrate the blood covenant I had with Christ, as this covenant also included angelic protection and personal protection from the Lord Himself (Ps. 91). I understand that it is not my strength, ability, or righteousness that forms this covering, but it's only the grace, mercy, and power of the Lord that protect us from these assignments.

FEAR ENERGIZES A CURSE

Haiti and cities in America such as New Orleans have been hotbeds for a religion called *voodoo*. Without going into details, this system consists of voodoo priests and priestesses who often mix a bizarre form of Christianity with old African tribal ritual and occult practices. There is much demonic activity linked to this practice, and it should be avoided at all costs.

However, one of the reasons voodoo holds such control over its followers is the power of both superstition and fear. When the disciples failed to cast out a spirit from a young boy, they asked Christ why their prayers failed. He replied, "Because of your unbelief" (Matt. 17:20). Obviously the spirit inside the lad sensed the unbelief of the disciples and thus retained its grip on the physical body of the child. Demons can sense both faith or unbelief and fear. Paul identified fear as a "spirit," saying God has not given us a "spirit of fear" (2 Tim. 1:7). This is why voodoo and other demonic-controlled systems have such a stronghold on the minds of people, as many followers are superstitious and fearful of what they have heard and seen.

Many years ago a pastor friend of mine, Larry McDaniel, was a missionary director living on the island of Haiti. He was familiar with the bondage voodoo had over millions of Haitian people, and he often confronted the voodoo priest on the island. On one occasion he entered a hut in which there were clay jars said to hold souls and spirits. Larry began crashing some of the jars on the ground to prove there were no souls or spirits living in the jars. Some people watching, of course, were fearful, but the fact that he had great faith and no fear prevented any unwanted and unwelcomed spirits from attacking him.

I personally discovered the power of fear when, as stated earlier, I experienced six months of a direct and very real demonic attack as a teenager. As the attacks persisted week after week and month after month, I became fearful to the point of anticipating and expecting these assaults, voices, and apparitions to continue. I eventually discovered that fear kept a crack in the door that allowed the unwanted invasions to continue. Only when I ceased to be afraid of either the spirits or the manifestations did the battle cease.

There are certainly generational cycles, patterns, and even spirits that we may encounter, but I believe the same principle exists in the *generational curse* realm. If I believe I am under a curse, acknowledge I am under a curse, and become fearful that a curse is following me, then fear itself can maintain the negative thoughts, emotions, and even physical attacks engaging me in spiritual warfare. The enemy will always enter any door where he is welcomed and permitted, but once exposed and divorced from your life, he will have no place in you (John 14:30; Eph. 4:27). Many alleged curses are simply works of the flesh (Gal. 5:19–21) that need to be exposed and dealt with through the discipline of the Holy Spirit. Paul wrote that he died daily (1 Cor. 15:31), meaning he found it necessary to discipline his flesh on a daily basis.

Should a person maintain that he or she is under a generational curse, that person must understand that Christ's redemptive covenant came to destroy the works of the devil and then develop a true understanding of how redemption brings freedom from the past. In Christ we become a new creation, as old things are passed away. Christ is not just a Redeemer and a Savior—but also a curse breaker!

Chapter 14

THE SELDOM-SPOTTED STRATEGY OF CALLING YOUR BLUFF

꧁ ꧂

ERSONALLY I DON'T play cards, but I recall hearing a term used in card games that actually is a strategy used in spiritual warfare. The term is *calling your bluff*, a term used in a poker game. When someone is *bluffing*, that person is pretending that the cards he is holding are better than they really are. This is done in hopes that the opponent will give up. It can also mean that you think someone may be lying, and you call his bluff to force him to prove what he is saying is true. An example would be a young person who is angry at her parent's discipline and says, "I am going to leave home and go get an apartment!" The parent knows the child has no money, no job, and no car. So the parent responds: "If that's what you want, I guess you are old enough to get a job and make your own way." Usually the child remains at home, and the issues eventually get settled. This is calling a person's bluff.

The term can also be used as a military strategy. I was in the Upper Golan Heights in Israel when a former Israeli commander related an amazing story. From October 6–25, 1973, Israel was surprised by a secretly planned invasion of Syria joined by an Arab coalition of Egyptian armies, in what would later be termed the Yom Kippur War. The Egyptian forces stormed in from the south, crossing the Israeli-held Sinai Peninsula, while the Syrians coordinated an assault from the Golan Heights in the north. The war occurred during the Jewish feast and fast day of Yom Kippur and the Islamic holy month of Ramadan.

Because the Israeli soldiers were in the synagogues praying and spending the day fasting, Israel was caught off guard, allowing Syrian tanks and troops to move swiftly and unrestrained from the border of Syria into Israel. There was a small Israeli community, called a *kibbutz*, located in the northern section of Israel, just over one of the large hills found in the Golan Heights. The men in the community discovered what was occurring and had no way of defending their community—except for one old tank with a few missiles. The Israelis moved the old tank near a ridge, and when the Syrian tanks made their move toward them, they shot one of the missiles! The Syrians were surprised and actually stopped their movements. Oddly enough, this one tank and the wise reaction of the men caused the Syrians to wonder if there were more tanks and if they were headed into a trap! This was an example of calling the bluff of the Syrians!

THE BLUFF MASTER

Our adversary is the master of the bluff. Using certain mental strategies and fiery darts against the human mind (Eph. 6:16), our adversary and his cohorts always attempt to make themselves stronger than they are, more important than they are, and more frightening than they are. They are masters of intimidation! They cause several thoughts to enter the minds of believers that are nothing more than spiritual bluffs. Take a look at some of these *spiritual bluffs*.

- You have been recently converted to Christ, and the enemy says, "You are not going to last long. You will be back in the same bondages before long!" This mental dart is sent to your mind to drag down your confidence and place a continual dread of failure in your mind.

- You have experienced a physical healing and are prepared to testify before others about God's goodness. But you may hear a still small voice in your mind say, "You better not testify. What if this disease comes back on you? You will look like a fool. Better just to keep your mouth shut." The enemy knows the power of your testimony, so he is calling your bluff and attempting to cause you to remain silent out of an unfounded fear.

- Perhaps you are preparing to give the largest offering or tithe you have ever planted in ministry. Suddenly you sense a gnawing sensation in the pit of your stomach, and these thoughts begin swirling: "You better not do that because you may need that. You know the economy is bad. What if an unexpected bill comes due?"

These continual bombardments of negative thoughts against your mind seem to never cease. They are ever present, especially when you are on the verge of a dynamic spiritual breakthrough.

During my earlier ministry I would hear a believer confess: "The devil is telling me such and such, and the enemy is lying to me."

I would respond, "So you know these mental thoughts are not from the Lord but are from the adversary?"

That individual would answer, "Yes, of course."

I would reply, "Are you aware Christ taught that Satan is a liar and the father of lies in John 8:44?"

Again the believer would reply, "Yes, I know that!"

I would then respond, "If you know the statement is a lie and the voice is coming from a liar, why are you even entertaining a lie when you know it is a lie?" After saying this, many times the person would look at me with a blank stare, then a gentle smile would slowly break across this face. It was as though light suddenly filled a dark room.

You cannot trust a perpetual liar any more than you would trust a kleptomaniac whose reputation is to steal each day and run off with your valuable possessions.

The Three Biggest Bluffs of the Enemy

I certainly do not underestimate the subtle and crafty deceptive influence of the enemy, neither do I ignore his influence in the lives of millions. However, there are three bluffs the adversary uses that we will expose with truth so that you may be able to disarm the misunderstandings caused by a lack of knowledge.

Bluff 1: He makes people think he is present everywhere (omnipresent).

Believers all know that God is a spirit (John 4:24) and that He is *omnipresent*—meaning that He can be everywhere at once. This divine ability makes God different from all other forms of creation. While angels are also spirit beings, they are only present at one place at a time and must travel from place to place at perhaps the speed of thought. Satan is a created being in the form of an anointed cherub (Ezek. 28:14), thus he is not and cannot be present in all places at once. His global influence is spread through a host of spirit rebels called "principalities...powers...the rulers of the darkness of this age...[and] spiritual hosts of wickedness in the heavenly places" (Eph. 6:12).

One reason some have a concept of Satan being all present is the conversation among believers when they are under a spiritual attack. A believer in Texas may comment, "The enemy is fighting me." At the same time a believer in Tennessee may say, "Satan is really hindering me." At that same moment another believer in Michigan may say to a friend, "The devil is on a rampage in my house." These are three different believers in three different states who are separated by hundreds of miles, yet all three are fighting *Satan*. These comments would imply that Satan seems to be everywhere at once.

However, the truth is that there is one chief fallen angel identified as "that serpent of old, called the Devil and Satan" (Rev. 12:9). He is only present at one location at one time. He came in the Garden of Eden in the form of a serpent (Gen. 3:1–6) and was later seen in the Book of Job attempting to penetrate Job's protective hedge (Job 1:10). Satan is the agent who stood up to provoke David to number Israel (1 Chron. 21:1) and is identified as the angel standing at the altar in Jerusalem attempting to resist the high priest (Zech. 3:1–2).

If Satan is one fallen angel, why do believers continually speak of Satan attacking them? It may be because the Hebrew name of *Satan* is *satan* and means "an adversary"; this is not just Satan himself but anyone who works adversely against the righteous. When Solomon disobeyed the Lord, the Bible reveals that "God raised up an adversary against Solomon..." (1 Kings 11:14, 23, 25). These adversaries were men who rose up against King Solomon during his reign. The

Hebrew word for "adversary" is also *satan*. Thus the Hebrew word for Satan is used two ways—indicating both the person of Satan and someone who is an adversary to a specific person. Satan and the ungodly are both opponents of righteousness and therefore are adversaries to godliness and righteousness. The contexts of the various passages clearly determine if the *satan* is the fallen angel (as in Job) or an opposing person (as with Solomon).

Therefore believers will often assign their warfare and extreme difficulty to the *adversary*, which can be both the invisible spiritual enemy and a fleshly human enemy. However, you must not accept the unfounded and unbiblical notion that Satan himself is all present, as this is a misconception he would love for you to accept.

Bluff 2: He makes people think he is all knowing (omniscient).

We call God *omniscient*, a word meaning that He is "all knowing." The word also indicates His knowledge is of past, present, and future events. Because God dwells outside of the human limitations of times and seasons, and dwells in the realm of eternity with its timelessness, He can actually see past, present, and future at the same time. For example, the Bible calls Christ "the Lamb slain from the foundation of the world" (Rev. 13:8). The foundation of the world would allude to the time when God created the earth, as penned in Job 38:4–7. Christ, however, was not slain at the time of Creation, but He came to earth about four thousand years after Adam was formed. What does this mean, "slain from the foundation"? Peter clarifies this idea of *slain from the foundation* when he writes that Christ was "foreordained [to shed His blood for us] before the foundation of the world, but was manifest in these last times for you" (1 Pet. 1:20).

Since God can see the past, present, and the future all at the same time, He had already seen the day when Christ would be slain as the redemptive offering for mankind. Thus, the all-knowing

God can speak of Christ's death *before* it happens as though it has *already* happened, because He knows it *will* happen!

The adversary desires to be like God (Isa. 14:14). Since God is all knowing, the enemy makes an attempt to convince a person during warfare that he knows all things about them—their situations, their plans, and how to prevent any form of victory or success from coming from their battles. When a person is in covenant with God, the real issue is when that person begins believing that the enemy knows all things. That fear may cause the believer to hesitate to make any positive move because of his fear that the enemy will block his actions before they ever begin!

If we go back to the birth of Christ, after the shepherds and wise men worshipped the future King at Bethlehem, Herod sent a hit squad of Roman assassins to slay all infants under two years of age (Matt. 2:16). Herod had no clue, and neither did the soldiers, which child was the true King. Joseph was warned to take Mary and Christ to Egypt to spare the infant's life. If Satan was so full of knowledge, he would have revealed the travel plans of the infant, and Christ would have died young.

Another question that has been asked is this: If Satan knew the final and ultimate defeat he would endure with the crucifixion and resurrection of Christ, why did he allow the crucifixion to occur and not prevent it? Early in Christ's ministry He revealed that He would suffer, be killed, and be raised on the third day. When Simon Peter heard Christ assert this, he immediately rebuked Christ, resisting the idea that this could happen. Jesus rebuked Peter by saying, "Get behind Me, Satan! You are an offense to Me, for you are not mindful of the things of God" (Matt. 16:23). The word *offense* in Greek is *skandalon* and indicates the bait placed on a trap to entice an animal to fall into a snare.

Satan was using Peter to set some form of a trap for Christ that would confuse Peter concerning Christ's future. Just prior to the crucifixion Christ interceded in intense prayer in the Garden of Gethsemane, praying until His sweat became as great drops of blood (Luke 22:44). This intensive inner struggle was further enhanced by the fact that the "prince of this world" (Satan) was somewhere present but had no part with the suffering. Christ said, "The ruler of this world is coming, and he has nothing in Me" (John 14:30). The prince of the world is also the "god of this age" (2 Cor. 4:4) and the "prince of the power of the air" (Eph. 2:2)—Satan!

The Bible indicates that Satan and the leaders of this world's system were unaware of the conquest that Christ's death and resurrection would initiate. We read:

> But we speak the wisdom of God in a mystery, the hidden wisdom which God ordained before the ages for our glory, which none of the rulers of this age knew; for had they known, they would not have crucified the Lord of glory.
>
> —1 Corinthians 2:7–8

Obviously had the adversary known his defeat was in the nail-scarred hands of the suffering Messiah (Isa. 53), he would have prevented the crucifixion! Thus, the archenemy of mankind does not have all knowledge. He is just as we are and has no clue as to when Christ will return. Not even the heavenly angels know the day or the hour, but the Father only (Mark 13:32). According to Revelation 12, when Satan and his angels are expelled from heaven and cast to the earth during the Tribulation, Satan will then know that he has "but a short time" (v. 12).

Bluff 3: He makes people think he is all powerful (omnipotent).

God is often called *omnipotent*, a word meaning that He is "all powerful." This power is witnessed in Genesis chapters 1–2 when God is introduced as the Creator of the cosmos, the earth, and all living things, including man. The Book of Psalms is filled with beautiful songs and poetry describing the greatness of God's unlimited power (Pss. 60, 63, 66, and so forth). God's greatest power is found in His spoken word! Since Creation He is "upholding all things by the word of His power" (Heb. 1:3).

The adversary would love for believers to think that *his* power is on equal footing with God Himself. If we are deceived into accepting this lie, then all of our prayer and rebuking of Satan is merely a "feel-good formula" that actually has no impact. In fact, if he were all powerful, he would never have needed to ask God for permission to test Job (Job 1). The opposite is true, as it was God who placed Satan on a *leash*, limiting him to what he *could* and *could not* do against Job. Satan would inflict Job with boils on his flesh, but he was restrained from taking Job's life (Job 2:4–6).

Christ promised spiritual authority over "all the power of the enemy" (Luke 10:19) and gave believers a special power through the infilling of the Holy Spirit (Acts 1:8). In the Gospels and Acts the apostles rebuked evil spirits, and they departed from the afflicted (Matt. 17:18). If we submit ourselves to God, we can "resist the devil and he will flee from you" (James 4:7). Peter added that you must resist the enemy, "steadfast in the faith" (1 Pet. 5:9). Obviously the enemy is not all powerful.

The enemy wants you to believe that he is stronger, smarter, and greater than he actually is. This deception often feels confirmed to us when we look around and see the influence evil has over society and throughout the world. Satan is not more powerful than the Almighty; he simply has a massive population pull from those who are willing to submit to him instead of resisting him. Neither is he smarter than you; he's just more experienced than you. He has played the game longer and has a playbook full of strategies and tricks that have been effective for many millennia. His bluff is that one trick played in the game of life where the formation reads, "This is a run," but the result will be a pass when you least expect it. He pulls off the onside kick at the beginning of the game instead at the conclusion when the game is tied. This is why we cannot be ignorant of his devices or methods (2 Cor. 2:11).

The Bible is God's game plan for living on earth when your heart is actually in heaven. Your affections are set on things above (Col. 3:2), but your directions are for life below. Since the Holy Spirit can show you "things to come" (John 16:13), He is our *bluff detector*, exposing strategies before they can occur. He has access to the entire spirit realm of both angelic messengers and demonic entities and can reveal the secrets of God (1 Cor. 14:2) and the strategies of the adversary.

CHAPTER 15

PORNOGRAPHY—THE SEDUCING SPIRIT BEHIND THE HINDERING SPIRIT

❦ ❦

Paul wrote to the young Timothy, "Now the Spirit speaketh expressly, that in the latter times some shall depart from the faith, giving heed to seducing spirits, and doctrines of devils" (1 Tim. 4:1, kjv). We see that happening today.

There are few men living in this generation who do not know the meaning of the word *pornography*. The word *pornography* can be derived from the modern Greek word *pornographia* (from the root words *pornē*, meaning "prostitute," and *pornea*, meaning "prostitution") and the root word *graphein* (meaning "to write or record something"). The word *pornography* indicates both "a written description or illustration of prostitutes or prostitution."[1] Prostitution existed in the pagan cultures in the time of both

Testaments, from the earliest days even into the New Testament era. While visiting the ruins of Pompeii in Italy, our tour guide took our group into a building that was once covered by volcanic ash. He stated there were over twenty-seven houses of prostitution throughout the city before the famed volcanic eruption covered the city. Inside this house—still intact—were paintings on the wall of various sexual acts that a person could request and pay for. After the group heard a detailed discussion of the idolatrous worship and perverted wickedness of the city, one tourist commented, "I'm not surprised that this city was destroyed."

Throughout history erotic statues, art, and personal contact with female prostitutes have been common in pagan Gentile cultures. Men tend to be sight oriented and can be emotionally and physically stirred by certain pornographic images. As a child aged five to nine growing up in rural southwestern Virginia, the only pornographic magazine was *Playboy*, and this magazine was kept under the counter in drugstores (there were no convenience stores). While I never saw one at that age, I would occasionally hear old men, in disgust, wondering what society was coming to for allowing a publisher to print and sell nudity in local stores. Eventually, over the past forty years, the pornographic printed images went from under the counter to the counter, to the television cable networks, and now to the easy access of the Internet.

Pornography at Age Eleven

I have only shared this story publicly once, and I believe it would fit the context of this chapter. When I was age eleven and in middle school, my father pastored in Northern Virginia. We lived in a neighborhood with many young people near my same age. We would spend a lot of time engaging in sports, making clubhouses, playing street football, and going to a sports area near the house with ball fields and basketball courts. There was a beautiful flowing creek behind the house, and many days were spent playing pirate and imagining finding buried treasure.

One evening I and another young man were near the main road, a four-lane highway near a large concrete bridge. We crossed the road and found ourselves in the medium, where several large evergreen trees formed a circle. There, in between the trees, was a large garbage bag with something in it. Our curiosity got the best of us, and to our shock it was numerous magazines, all with pictures of nude women.

At age eleven I had never seen any woman without clothes, being from a strong Christian home with very modest parents, and I was embarrassed at what I saw. The young fellow with me advised me that we should drag this bag of magazines into the woods near our house and look through them in that setting, as cars were whizzing by us where we were. When the road was clear, we carried the bag with what appeared to be twenty or more magazines into the woods and secured the bag under leaves. For several days young men ages eleven to thirteen would sneak into the woods and look at the pictures. At the time we were very innocent, and as young *church boys* with Christian parents who sheltered us, we had no idea how these images could bring a terrible bondage into a young man's life. To us it was a challenge and fun to sneak around doing this. We even called our secret meeting place, *The Playboy Club*.

However, to show you how an image can impact the mind of a young child or young man, the first image I saw at age eleven is still clear in my mind. To this day I cannot recall any other pictures in those magazines except the first one I saw. This reveals the literal impact and imprint on the mind through the visual pictures identified as pornography. In retrospect I believe that the discovery of these magazines was not an *accident* but a well-planned *setup* initiated by some type of a unclean spirit with the hopes that as a young child I would become addicted to pornography and experience a chain of bondage that would lock my mind into the cycle of lust of the flesh. However, later that same year at a church youth camp in Roanoke, Virginia, I totally dedicated my life to Christ and received the baptism of the Holy Spirit. This dynamic spiritual encounter set my heart on a path to pursue the Lord, study the Bible, and spend time with believers.

The brain is a neurological miracle that operates with the help of the five senses of seeing, hearing, smelling, tasting, and touching. The brain uses the information from the five senses to store and retrieve images and information that it receives. Our thoughts, feelings, and memories made by images exist in the brain as patterns of nerve messages. Each message and image actually burns a pathway into the brain through billions of axons and dendrites. The axon (also called a nerve fiber) is a long threadlike part of a nerve cell along which electrical impulses are conducted away from the neuron's cell body. The dendrite works like the branches of a tree and is the cell in which the electrical impulses are received and transmitted to the cell body.[2] If a person persists year after year in viewing pornography, they literally dig a channel in the brain that moves only in one direction. Thus they have difficulty after many years of reversing the process. This is why we say a person set in their ways has a "one-track mind." Individuals are able to recall images from many years ago as they are imprinted in the brain.

Thankfully, those magazines from my childhood experience were destroyed and the possible cycle of mental captivity was broken early. However, in the lives of many young people in our generation, the visual aspect of sexual images is literally in everything they read, see, and hear in the secular world—from television to movies to the Internet.

THE *PONEROS* SPIRIT
OF THE LAST DAYS

When Paul revealed the spiritual armor of God for a believer in Ephesians 6, he instructed believers, "Therefore take up the whole armor of God, that you may be able to withstand in the evil day, and having done all, to stand" (v. 13).

Paul spoke of the *evil day*, not just *evil days* (plural). Had he said "evil days," it would refer to a series of times and seasons in which evil would be continually released. He did allude to those times in 1 Timothy 4:1 when he spoke of seducing spirits that would be unleashed in the last days. However, in Ephesians 6:13 he was speaking of a specific day (the evil day), which would be very difficult for the *individual* believer. This "evil day" in Paul's time could refer to arrest by Roman government officials, persecution of the righteous, or of general temptation and spiritual attacks that can impact a believer's walk with God.

The Greek word for "evil" in Ephesians 6:13 is *poneros* and is used in a wide sense of "bad, evil, grievous, harmful and lewd."[3] We see a form of this word in the word *pornography*. In the Book of Revelation the King James Version speaks of a "whore" (Rev. 17:1, 15–16), which is from the Greek word *pornē*, meaning a "prostitute." The evil day of Paul's warning is a day that includes lewdness, sexual immorality, and perversion. In Roman times sexual promiscuity was common. When a person visits Rome, Italy, and the museums holding Greek-Roman art, full nudity was consistent with the Roman culture in paintings, sculptures, and in the bathhouses of that day. There was an obsession with gods and goddesses of fertility, which led to further immorality in the name of a god or a religion. In Corinth there were hundreds of temple prostitutes to "serve the worshippers" at the temple of Diana. This type of perversion assisted in the eventual fall of the Roman Empire, and the fall began morally, spiritually, then economically, then finally politically as ten heathen tribes overtook the western half of the empire.

In Ephesians 6:12 Paul list four types of active spirits in the satanic kingdom that operate in the earth at various levels, working against the kingdom of God. While each level of spirit has a realm of authority—from high governments to the lower workers of darkness—each has a main assignment, which is to possess or control the human flesh for the purpose of sinning against God. As I have often taught, spirits can take on the name of the disease or problem that they create in a human being. While there may not be a *spirit of pornography* by name, there is an "evil day" (*poneros*) and also lust of the flesh (1 John 2:16), which includes sexual addictions. These addictions become an obsession with people who are chained and addicted to the spirit force behind the bondage.

Today there is an obsession with sex and sexual perversion. America is literally enamored with same-sex relations, as liberal educators are making sure the upcoming younger generation accepts these "alternative lifestyles" with no opposing ideas or spiritual convictions. Not only has the *fatherless generation* produced a more *effeminate male* in the nation, but this has also rubbed off in the churches where ministers coddle ultrasensitive members to ensure no one is offended at the song, message, or type of service they have encountered. The obsession with pornography is only one of those bondage traps that has impacted millions of men, some of whom, although they reject any form of homosexual behavior, have confessed to being *comfortable* with viewing two women conducting lewd activities.

So outside of living in an *evil day*, what are some of the less discussed or least understood root causes of a continual addiction to pornography?

THE DOPAMINE HIGH

Why does an erotic picture of a strange woman have such an impact upon a man? The original and pure intent for a male and female was for a man to fall in love with a woman, enter into a marriage covenant, and for the husband to become emotionally and physically *excited* to see her in their intimate moments. The ability for a married couple to experience sex was for both procreation and pleasure.

There are numerous naturally released chemicals connected with the sight of your wife and also released during the intimate act. During your honeymoon as a man, testosterone, oxytocin, serotonin, and dopamine are released, which cause the feeling of euphoria. One of the most noted chemicals in the body is dopamine, a brain-released chemical behind all forms of motivation, including the desire to date, have intimate relations, and even eat. Dopamine is an important *feel-good* chemical.[4]

A test with rats reveals the importance of dopamine in the process of sexual relations. A male rat was placed in a cage with a very aggressive female rat. The male rate copulated six times, but eventually he settled down and would not respond to the female rat. When a new female was placed in the cage, within seconds the male rat was aggressive again, as his tiredness departed and his aggressive nature returned. In each case he eventually became tired of the female, until a new female rat was placed in the cage. With each new female, his aggression returned, as the rat received a new dose of the chemical dopamine to its brain. When your dopamine levels drop, so does your motivation.[5]

Thus, if the natural God-made chemicals are not flowing in the body of a man, then instead of renewing his mind and body, the man may begin to look outside of his marriage for a person who gives him that renewed feel-good moment, which can also lead to alcohol and drug addiction, along with pornography addiction.

Even certain foods, such as chocolate, release dopamine, which causes that mellow, chilled-out, and relaxed feeling.

The rat study demonstrates the effects on a man who continually views pornography. He eventually loses interest in his own companion, only receiving his thrill from the visual or physical contact of a new female, which releases numerous feel-good chemicals into his brain. The deception is that the man will think he has lost his love for his wife and is now "in love" with this new woman. Often it has nothing to do with love but everything to do with the chemicals bombarding his brain, which cause him to swoon with excitement. I have encountered husbands who left their wives because they were "in love" with another woman they met over the Internet. In reality, it was not *love* but a release of feel-good chemicals. Thus the enemy of the soul used the circumstances and the feelings to deceive the person into thinking he was in love when, in reality, he was *in lust*.

I have heard people say that when they saw a person the first time, it was *love at first sight*. I tend to believe it was actually *attraction at first sight*, as real love must be built upon a foundation of relationship and commitment. This is the danger when youth begin dating at an early age. Parents often allow their sons and daughters to date at age sixteen, which is the time when the raging chemicals are surging through the bodies of both sexes, but especially young men. As a young man and young girl hold hands, hug, and eventually kiss, every type of feel-good chemical is pouring through their bodies. They only "feel good" around this person, and soon, they are "in love" at age fifteen or sixteen and ready to run away to be married! I have watched young teenage girls become heartbroken, depressed, and ready to give up on life when their boyfriend "fell out of love." In reality, he found another female who stimulated his chemical levels higher, and he chose to replace his previous girlfriend with a new one.

In our youth ministry, we encourage our youth to *court* and not to *date*. In the courting process they go to each other's home with adult supervision or only go out together when there are other trusting youth present. We also encourage them not to get physically involved, as this only adds to the temptation and confusion. The Lord has a mate for each person, and when he or she finds that mate, they will be attracted first spiritually, then emotionally, and finally, at marriage, physically. Men especially must be aware of how their body works to ensure they maintain a strong marriage from the wedding day to the final moments when death parts them from their companion and lover.

THE PERFECT "10"

Many men who view images of what they believe are the *perfect woman*, called by some the *perfect 10*, are clueless to the fact that by using computer-enhanced special effects, the lines in the face and around the eyes are removed, the blemishes are erased, and the skin tone can be darkened. Even areas of additional weight can be manipulated to form a perfect curve. The image is enhanced to create a perfect 10. Then, after viewing the images of these *Photoshop-enhanced women*, the porn viewer returns to his precious wife, who cleans his clothes, keeps the house, and raises his children, where he sees her without makeup, with that additional "baby weight" she can't lose, and her hair a little disheveled. His interest is gone just like the rat's, because he has low testosterone and no dopamine being released, having used it all up viewing the pornographic images. Thus his new excitement comes from the emotional high he is experiencing from pornography. Pornography is popular because it tends to give a man a fantasy world without going outside of the physical bonds of matrimony. Yet Christ informed the people of His day that if a man looked on a woman to desire her in his heart, he had already committed adultery (Matt. 5:28).

Emotional feelings are a normal way of connecting us with our companion, family, and friends. True love produces a wonderful feeling of security and peace for a couple enjoying their covenant of marriage. However, emotions can fluctuate with surroundings and circumstances. When the money is in the bank, the new house is paid for, and you received a bonus at work, you are smiling, happy, and singing, "God is good all the time!" With a job loss, a child afflicted with a sickness, and the house needing repairs, you must rely on your covenant and vows to sustain your emotions.

REACTION TO A MARITAL FAILURE

When a woman discovers her husband has been two-timing her with an Internet fantasy or a flesh-and-blood woman, she reacts differently toward her husband. Some women immediately leave, while others seek counseling to restore their marital relationship. Without understanding the impact of these chemicals and how they affect the brain, a man who has fallen into a sexual sin is often considered by his companion to be an unfaithful partner who was *eaten up with lust* and not worthy of being loved ever again, since he broke her bond of trust. Some time back a noted minister fell into a moral failure for a period of time. When his wife discovered the situation, many thoughts went through her mind of how to handle this broken covenant. However, after praying, the Lord spoke to her and said, "He is worth saving," meaning he was worth rescuing from the trap and restoring their home and their marriage. His heart felt repentance, and the desire to be a good husband was a motivating force for her to work with him to prevent the enemy from gaining a trophy from the battle. To this day their marriage is stronger than ever.

I have had several friends in the past who engaged in adultery. In several cases the husband confessed his sin and asked for forgiveness. In some instances, after the confession, the wife felt the husband had "fallen in love" with the other woman, and this became the most difficult perception to deal with during the counseling session. At times this does occur, but after asking many men in private what actually happened and discussing their true feelings, several have said, "My wife thinks I am lying, but I never lost the love for my wife and actually felt heavily convicted of the Lord when I was sinning. I never wanted to hurt her, yet I was driven by an uncontrollable force." That *force,* many times, is a combination of three things: the release of feel-good chemicals, the power of a seducing spirit (1 Tim. 4:1, KJV), and the *thrill of the chase,* meaning the same thrill Eve experienced with the idea of eating from a forbidden tree—something the Bible calls *temptation.*

THE THRILL THAT CAN KILL

Adam and Eve discovered the *thrill that can kill.* The temptation to be as God and know good from evil was an overwhelming concept to Eve (Gen. 3:5). However, Adam was seduced by his beautiful wife into tasting what was forbidden, and eating from the tree of the knowledge of good and evil brought death to the first couple (v. 19). By nature men are thrill seekers. Some thrills come through sports, roller coasters, bungee jumping, and even sky diving. These activities produce a rush of a chemical called *adrenaline,* which, when released, causes the heart to race, breathing to increase, and, at times, the palms of the hands to sweat. Men are more likely than women to be thrill seekers and risk takers—in more ways than one.

In the beginning God gave Adam "dominion" (Gen. 1:26). In Genesis 10 Nimrod was a "mighty hunter" (v. 9); Esau was also a man of the field who was a hunter (Gen. 25:27). I was born and raised in West Virginia, the place I call *world headquarters* for deer hunters! Personally, hunting never appealed to me, as I had difficulty imagining the *boredom* (actually my impatience) of sitting for hours in one spot waiting for a deer to cross my path. However, hunters from the mountains will put on camouflage, take snacks and a thermos of coffee, bring their best rifles, and sit in a deer stand for hours of a day, days on end, to get that prize buck, and stuff its head, mounting its rack on the wall in their living rooms. The bragging rights last until the next year, when the process is repeated.

This hunter nature in men kicks in and motivates them to pursue deer and occasionally a *dear*—a two-legged female. My wife and I have been puzzled when seeing a rather average-looking man with a beautiful wife become unfaithful with a woman who is, as we should say, rather homely in her physical appearance. Those who knew the situation pondered as to how a man could be so *deceived* as to fall for a female who was far less attractive and with less personality than his beautiful wife.

One of the answers is a simple phrase: *the thrill of the chase*. Certain things appeal to the *hunt* in men. They will hit, tackle, jump, and scream until they drive their team into the end zone to score six points! Then they will slap each other high fives and yell like they are dying, reacting to the touchdown that will lead them to victory. Some call this a *testosterone rush*, but others simply call it *a football game*. This competitive spirit runs throughout the entire world and motivates companies to expand, teams to win, businesses to add new products, and men, at times, to chase the wrong *dear*. There is a danger in getting *bored of the rings* and having a droll marriage without a little spark to light the wet wood. Thus, the hunter spirit in a man entices him to leave his own camp and seek out the *dear* in the other man's woods.

A Sign of the Last Days

These forms of attacks on marriages and men are a part of the end-time arsenal of the enemy. In Matthew 24 the writer records where Christ listed numerous "signs of the times," which were significant and specific events to occur prior to His return. One of the premier warnings reads:

> And because iniquity shall abound, the love of many shall wax cold.
> —MATTHEW 24:12, KJV

It is significant to note that Christ did not say because "sin" would abound, but that "iniquity" would abound. Christians often used the words *sin* and *iniquity* interchangeably as though both words hold one meaning; however, the words are different both in the Greek New Testament and in the context of the level of disobedience linked to each word.

The common Greek word for "sin" in the New Testament is *hamartia* and actually means, "to miss the mark."[6] It alludes to a person shooting an arrow at a target and the arrow going completely off course. Sin takes a person off course, away from God's Word and God's will for that person's life. The Greek word for "iniquity" in Matthew 24:12 is *anomia,* meaning, "a violation of the law and wickedness."[7] In the Old Testament a sin was any act of disobedience against the law of God. However, iniquity was a higher level of sin, in that a person could be overcome by a temptation that caused him to fall into a *sin* (1 John 2:1), but *iniquity* was a willful and premeditated transgression of God's commands. Iniquity is the level of continual sinning that eventually leads to a lifestyle of disobedience and eventual perversion. David sinned with Bathsheba, but when he set up her husband to be killed so he could marry the wife who was now pregnant, the sin moved to the level of iniquity.

In the last days "iniquity shall abound." The word *abound* is the word for *increase*; iniquity will be on the increase prior to the return of Christ. The iniquity in the heart could then cause the "love of many [to] wax cold" (Matt. 24:12). The term "wax cold" is from a word that figuratively means to reduce the temperature by evaporation, or to reduce the temperature by turning down the heat and producing air that is chilled. Have you ever heard someone say, "They are as cold as an icicle"? This is the imagery in this verse; iniquity will eventually take the fire out of your love (and love life), leading to a frigid and cold relationship! We are surrounded by both sin and iniquity in people we work with and perhaps with family members in our blood line. The end-time spiritual powers work through the iniquity that is increasing in our world today.

THE HINDERING SPIRIT BEHIND THE ASSAULT

Such activities as viewing pornography may not begin with a spirit linked to the initial moment, but the adversary is clever to discover how to use each situation to his advantage. An unclean spirit can easily work like a magnet, attracting another magnet, pulling in images that make imprints upon the brain. Demonic spirits can be resisted and rebuked, but the source of images and information entering your eyes must be cut off to prevent further bondage. This is *closing the door* and cutting off any spirit's ability to feed off the sin or negative actions of a person.

Scientists, researchers, and the medical profession have noted that pornography and certain drugs such as crack cocaine actually affect the same areas of the brain. Yet some suggest that pornography may be more addictive than crack, as through rehab and other medical and spiritual methods the drugs can eventually be extracted from the body, but the images created by pornography cannot be removed and are impressed upon the memory for the long term.[8]

There is no easy way to break such a stronghold, as the pornography impacts the same area of the brain that certain feel-good drugs impact. The desire for that emotional high and care-free feeling and living in a fantasy world to escape reality becomes a draw to stay connected to the images or persons. Having had close friends who confided in me and were later helped, I will suggest several of their suggestions.

1. *It's not reality.* The entire world of pornography is not a real world, but one designed for fantasy. It is your wife—who cleans your clothes, cooks your food, keeps your house, picks up your dirty clothes, takes care of the children, and in many cases pays the bills—who is your *real helper*, trusted companion, and proven commodity! You cannot live the real life sleeping in a bed all day with your *fantasy pick*, as the real world has responsibilities, jobs, bills, and good and bad times. Get back to the real world.

2. *Never lose your first love.* If you ever feel your love is waning or is being consumed by the cares of life, then do something fun together with your companion—mini-dates, going away for a weekend, chilling out on a lake or private beach, eating dinner at a nice restaurant, or, as my wife and I do, driving through the mountains in nice weather, holding hands, and laughing. Do what you used to enjoy and leave the phones turned off!

3. *Go back and see old pictures and videos of all your good times.* Every few months I will pull out the old family pictures and begin to go through each book. When I see that beautiful little Alabama girl I married in those early pictures, two things cross my mind—"WOW, I know why I married her, because she was a *fox*." Second, I say to myself, "You are sure a lucky man to have her." That's when I recommit that I want to grow old with her and have her at my funeral talking about me, and not some

other person who didn't build a life with me. Good memories need to be recalled, and not the negative moments or discouraging times.

4. *Be open to talk about problems.* Women, let me say this, and please take notice. Men who fall into pornography or other sexual sins have told me they wanted so badly to tell their wife but were afraid she would either reject him, criticize him, leave him, or become cold in the marriage bed. If you truly love your man, you should have a clear understanding that he can come to you and say, "I'm having a struggle with this." Your reaction should not be to call him a *pervert*, but it should be to pray for him and get closer to him at this time. The Bible teaches that Satan can tempt a husband and wife if they do not meet one another's sexual need (1 Cor. 7:5), and rejecting your husband (or wife) when they are in a struggle is a weapon Satan will use to divide and conquer. His or her confession of being tempted must not be read as a desire for unfaithfulness but as an attack that must be thwarted through love and prayer.

5. *Take a stand and rebuke the spirits.* Years ago I battled with a terrible mental attack for several months, but never told my wife as I felt I could handle this alone and it was a season that would pass. Finally I exposed the assault and later received complete freedom. Months later when I told her my battle, she cried and said, "Why didn't you tell me? I knew something was wrong but didn't know what. You should have to me so I could pray for you." Since that time when I am under what I believe to be an attack from the enemy, I ask her to lay hands upon

me and pray. It does work. When you discern a spirit is involved, then rebuke the spirit and command it to loosen its hold and be removed! There is also additional authority released when at least two are in agreement (Matt. 18:19).

6. *Shut out and remove the source.* You may need your companion to serve as a watchperson over your actions, assisting in guarding you or removing any cable networks or perhaps placing a filter on the Internet. Just as in the case of alcohol and drugs, someone addicted to porn must have a long period of time in which he or she cannot see these images in order to provide time for healing to occur. Then to remain healed that person must maintain discipline.

7. *Be filled with the Holy Spirit.* The power of the Holy Spirit brings righteousness, peace, and joy to a believer (Rom. 14:17). Former addicts reveal that the powerful infilling of the Holy Spirit and praying in the prayer language of the Spirit brings such spiritual and emotional fulfillment that they no longer crave or need the chemical substances that held them captive. The presence of the Lord manifested through His Spirit brings such companionship, fellowship, and fulfillment that He becomes the emotional *high* that fills the empty places of the heart.

Without doubt, one of the main game plans in the playbook of Satan is to place an individual under the bondage of pornography, which, as a believer will produce condemnation, guilt, and shame, thus hindering your spiritual walk and confidence in your prayer life. It is the will of God for you to walk in power, love, and a sound mind (2 Tim. 1:7).

CHAPTER 16

BREAKING HABITS THAT CREATE HINDRANCES

❦ ❧

I F A CHRISTIAN has never indulged in or felt a sense of bondage from some form of a habit that became addictive, it is often difficult for that person to understand why a person who has, for example, a smoking habit, can't just quit cold turkey and lay aside the weights (or, at other times, certain sins) that are easily besetting them (Heb. 12:1).

It is because within certain habits there is a mixture of chemicals or addictive agents that cause the neurological system to depend upon the continuation of the habit in order for the person to maintain that feel-good feeling. Often it is not until a medical report reveals that, for example, a smoker has been stricken with a disease or physical malady resulting from the habit that the *motivation* arises from within to seek freedom from the particular habit. I have known of many people who truly love the Lord and regularly attend church but who have a smoking habit. At times the individuals have approached me, wondering if the habit can actually be a roadblock to certain spiritual blessings, including having their prayers answered.

Let me first confess that, thankfully, I have never had the desire at any time in my life to smoke or use tobacco products. I am actually *allergic* to cigarette and cigar smoke, and when entering a room where any smoker has been, my eyes water, my sinuses close up, and I become very uncomfortable. I also have a sensitive nose, which I teasingly say is as sensitive "as a dog," and can smell the smoke at a long distance. This has worked to my personal advantage as a teen, since I could have never smoked because of my body's reaction to it. However, others have no such reaction to tobacco smoke.

When we were growing up in the Full Gospel churches, no one in the congregation was received as a member into the church if he or she had a smoking habit. However, once the person was *sanctified* and the habit was broken, membership was permitted. One reason given for withholding membership was that the habit was defiling the temple of the Holy Spirit: "Do you not know that you are the temple of God and that the Spirit of God dwells in you? If anyone defiles the temple of God, God will destroy him. For the temple of God is holy, which temple you are" (1 Cor. 3:16–17). Another reason was that it was not a good *testimony* to the youth in the church or to those in public. The denomination had a sincere desire that their members live a life of sanctification and holiness not only within the church walls but also outside the church in the community.

The only challenge I saw with this teaching while growing up was that often a feeling of guilt or condemnation arose in the person smoking, especially if he or she had difficulty breaking the habit. Also, at times it could cause a nonsmoker to be more judgmental toward a smoker, and this attitude of being more righteous than another person was certainly Pharisaical and not from the Holy Spirit. I also noticed that instead of a smoker being in church where he or she could receive help and freedom through the power of the Word, the person often felt so guilty that he or she never attended church for fear of being judged by the congregation as unworthy of God's blessings.

As a teen I heard ministers, when preaching against habits, announce that "God will destroy" the person who defiles his body. It was common medical knowledge that smoking for a long period of time could cause various forms of cancer. Certainly I do not take this verse (1 Cor. 3:16–17) lightly, and I understand that the human body is the dwelling place of God and His Spirit on earth. However, if a person eventually gets a form of cancer from smoking, it was *not God* who *destroyed* the temple; it was the chemicals in the smoke that caused the damage. In other words, God is not using a habit to take the life of someone early in their prime.

When writing this manuscript, I was meditating on these verses with the emphasis on the phrase, "God will destroy him." The word *destroy* is used in the 1611 King James translation thirty-two times, and the particular Greek word used in this passage is different from the other thirty-one times the word *destroy* is used. The common word for destroy used in numerous passages is *appollumi*, and means, "to fully destroy, die or perish." (See Matthew 10:28.) In 1 Corinthians 3:17, it is the word *phtheiro*, which means, "to wither away, to shrivel or to spoil over a process of time."[1] Hearing this passage preached the way it was while growing up, we could see God trying to kill the person who was smoking or defiled their temple (their body) in any way. Actually, the Greek interpretation can mean that God will allow the person to begin to wither away and be spoiled over a process of time—*without preventing it.*

Let me say it this way. If a believer persists in any action that brings moral or physical corruption that impacts his or her physical body, God will not intervene to stop the destruction (for example, a disease) from entering the body as a result of that person's actions. A good example is someone who is morally careless and through fornication or adultery receives a sexually transmitted disease. The person cannot cry out, "God, why didn't You prevent this from happening to me?" or "Why didn't You stop this?", because the person walked into a situation with some knowledge that there are repercussions to certain lifestyles. If a believer persists and does not get victory over a habit such as smoking, the body will eventually succumb to the effects and the person's life can be taken prematurely through the diseases (cancer, heart trouble, or stroke) caused by putting a substance within the temple that can harm. Smokers will often point out, and it is true, that others abuse their body through overeating or by eating foods that will clog the arteries, cause unhealthy weight gain, and eventual heart attacks. I would suggest we must all examine our physical lifestyles and make adjustments to maintain a strong and healthy temple if we wish to live out our days.

Certainly in any believer's life there can be both sins and weights that *beset*, or weigh a person down from effectively running the race of faith (Heb. 12:1). We know from reading the Scriptures there are certain practices that are sin. No gray lines—simply sin. Lying, stealing, fornication, murder—all these are sins (Gal. 5:19–21). There are also weights that can easily slow us down. Hebrew 12:1 (KJV) says:

> Wherefore seeing we also are compassed about with so great a cloud of witnesses, let us lay aside every weight, and the sin which doth so easily beset us, and let us run with patience the race that is set before us.

In this passage the Greek word for "weight" is *ogkos*, and it means, "a burden that causes you to be bent over or that weighs you down spiritually or mentally."[2] Figuratively it can allude to a hindrance that distracts you from fully running your race to gain the prize. The word *beset* is an old English word that, in Greek, refers to someone standing near a runner attempting to thwart, distract, or disrupt the race in whatever direction the runner is running. A smoking habit, like other habits, can weigh a person down in several areas: in the *cost* of purchasing the cigarettes, which is an added *weight* of expense; in the *odors* that cling to your clothes, in your car, and in your home (especially distasteful for nonsmokers); and the eventual *damage* it will cause to your lungs, heart, and arteries. When I was talking with a youth group on one occasion, several of the older girls stated that when they dated a young man in the past who was a smoker and kissed that person goodbye, it was like *kissing an ashtray*. (Single fellows, this is a good *motivation* to quit now!) Whether this was an exaggeration or not, I am uncertain. However, my subject is not intended to condemn someone struggling with the habit, but to bring knowledge and understanding to the subject.

FACTS ABOUT SMOKING

According to the American Cancer Society's research on smoking, tobacco smoke contains more than 7,000 chemical components, with more than 250 of these known to be harmful and at least 69 known to cause cancer.[3] Out of all of the lung cancer deaths in the world, smoking is the cause of 90 percent of those deaths.[4] I have spoken with several nurses who have watched lung cancer patients pass in the hospital, and they have told me it is one of the most horrible types of death as the individual struggles to breathe. Every day 1,200 Americans die directly from smoking, and more than 435,000 Americans die from tobacco-related illness every year.[5] These facts alone should cause someone who has never smoked to think twice before beginning the habit. But what about those who already battle with this habit? Why is there such a craving for a cigarette?

The Craving—Nicotine

Just as coffee contains caffeine, cigarettes contain a substance called *nicotine*, a natural drug in tobacco that is highly addictive over time and is the main substance that leads to dependency. Nicotine is an *analkalois*, a colorless and highly addictive chemical. In the past, when farmers would plant their crops, they would take tobacco and mix it with water and spray their plants to protect them from insects. This was one of the ways in which my grandfather William Stone, from West Virginia, kept insects from eating his plants; the nicotine killed the *bugs*.

As a person inhales the smoke, the nicotine is carried into the lungs and absorbed into the bloodstream and up to the smoker's brain within a matter of seven to ten seconds after being inhaled.[6] Tobacco is also chewed or dipped; snuff is made to be placed directly in the mouth. Research indicates that nicotine affects the heart rate, the blood vessels, the hormonal system, and a person's metabolism. When a woman smokes, nicotine can be found in the breast milk and the cervix mucus.[7] When nicotine is released in the blood, it impacts the neurotransmitters in the brain and releases dopamine in what is called the *reward circuits* of the brain, giving the person that sudden sense of relaxation or that *good feeling* a smoker claims to experience.[8] However, the nicotine acts as a depressant and actually interferes with the information that flows between the nerve cells. This is why the longer a person smokes, the more that person begins to increase the number of cigarettes to maintain the nicotine levels in the body. Smoking also causes the heart to beat faster, requiring more oxygen. Smoking actually causes hypertension in many smokers, as the chemicals cause the blood vessels to narrow, causing blood to move slower.

Research has now proven that there is also great danger in *secondhand smoke*. Other individuals in the family who are not smokers, by being in a car or a room with a smoker, breathe the secondhand smoke—the smoke coming from the lit cigarette in the room and out of the mouth of the smoker. Secondhand smoke is just as dangerous as the smoke entering the smoker's lungs. This alone is a great motivator to break the habit. According to American Cancer Society resources, each year there are an estimated forty-six thousand deaths from heart-related diseases linked to second-hand smoke. Secondhand smoke also causes an increase in asthma and asthma-related problems, including respiratory infections in children. The bottom line is that secondhand smoke can actually kill children and adults who are nonsmokers but are present in the house, room, or car with a smoker![9]

When Trying to Quit

Many Christians picked up the smoking habit prior to their conversions. I have met many individuals over my many years of ministry who were instantly delivered from the habit, either at the moment of their conversion to Christ or at the time they were baptized in the Holy Spirit. The Lord did a wonderful work of what the old-timers called *sanctification*, which simply means, "to set apart something or someone for a holy purpose." This sanctification process includes but is not limited to separation from various unclean habits. However, there are other Christians who have made a sincere effort to quit, yet when the craving for the nicotine kicks in, they return to smoking. After making several attempts to quit, they eventually give up. This is because the nicotine is in the blood-stream, and the numerous feel-good chemicals in the human body that are released are craving another hit from the nicotine. It is this craving that some are unable to resist, and they return to smoking after attempting to lay aside the weight of the habit.

Reasons for Quitting

There are many reasons a Christian, or for that matter anyone, with the smoking habit should desire to kick the habit. The first reason is to live out the full number of your days, living to see your children and your grandchildren. In Ecclesiastes 7:17 the writer asked the question as to why we should foolishly sin and "die before your time?" It is possible that fleshly habits can send us to a premature grave when, if we would have been free from the dangerous chemicals, our bodies would not have suffered the disease that *took us out*. The fact that secondhand smoke is dangerous to your companion and all of your family members can also serve as a motivating factor in increasing your desire to quit. As Christians, it is not a good *testimony and example* to others, especially children or visitors, to have a *smoking break* for the elders and the board members on the front steps of the church as people are trying to get through the puffs of smoke to enter the congregation! Another reason is the physical effects smoking has on a person's breath, clothing, teeth, and so forth. The single most important reason, however, is for your health's sake and respect for the temple of God—your body.

People have often said, "Well, people are also addicted to coffee, so what's the big difference?" I have never visited a hospital where a person was struggling to breathe because he or she drank too much coffee or who had developed cancer from the caffeine. I will tell you that too much caffeine is not good for a person, and some people should come off of coffee if it has become addictive to them. Too much caffeine keeps you from resting well and gives you the jitters. Years ago I was drinking about three cups of coffee a day as well as iced tea every time I ate lunch or dinner. Eventually I began losing my voice. I thought it was caused by small cysts on my vocal chords. It turned out that the years of drinking caffeine had begun drying out my vocal cords, which I did not know could occur. I immediately came off of coffee and began drinking water in place of the tea. Within about one month my full voice returned, and I felt much better.

WHAT SHOULD YOU DO TO HELP KICK THE HABIT?

Individuals who have quit smoking state there are several things a person desiring to stop the habit should do to assist in their desire to quit. First, allow two weeks for cutting down. During that time make yourself cut back on the number of cigarettes you are smoking. As you begin cutting back, there will be thirty to sixty days in which the craving will be strong, but mentally resist the craving by keeping your mind occupied. Second, remove all packs from the house during this time period. As long as you are hiding packs, you will be tempted to go to them for "just one more smoke."

Today there are numerous antismoking helps that can assist you in reducing the craving for nicotine. Of course a person should always consult a health professional if they are taking any medications to ensure that the medications will not clash with any antismoking drug. Some sources suggest taking vitamins C and B to help reduce irritability. It is also important to avoid places where you know a group will be smoking. It is also important to tell friends who may smoke that you are trying to quit and to ask them to please not smoke around you. Any urge to smoke should be met with something to be placed in your mouth, such as water and, as strange as it sounds, sucking on a prune and keeping the pit in your mouth up to an hour. It is also important to stay in touch with someone you know who has quit to encourage you in your process.

With all of the above instruction, we must not leave out the spiritual side of your freedom! The anointing of the Holy Spirit is able to "break the yoke" of any bondage in a person's life (Isa. 10:27). When a person makes up his or her mind that he or she *wants* to quit, the Lord will help that person quit.

How to Pray for Freedom

There are two prayers that I prayed in my early revivals when I was impressed to pray for those desiring freedom from the smoking habit. Since nicotine is the root cause of the addictive nature of smoking, I would ask the Lord to remove all traces of nicotine in the person's bloodstream through the power of the blood of Christ—a type of spiritual *blood transfusion*. This prayer also included that the desire for the habit would be broken. I know that if the craving for the nicotine is gone, the desire to smoke will be gone.

The second prayer seems a little radical. However, I saw it work on many occasions. I would pray that the cigarettes would begin to make the person feel sick when he or she smoked them and that the person would literally become *sick of smoking*. Amazing things can change when you get sick and tired of being sick and tired of something!

I have never forgotten a rather odd incident in Daisy, Tennessee, in 1981 during an eight-week revival. A wife brought her husband's cigarettes in a paper bag and asked me to "curse the tobacco" to make him sick and quit the habit. She couldn't take the smoke in the house anymore and knew it was a danger to her and the children. I earnestly asked the Lord to make them *bitter* when he smoked them. She took them home and laid them on his normal spot—the top of the television. The next day he came home, saw the new pack, opened them, and took a smoke. He began coughing violently. He put that one out and lit up a second, with the same effect. He yelled, "What's wrong with the cigarettes? They are terrible!" After lighting a third, he suddenly ran outside coughing. She found him rolling on the grass trying to breathe!

She was frightened until he said, "Man, these cigarettes are terrible. They're bitter!" She laughed and told him what she had done. He went to smoke another one to prove it was a *fluke*, and it was bitter. So were the next few he tried. He decided to attend the revival to see the young preacher who could curse a pack of cigarettes, and he was touched by the Lord that night and set free! While this is a rare and unusual story, a person's faith can certainly bring deliverance in every area of their lives, as it is the will of God for the Son to set you free (John 8:36). In our early ministry when smokers desired to quit, we would pray that they would become *sick* of the smoke. I received reports that this began to occur in believers who sincerely desired to stop. Thus, prayer is very significant and a powerful weapon for this struggle.

Continual smoking is a habit, and it will eventually cause you and even those living with you serious health problems. I believe it is the will of the Lord to give you a long life and to remove from your life any habit that could reduce the number of your days. As a believer, your body is the temple of the Holy Spirit, and God desires His temple to remain clear from impurities. We agree with you that God will bring an anointing to break the yoke and give you strength to be free from this habit!

Various habits of the flesh can certainly be a hindrance to a believer. There will be great relief, release, and rest in the Spirit when a believer receives complete deliverance. We should make every effort to care for our body, since it is the temple of the Holy Spirit. This includes proper food, exercise, and rest. God instructs us to do this to care for our bodies and give us a longer and fuller life.

CAN MY PRAYERS BE HINDERED?

At the beginning of this chapter I posed a question that was asked me by a person with a smoking habit: "Can smoking hinder my prayers from being answered?" According to Scripture, I do know that unrepentant sin and iniquity will most certainly impact your prayer life, as we read: "If I regard iniquity in my heart, the Lord will not hear" (Ps. 66:18). In reading the New Testament approach to God through prayer, the one thing that does and will hinder your prayer life is your lack of confidence in your prayer through a spirit of condemnation. We read:

> My little children, let us not love in word or in tongue, but in deed and in truth. And by this we know that we are of the truth, and shall assure our hearts before Him. For if our heart condemns us, God is greater than our heart, and knows all things. Beloved, if our heart does not condemn us, we have confidence toward God. And whatever we ask we receive from Him, because we keep His commandments and do those things that are pleasing in His sight. And this is His commandment: that we should believe on the name of His Son Jesus Christ and love one another, as He gave us commandment.
>
> —1 John 3:18–23

When you sin, there will be a sense of conviction—where the Holy Spirit will *arrest* and seize your attention to call you to repentance. If you obey and repent, you will be released from condemnation, which, in the Greek thought, is a sentence passed upon a person who was found guilty of a crime. Thus conviction is the arrest and condemnation is the penalty for the unrepentant sin. If a person's heart senses condemnation when he prays because of a known or hidden sin, then he has no confidence in his prayer. This may be why many believers always desire someone else to pray for them and their specific needs. They have little confidence in their own prayers.

If you are engaged in any type of activity in which you always have a feeling of conviction, then your prayers will be hindered, as the conviction is a sign of some form of disobedience in your life. If you are making every effort to be released and free from those things that are a spiritual hindrance, then I believe the grace and mercy of God will be extended to you, even in the midst of your struggle, as God's will is for you to be free!

These types of habits are not healthy, and God desires you to live a long life and live out all of your days. The playbook strategy of the adversary holds a strategy to cut your life short by using whatever methods available at his disposal. However, the playbook of God (the Bible) indicates that Christ came to set men free indeed (John 8:36), and I believe this freedom includes freedom from habits of the flesh.

CHAPTER 17

WHY AM I STILL TEMPTED—EVEN AFTER I HAVE RECEIVED CHRIST?

T HERE MAY BE a slight challenge in the way we introduce a redemptive covenant to the unconverted souls. When we present the gospel in a manner to *imply* that once we have received Christ, many of our problems will cease and difficulties will subside, we do an injustice to both the message and the seeker. Some young converts are surprised to discover that the same darts of temptations that were shot into their mind tempting them to sin before conversion are still flying in their direction after receiving Christ. In light of the fact that temptation never ceases, even after you are converted to Christ, two things must be understood: the *psychology* of satanic temptation and the *power* of the Holy Spirit to renew the mind using the "shield of faith," that quenches Satan's burning arrows (Eph. 6:16).

Trouble Is a Part of Living

An important truth to understand is that trouble comes to both believers and nonbelievers. Not all trouble is the result of temptation; difficult times come to all people.

> I am not at ease, nor am I quiet;
> I have no rest, for trouble comes.
>
> —Job 3:26

> Yet man is born to trouble,
> As the sparks fly upward.
>
> —Job 5:7

> Man who is born of woman
> Is of few days and full of trouble.
>
> —Job 14:1

The Hebrew word used for "trouble" in Job 14:1 is *rogez*, and it refers to some type of commotion. It is also used in connection with the restlessness of a horse and the sound of the crashing of thunder. When a horse is restless, it can become aggressive and can throw a rider off its back to the ground. The sudden and unexpected crash of thunder can shock the hearer and create an increase in the heart rate. This is often the same reaction when unexpected trouble strikes. It is sudden, causes restlessness, and can create fears—both founded and unfounded.

When I was growing up, there was a common saying that stated, "Trouble comes in threes." In the case of Job, he lost three things—his children, his livestock, and eventually his health (Job 1–2). Job's troubles were then *judged* by three friends, each giving his own opinion of the reasons for Job's losses (Job 2:11; 32:1–5). If trouble comes in threes, then spiritual authority and unity are increased when three agree. Solomon alluded to this in a rather poetic manner when he wrote, "Though one may be overpowered by another, two can withstand him. And a threefold cord is not quickly broken" (Eccles. 4:12). It was Christ who said that if two or three were gathered in His name, He would be in their midst (Matt. 18:20). Actually, there are three main methods in which trouble manifests:

1. Self-invited trouble, which is created by personal actions and wrong decisions you make

2. Uninvited trouble, which comes as a result of outside people or situations that were unseen and unknown

3. Natural trouble, caused by a storm, tornado, flood, drought, volcano, earthquake, or other natural disaster

Uninvited trouble is what Job endured when he was targeted by Satan, an uninvited intruder (Job 1:1–12; 2:1–7). Trouble impacts us both *within* and *without*. In 2 Corinthians 11 the apostle Paul lists twenty-two different situations that were the result of evil or wicked men persecuting him or of circumstances that caused difficulty in his global travels. He called these "things that are without" (v. 28, KJV). In the same verse he then spoke of the "care of all the churches," which would have been situations from *within*. Our *within problems* include internal emotion, spiritual or health conflicts, and the outside difficulties and negative circumstances that are not of our making and beyond our control. Temptation is a pressure that often initiates from *without* (with what we see or hear) and impacts us with pressure from *within*. The testing without often enters through the five senses of hearing, seeing, tasting, smelling, and touching, and the flesh is dominated by these five sense gates. The testing within is caused by the thoughts that are birthed on the image screen of the mind.

The Power of Temptation

The word *tempt* refers to something being tested or even scrutinized under some form of pressure. The word *tempt* in Hebrew can have the connotation of, "to assay, or to purge metal by using fire, such as when impurities are removed from gold and silver through hot flames burning out the dross and leaving the pure precious metal." Temptation begins in the form of a thought to do something contrary to the laws or ethics of God. If the thought persists, it turns into a mental pressure and eventually stirs the emotions of the person being tempted. The great danger to a believer is when the *thought* becomes a *feeling*. Once a temptation moves from a simple thought to a feeling, it presses on the emotions of an individual. Then the individual emotions begin building mental images called *imaginations*. As the imaginations persist, they become mental strongholds. Mental strongholds tied to emotionally charged images are difficult to break, and the person finds himself in a mental battle. For example, men are sight oriented when it relates to the opposite sex. Pornographic images create emotionally charged feelings that impact the brain and imprint pictures on the mind. Eventually, viewing such images builds a personal bondage, or a stronghold.

All thoughts come on two levels: the conscious and the subconscious. The conscious temptation is rooted in things you can see and hear, but the subconscious temptation operates upon a mental fantasy of imagination you make up in your own mind. The enemy has the ability to send images into the thinking process, manipulating the emotions by using mental images. We think this only occurs to sinners and unbelievers or to believers who are living carnal lives. However, there are three examples from Scripture of individuals whose *thinking* was directly influenced by Satan.

SATAN CAN INFLUENCE THE
THOUGHTS OF BELIEVERS

Christ questioned His disciples as to who men said that He was. After several responses Simon Peter finally spoke up, saying, "You are the Christ, the Son of the living God" (Matt. 16:16). Christ responded that Peter was speaking a revelation directly from the heavenly Father. Immediately Christ began speaking of His future sufferings, but Peter began rebuking the Lord and telling Him that such suffering would not occur. Jesus responded, "Get behind Me, Satan..." (v. 23). By rebuking Christ, Peter was really saying that Christ's words were not true. Satan has always desired to prove God a liar with His words. On this occasion the subtle *thought* placed in Peter's mind may have been said to encourage Christ, but in reality it was a dart from Satan, who was intent on resisting the plan of the Almighty.

A second disciple of Christ, Judas Iscariot, was the treasurer among Christ's traveling ministry team, yet he is identified by John as a "thief" (John 12:6). He attended the Last Supper and drank from the Communion cup (John 13:26). Yet during this sacred moment when Christ was introducing a new covenant, we read that: "Satan entered Judas" (Luke 22:3). It was dangerous for Judas to drink from the cup while his heart was filled with evil. Years later Paul spoke of the Lord's Supper when believers receive the bread and the cup and noted that some in the church were "weak and sick among you, and many sleep [had actually died]," because they had partaken from the table of the Lord unworthily and had drank judgment (or condemnation) to themselves (1 Cor. 11:29–30). Judas had certainly drank from the cup of the fruit of the vine in an unworthy fashion, and thus he opened a door to Satan, later actually taking his own life (Matt. 27:3–5).

A third and very powerful event is recorded in Acts 5. A husband and wife sold a piece of personal property and committed to bringing the finances from the sale to the apostles to distribute among believers in need. They made a public commitment, but in private they formed a conspiracy to withhold part of the profits. Peter confronted the husband and the wife—each individually on the same day. He asked the husband why Satan had "filled your heart to lie to Holy Spirit" (v. 3). The result of this *money-laundering conspiracy* was that both Ananias and Sapphira came under the judgment of the Almighty and lost their lives.

Notice that Peter and Judas were disciples, and Ananias and Sapphira were members of the Jerusalem church. None of these individuals were *possessed* of the devil. However, in all three instances Satan is credited with giving the thoughts and actions to the individuals. These examples reveal the possibility of certain thoughts, which are contrary to the Word and will of God, actually being shot into the minds of believers by Satan and his invisible forces. This possibility is why Paul wrote, "Lest Satan should take advantage of us; for we are not ignorant of his devices" (2 Cor. 2:11). Satan's greatest device is fiery darts that are sent into the mind in the form of wrong thoughts (Eph. 6:16), creating confusion, division, and temptation.

THE MIND IS A BATTLEFIELD

The mind becomes a battlefield. Most choices we make are based either upon *information* or *emotion*. The Book of Proverbs is a biblical book of wisdom nuggets, the majority penned by Solomon who was noted for his gift of wisdom (1 Kings 3:28). In Proverbs there are three prominent words: knowledge, understanding, and wisdom. By definition, *knowledge* is the *accumulation* of facts. *Understanding* is the ability to organize and *arrange* the facts, and *wisdom* is knowing how to *apply* those facts. I have often stated that college can give you knowledge, but it is God who gives true wisdom.

When a decision is based upon proper knowledge, then a good choice can be made, which usually ends with a positive result. If, however, a decision is based upon how we feel at the moment or purely upon emotion, then this can lead to future difficulty and confusion. I can recall that when I was about sixteen years of age, I became close friends with a young girl in my dad's church. If I recall, she was about fourteen years of age but mentally and spiritually mature for her age. I remember buying a ring and giving it to her. I sat down with her father and told him my intended plans were marriage. I may not remember much about those days, but I do remember that he didn't smile or laugh. Now that I have children, I know what he was thinking: Where would I work? How much income would I bring in? Where would I live? And so forth. I did have a car, and that was a start! In my immaturity the idea was based upon emotion, not upon wisdom.

Six years later I met my soul mate and the woman who is, to this day, my girlfriend—Pam, my wife of more than thirty years. My decision to marry was not based upon emotion but upon revelation and information. Having met her during a four-week revival in Northport, Alabama, I knew by revelation of the voice of the Holy Spirit that I was to marry Pam, and I also had spent ample time weighing the *cost* of marriage, such as where we would live, the light and food bills, the car payment, the furniture needed, and the facts of life. Thus the decision was based upon mutual love and mutual knowledge of what it would take to make the marriage successful. It requires both proper emotional stability and correct knowledge to overcome the battles of the mind. Understanding the rational and emotional sides of men and women also reveals clues to the strategy of the enemy's temptations to both men and women.

How Satan Tempts
Men and Woman

The human brain houses two hemispheres: the left hemisphere and the right hemisphere. These two halves are connected by fibrous tissue called *corpus callosum*. Each hemisphere in the brain serves a different function in the human body. The right side is more visual and processes intuitively, holistically, and randomly. The left side of the brain is the seat of language and processes in a logical and sequential order.[1] When men and women are given the same challenge to solve, they often use different sides of their brains to come up with the same answer or solution. Most men tend to be rational and can come across as rather cold and unaffectionate, while women tend to be freer with their compassion, affection, and emotions.

These differences in the left and right sides of the brain are seen when in the shopping habits of men and women. Most men go to a mall and head directly to the store they want, buying what they came for within ten minutes and walking out with their choice. Women will try on five pairs of shoes before picking out a pair, as they must have exactly the right size, shape, color, and even brand! Men may spend time on a mathematical formula, while women prefer a romance novel. When giving details, the majority of men want the black-and-white version with the bottom line, but women are often very detailed when relating a story and when giving their opinions. Men are willing to take more risk with money (just look at the stock market), but women tend to be concerned with security and desire less risk. When men get lost while driving to a destination, they want to try to figure it out and will continue driving thirty minutes in circles, hoping to hit the right road any minute. Their wives will beg them just to stop and get a map or directions!

There have been many books and articles written on the differences between the rational/emotional reactions and brain functions of men and women. However, I have never read a book that described how our spiritual adversary tempts a man and woman by using the rational and emotional aspects of each human brain.

I believe one reason that opposites attract is that where a husband may be weak, the wife is usually strong, and where the wife may struggle, the husband can step up to the plate. I am a very reactionary person, but my wife is very stable and responds according to knowledge and not just emotion. I do not conduct the staff meetings, but she is in charge, and believe me, the staff would rather meet with her because she listens when I am quick to react. These opposites between a man and woman are very useful for bringing balance into the relationship. However, it is the fact that at times the enemy uses these differences to drive a wedge between a husband and wife.

This has been played out thousands of times in marriages. If one marital partner is totally rational and expresses little emotion, that person may also struggle in expressing affection, such as hugging, holding hands, and touching. If his or her companion is very affectionate, this difference can become a future trap of the enemy to ensnare the more affectionate or touchy-feely type of personality, as the enemy magnifies this difference. Often affection and touch are a form of a *love language* in the DNA of a person, and a lack of this can cause the enemy to forge a dart of temptation. Paul understood the importance of a husband and wife's physical relationship when he wrote in 1 Corinthians 7:5:

> Do not deprive one another except with consent for a time, that you may give yourselves to fasting and prayer; and come together again so that Satan does not tempt you because of your lack of self-control.

The phrase "deprive one another" refers to the physical act of marriage. Paul said when a husband and wife agree to spend time in fasting and prayer, they should also avoid sexual contact, but only for a time, and then they should come together again. If they refuse to meet one another's physical and emotional needs, Satan will tempt them.

The same is true if a companion is extremely emotional and uses little rational reasoning in his or her life decisions. I have known of women, or even occasionally of men, whose weakness was the compulsory purchasing of clothes and other items. They literally experienced an emotional *high* and fulfillment through shopping. At the end of each month their spouse sat at the kitchen table with bills from two to five different credit cards and tried to figure out how to break this *spending spirit*. Many divorces have been rooted in the lack of money necessary to cover the debts and high balances on credit cards caused by unwise spending habits. These debts can make it difficult to meet even the most basic needs of the family.

All emotional feelings must be balanced with real facts. If we are all facts and no feelings, our personalities will be very boring to others. However, if we are all emotions, we may become a roller coaster of highs and lows depending on our circumstances or feelings at the moment, and we will be very difficult to live with and understand.

Jesus is the perfect example of a person who balanced rational understanding with emotion and feelings. We read where Jesus was "moved with *compassion*..." (Matt. 9:36, emphasis added), is "touched with the *feeling* of our infirmities," and was "in all points *tempted* like as we are, yet without sin" (Heb. 4:15, KJV, emphasis added). At the tomb of Lazarus "Jesus *wept*" (John 11:35, emphasis added). On other occasions He became agitated and amazed at the unbelief of the people (Mark 6:6). Christ used effective *reasoning* when debating the religious leaders and flowed in *compassion* when ministering to the sick and afflicted.

THE POWER OF A WOMAN

It is no secret that great men have been brought down from important positions of power or authority through the strategy of PMS, which, spiritually speaking, is pride, money, and sex. A roaring lion and a thousand Philistines could not defeat Samson, but one Philistine woman with a pair of hair salon scissors took out God's champion (Judg. 16). Eve influenced her husband to eat from the forbidden tree (Gen 3:6), and Sarah influenced Abraham to have a child through Hagar (Gen. 16:1–3). Delilah vexed Samson until he revealed the secret of his Nazirite vow (Judg. 16:4–18). Bathsheba was so beautiful that David was willing to risk his influence and kill her husband to make her his wife and cover his sin (2 Sam. 11). Strange wives were able to override the wisdom of Solomon and turn his heart away from God (1 Kings 11). When a young woman danced in front of King Herod, he offered her half of his kingdom and was influenced by the mother of girl to behead John the Baptist (Mark 6:22–25). A woman can stir up a *passion, emotion,* and *excitement* in a man and tap into his *emotional side,* overpowering the rational thinking.

How many times have you heard someone say, "What was he thinking of when he did that?" From presidents of nations and professional athletes to preachers and church members, at times the rational has been thrown out the window and replaced by a momentary thrill of the flesh. If a man is unguarded, a seductive woman can stir such passions in a man that he is willing to leave his wife and children and work two jobs to maintain two families, all because the opposite sex tapped into his hormones, emotions, and affections.

The adversary knows how to tap into both sides of the mind, including knowing how to manipulate a woman into temptation. In traveling to thousands of cities since I was eighteen years of age, it has been sad to hear the hundreds of stories of church-attending, dedicated women who end up in a physical or emotional affair with the pastor or a man on staff. Not always, but many times, the *fallen* woman had a husband who was either unconverted, did not attend church, or did not meet her expectations. God created the woman to be geared to what she hears and what is spoken. Thus words are very important for women. One of the main needs a woman has is the need to feel safe and secure. This includes the need for the finances to pay the bills, having a safe place to live, the need for attention and care, and the need for verbal communication.

Look back at the affair between David and Bathsheba. David's *original* wife was Michal, the daughter of King Saul. Their marriage had been arranged by Saul and had been a rocky road from the start. Saul had made twenty-one attempts on David's life, and Michal was given by her father, Saul, to another man! When David became king, he brought Michal to his palace. Later, on one occasion, when David was bringing back the ark and was dancing before the people near the palace in a linen ephod, Michal was watching from the palace. When David returned, she criticized his actions. We read in 2 Samuel 6:23, that from that moment forward, "Therefore Michal the daughter of Saul had no children to the day of her death." It appears David completely cut off his relationship with her.

Sometime after this incident the kings were at battle, and David was lying around the palace. He saw a woman bathing herself and invited her into his bed chamber. She was the wife of one of David's mighty man, Uriah, who was a mighty warrior (2 Sam. 11). After she became pregnant, David called the husband from the front lines and told him to sleep with his wife, but his loyalty to David and the army of Israel was so strong he refused. After two attempts to get Uriah to do so, David then sent him to the front line, where the husband was slain.

Why would a beautiful married woman engage in adultery with the king? Theology will suggest that God would not cover

David's sin, thus not allowing Uriah to sleep with his wife. This may be a correct observation; however, I also suggest that Uriah is an example of a husband who is too busy for his wife. If I were invited from a battlefield to stay two nights with my lovely wife, Pam, I would remain in the house and not come out for two days! Perhaps Bathsheba was like some wives today, desiring attention and not always getting it. David's being estranged from his queen wife, Uriah being one of the chief soldiers, and the idle time on David's hand formed a combination for a moment that caused great difficulty for David the remaining days of his life.

Men can be tempted by sight, by affection, and by emotional manipulation; women can be tempted by attention, word, and the position of the person. The adversary of mankind was successful to bring sin and separation from God into the life of the first couple, Adam and Eve. After six thousand years of experience in battle strategies, the lust of the flesh, lust of the eyes, and the pride of life are the three main missiles from which all other darts originate (1 John 2:16).

CONFUSION BETWEEN TESTING AND TEMPTING

At times there is confusion in the body of Christ between the meaning and purpose of testing and temptation.

A test can be a trial of your faith that God permits to bring you forth as gold being purified in the fire (1 Pet. 1:7). Temptation can become a burning fire, but the purposes and end results of the two are different.

God allows a testing of your faith, but Satan is the tempter initiating temptation (Matt. 4:3). James 1:13 reminds us that God cannot be tempted with evil and does not tempt men. When the Israelites were journeying in the wilderness, God put them to a test to reveal to them what was really on the inside of their souls (Deut. 8:2). They were out of Egypt, but the thinking of Egypt remained in them, evidenced when they worshipped a golden calf (Exod. 32) reminiscent of the idol god Apis, a bull deity worshipped among the Egyptians. No one knows what weakness lay hidden deep within their spirits until pressure squeezed them and what was hidden began to surface. The same is true for us. It may be a bad temper, depression, or negative words that pour forth. Since "out of the abundance of the heart the mouth speaks" (Matt. 12:34), pressure on the inward man of the heart will force words out of the mouth that at times people regret. God's test is to prove you, but Satan's temptation is intent on destroying you (John 10:10).

When a believer endures a trial of faith, it builds character and integrity. When Satan succeeds in a temptation, the fruit is guilt, condemnation, and shame. I have encountered numerous trials and tribulations during my many years of walking with God. In retrospect, each time I overcame and moved forward, it only added to the foundation of my faith, as it built more trust that God could see me through anything (Phil. 4:13). Satan's temptations are designed to have the opposite result. When Satan assigned himself to go after Peter, the plan was to sift him as wheat to cause his faith to fail. Christ interceded for Peter prior to this attack and prayed that his faith would "not fail" (Luke 22:32). After many years of ministry and more than seventy thousand hours of study in the Word, I have learned that all of our temptations are designed to wreck our faith and cause us to fail God. This was Paul's warning when he wrote in 1 Thessalonians 3:5:

> For this reason, when I could no longer endure it, I sent
> to know your faith, lest by some means the tempter had
> tempted you, and our labor might be in vain.

As believers, it is important that we never judge others based upon the temptations and pressures they face. When we judge others, we are then subject to experiencing the same difficulties they are encountering.

> Brethren, if a man is overtaken in any trespass, you who are spiritual restore such a one in a spirit of gentleness, considering yourself lest you also be tempted.
>
> —GALATIANS 6:1

Among the differences between a test and a temptation, the one difference is that the test God sends our way will eventually have a conclusion, but the temptations of Satan will never end as long as we live in a fleshly body. When Christ was tempted during His forty-day fast, Satan departed from Him, but only "until an opportune time" (Luke 4:13).

THREE MAIN INSTRUCTIONS RELATED TO TEMPTATION

There are three important instructions related to temptation.

1. Watch and pray against temptation.

In the Gospels the word *watch* has three general meanings. In Christ's day time was divided up into *watches*, which were divisions of the day and night. For example, Jesus was praying during the "fourth watch of the night" (Matt. 14:25), which in Roman time would have been between three and six o'clock in the morning.

The second meaning of the word relates to a series of Roman guards being assigned to a specific location, called a "watch" (Matt. 27:65, KJV). This meaning comes from the Greek word *koustodia*, which is a word from the Latin word for keeping custody, or guarding something. In Matthew 27:65 Pilate placed a watch of Roman guards at the tomb of Christ.

The third meaning of *watch* is used in Matthew 26:41:

> Watch and pray, lest you enter into temptation. The spirit
> indeed is willing, but the flesh is weak.

This word *watch* means to stay awake and be alert. Christ was in the garden prior to His arrest and was warning the disciples to stay awake (while He prayed) to prevent temptation. In the story Peter, James, and John were with Christ, and all three were sleeping during Christ's agonizing moments of intercession (Luke 22:45). When the Roman soldiers arrived with swords and lanterns, Peter arose swinging a sword and cut off the ear of the servant of the high priest (v. 50). He neither watched (stayed alert) nor prayed, but he slept, and without Christ's intervention of healing by placing the ear back on the head of Malchus, Peter could have been arrested—and that would have been the end of his ministry!

Notice we don't watch to prevent temptation, as temptation is a part of our spiritual development, but we watch that we enter not into temptation (Matt. 26:41). This means to watch and pray that we do not enter through the door and perform the acts and actions that the tempter is throwing at us. By watching you will say, "I am not going there," and by prayer you will sense the movement of the enemy before he arrives on your doorsteps. Watching and praying lead to the second important instruction.

2. Pray that you will not be led into temptation.

One of the significant lines in the Lord's Prayer, which Christ instructed us to pray, is:

> And lead us not into temptation, but deliver us from evil:
> For thine is the kingdom, and the power, and the glory, for
> ever. Amen.
> —MATTHEW 6:13, KJV

When was the last time you prayed, "Lead me not into temptation, and deliver me from evil"? This line of the prayer may seem to be a contradiction when we read that God is not tempted with evil and does not tempt any man (James 1:13), and yet we read where the Spirit led Jesus into the wilderness to be "tempted of the devil" (Matt. 4:1). In Christ's instance He was required to be tested with the lust of the flesh, lust of the eyes, and pride of life and to overcome Satan's testing by using the Scripture and resisting the adversary. The first Adam failed, but the Second Adam, Christ, was successful against Satan's assault.

The prayer of Christ must be understood in light of praying that the Lord will not allow you to walk into a temptation but will deliver you from it. Every believer should pray that we would avoid Satan's temptation and be freed from any evil set against us. We have this promise:

> No temptation has overtaken you except such as is common to man; but God is faithful, who will not allow you to be tempted beyond what you are able, but with the temptation will also make the way of escape, that you may be able to bear it.
>
> —1 Corinthians 10:13

When Joseph was tested by another man's wife, instead of looking for the bedroom, he looked for the exit and thus saved his integrity.

3. The spirit is willing to resist.

The third important truth is found in the same verse that instructs men to watch and pray:

> Watch ye and pray, lest ye enter into temptation. The spirit truly is ready, but the flesh is weak.
>
> —Mark 14:38, KJV

In the New Testament when we see the word *spirit*, we must examine the text to identify if it is the spirit of a man or the Spirit of God. Usually when the verse refers to the Spirit of God, the *S* in Spirit will be capitalized in the English translation. In this verse Christ reveals that the spirit within us is willing to watch and pray, but our flesh is weak. It is the flesh that wants to eat when your spirit desires to fast. The flesh would rather sleep than get up early and pray. Your flesh would prefer to sit in your pajamas watching Christian television on Sunday than getting dressed and "not forsaking the assembling of ourselves together" (Heb. 10:25). Your flesh wants to be fed carnal and fleshly images and talk, but your spirit desires that you control your imaginations and your conversation (1 Pet. 1:15–16).

It is the redeemed spirit of a believer that needs to be fed the spiritual energy of the Word of God and be sharpened by the Holy Spirit on a daily basis. When your flesh is strong, your spirit is weak, and when your spirit is strong, your flesh will lose control.

The following verse sums up how to defeat the numerous temptations of the enemy:

> Casting down arguments and every high thing that exalts itself against the knowledge of God, bringing every thought into captivity to the obedience of Christ, and being ready to punish all disobedience when your obedience is fulfilled.
> —2 Corinthians 10:5–6

Since we live in an earthly body on a flesh-and-blood planet, and the adversary has access to our information, including strengths and weakness, we will from time to time experience temptation. However, being tempted is not a sin, for Christ Himself was tempted and yet never submitted to the voice of the enemy. Numerous provisions have been given in the Word to help to prevent you from falling into a trap, to help you escape when you have entered a trap, or to bring you forth from the snare of the enemy when you are in the trap. The best method of battle is preempting the warfare, and this is done when we avoid falling into temptation.

LEAD YOURSELF NOT INTO TEMPTATION

There is one more important thought concerning temptation, and that is avoiding your own setup. First of all, never determine what you do and do not permit, or can and cannot do, based upon another person's commitments or convictions. I have a board member who, before his conversion, was a high-rolling gambler in Las Vegas and would even take people to the city for gambling. After his conversion he was unable to even pick up a pool stick and play a game of pool, as it reminded him of his days of gambling and a competitive spirit rose up in him. I have another friend who would never allow his children to play the arcade games in the mall for personal reasons. Over many years I too have had personal convictions that some have laughed at and said, "That's silly," but for me it was a personal issue.

Let's be clear. The Bible identifies specific sins, and there must be no compromise in this area. However, from a practical perspective, we are to "work out your own salvation with fear and trembling" (Phil. 2:12). In the Christian walk there are a few *gray areas* where the Bible does not indicate one way or another about a specific issue. One such example is cremation. Some believers are fine with the process, and others would never permit a loved one to be cremated. This is an area of working out your own convictions. If a believer holds to a conviction, even though others may not hold the same belief, each believer should maintain his or her own convictions and not compromise for the sake of another person's opinion or pressure or to gain another's approval. It is possible that compromise could lead to a temptation that could open the door to sin.

It is important not to lead yourself into temptation. As an

example, when we hire a person to work in our ministry, every person must be approved by my wife, Pam, especially any female worker. We must know about their level of spirituality, work ethic, and their relationship with their companion. Many years ago a fellow minister was going to move to town and had asked if his wife could work part-time in the ministry. They were a very sweet and personable couple; however, I sensed something about the woman that made me uncomfortable. I told Pam, "I'm not sure what it is, but I don't think it would be good for her to work here, or, for that matter to work around me." Pam had already sensed the same, and we turned down the offer. Several years later there was a situation that occurred, which, when we heard of it, we knew why there had been a check in my spirit.

Another important issue is that a husband must learn to trust his wife's discernment and give her the liberty to protect him from members of the opposite sex who may have the wrong intentions. This is true in the area of the attire women wear who work, especially in the ministry. Years ago I was ministering in a large church, and Pam and I both noticed the women on staff all wore short skirts and rather low-cut dresses. I warned the pastor's wife that she should take control of the appearance of the women, as it would eventually cause her husband to be tempted. My suggestion was blown off, and today the couple is separated and the husband has fallen into sexual sin.

A man may act super spiritual, as though a seductive woman has no influence over him, but I would suggest, "Why bring a temptation upon yourself or fight a continual mental battle by having the wrong type of people working in or around you?" The power of temptation is too common and too strong in our addiction-seductive culture. Don't set yourself up to *fellowship* with your old drug partners who still sell dope or to eat in restaurants with your old drinking buddies who still take a *toddy for the body* and where underdressed females prance around like show dogs at a contest. It is far simpler to prevent a temptation by controlling the circumstances from occurring than to fight a temptation with the circumstances you have permitted. Satan is the tempter, and we can be given a way of escape—if we are willing to take it. It is better to preempt the warfare than to engage in it.

CHAPTER 18

THREE SECRETS SATAN HOPES YOU NEVER FIND OUT

❧ ❧

T HE PERSON WHO said, "Ignorance is bliss," must have been living in a deep forest where simple life sustained itself with animals and raw vegetation, and there was no contact with human beings. Actually, ignorance can kill you. If you continually stop at a green light and go on a red light, you are either severely color blind or super ignorant. If you cross a train track with an oncoming train blowing its whistle, then you are either deaf to the sound or having serious thoughts of suicide. Either way, ignorance is not bliss—ignorance can be deadly. The same is true about understanding the devices of the enemy; we read, "Lest Satan should take advantage of us; for we are not ignorant of his devices" (2 Cor. 2:11). The word devices can actually allude to the enemy's perception of a situation. His perception of what he sees will help determine the type of weapon he releases from his arsenal.

Deception is a major tool in the time of the end against even the righteous. Deception can be a *perverted perception*. A person with facts and a clear picture will call things as they see it. A deceived person will read into a situation, misread a situation, and rewrite the facts according to a twisted perception. Deception always involves perception. To defeat lies, you must know truth, and to receive truth, you must know the fact.

There are three very important facts that the adversary hopes you never find out, as this information will change your perception of the enemy.

Perception Deception 1: Satan Wants You to Think He Has No Limitations

Years ago while researching a message for a main conference, I came across some biblical research so fascinating that for the past twenty years I have been sharing it in churches. It deals with the fact that God placed limitations on Satan at the very moment of his creation. In God's foreknowledge He knew that Satan would lead a heavenly rebellion with a third of the angels. He also knew that man would be created as a *replacement* for the fallen angels. Thus God placed a limitation on Satan at the time he was created. This limitation is revealed in a study of Ezekiel 28.

Satan's limitation

From the beginning of God's angelic creation, I believe the Creator placed specific limitations upon His highest-ranking angel, identified as "the anointed cherub" (Ezek. 28:14). In God's fore-knowledge He knew that this cherub named Lucifer (Isa. 14:12), or Satan (Luke 10:18), would led a cosmic rebellion at the heavenly temple, deceiving a third of the angels in following him in a rebellion that initiated their expulsion from the highest heaven (Luke 10:18; Rev. 12:4).

In Ezekiel 28:13–14 (KJV) the prophet describes this anointed cherub this way:

> Thou hast been in Eden the garden of God; every precious stone was thy covering, the sardius, topaz, and the diamond, the beryl, the onyx, and the jasper, the sapphire, the emerald, and the carbuncle, and gold: the workmanship of thy tabrets and of thy pipes was prepared in thee in the day that thou wast created. Thou art the anointed cherub that covereth; and I have set thee so: thou wast upon the holy mountain of God; thou hast walked up and down in the midst of the stones of fire.

In Exodus 28:17–20 Moses lists the twelve precious and semi-precious stones placed on the foursquare breastplate of the high priest. Using the description found in the traditional 1611 King James translation, we discover the twelve stones on the four rows:

- The first row: a sardius, a topaz, and a carbuncle
- The second row: an emerald, a sapphire, and a diamond
- The third row: a ligure, an agate, and an amethyest
- The fourth row: a beryl, an onyx, and a jasper

The cherub in Ezekiel 28 has *nine* stones that are the same stones identified on the stones embedded on the priestly breastplate. If the high priest was given *twelve* and the cherub in Ezekiel 29 has *nine*, then there are three stones missing from the covering that was placed on the anointed cherub. Several years ago while researching which stones were missing and why they were omitted, I discovered it was the third row of the high priest missing on the covering of the cherub—the ligure, agate, and amethyst. (Compare Exodus 28:17–20 with Ezekiel 28:13.)

I then began researching the twelve tribes and each stone that identified each tribe. The third row would be the tribes of Gad, Issachar, and Asher. The next step was to discover why these stones were missing. After much research to confirm something I was told, it appeared that the answer was found in Genesis 49. Jacob was blessing his sons and releasing a prophecy for each one. If we take the three sons mentioned above, we read:

> Bread from Asher shall be rich, and he shall yield royal dainties.
>
> —Genesis 49:20

> Gad, a troop shall tramp upon him, but he shall triumph at last.
>
> —Genesis 49:19

> Issachar is a strong donkey, lying down between two burdens; he saw that rest was good, and that the land was pleasant; he bowed his shoulder to bear a burden, and became a band of slaves.
>
> —Genesis 49:14–15

Looking at these three predictions, consider the possibility as to why the third row of stones were never placed upon the breastplate covering of "the anointed cherub." It seems to me that God was placing certain limitations upon him from the beginning. First with Asher, the adversary would never produce a royal seed, as the Messiah would be both a priest and a king—from the seed of David! With Gad, the enemy would from time to time overcome God's people, but God's people (Gad) would overcome the adversary in the end! The theme of Issachar is more complicated, but simply Issachar could bow his shoulders and bear (carry) a burden, but the adversary is a burden maker and not a burden bearer. Christ can carry our load for us and with us!

PERCEPTION DECEPTION 2: SATAN DOESN'T WANT YOU TO KNOW HE IS RUNNING OUT OF TIME

This is a powerful truth! As we get older, we often say that we need to accomplish what we can quickly because we are running out of time. In reality, we will never run out of time; we will simply step out of time and into eternity—the land of no time. The only people running out of time are those unconverted souls whose lives are ticking away on a road to eternal destruction and the devil himself, whose time is shorter than he might think. Satan would like you to think he has an unending forever on earth, but his time clock is ticking ever closer to his end.

Something happened the moment that Satan and his angels were expelled from heaven; they left a land of no time and entered a cosmos where the sun, moon, and the stars set the day, month, and year on a calendar that counts time. When entering the earth reality, the adversary understood that he would be placed on a certain time with a *limited amount of this human commodity* to fulfill his desires and make numerous attempts to disrupt God's plans for man and the earth. Because we are living in the time of the end and the prophetic signs are evident all around us, Satan knows his time is running out. This reality will be self-evident the day when he is cast out of the second heaven to the earth during the Tribulation—for which God has assigned him an additional forty-two months to work in coordination with the Antichrist and false prophet; *then* he is cast into the lake of fire.

Perception Deception 3: Satan Doesn't Want You to Know the Importance of Time Limitation to a Believer

The fact that the enemy must work with limited time reserves is also important in the life of a believer, especially when the war is on and the attacks are strong. The first truth nugget to understand is that a battle cannot go on forever; it has to have an ending at some point in the near future. The second truth is that every attack is time sensitive, meaning that the enemy only has a certain amount of time that he can give to the assault. Paul understood this when he wrote of his pressing conditions and reminded the church that, "Our...affliction...is but for a moment" (2 Cor. 4:17). The fact that during Jesus's forty days in the wilderness Satan did not continually follow Christ around each day, but "departed for a season," indicates that the attack ran out of steam because Christ initiated the ultimate weapon in the conflict—the "sword of the Spirit," the Word of God! When Christ began quoting the Word of God, the adversary departed, as he is only able to take so much of the spoken Word being thrown at him in one particular setting.

A third important truth to remember is that your reaction to the conflict can actually reduce or add additional time to the attack. If you submit to God and resist the devil, your enemy will flee from you (James 4:7). However, the opposite is also true: if you resist God and submit to the devil, he will remain near you! Your lack of resistance or lack of a will to fight back using the Word and prayer can actually lengthen the amount of time given to the enemy to battle for your soul. We know that the human immune system is usually strong and can resist and fight an illness, but when the immune system is weak, a person is more subject to a virus, a cold, or even a disease. All diseases can be traced through the blood of a person, for "the life of the flesh is in the blood" (Lev. 17:11). The power that is in Christ's blood is the life force and life source that strengthens the believer's spiritual immune system to resist the onslaught of Satan's devices!

A fourth and very important truth is that you cannot ever out-think your spiritual enemy, as his greatest strength is in his control over the power of the air (Eph. 2:2) and the fiery darts sent against the mind (Eph. 6:16). As you begin to think, foreign thoughts begin flying over your head like a flock of birds headed south for the winter. As you expel one thought, a second dart seemingly comes out of nowhere.

You may not be capable of outthinking your enemy, but you can certainly outtalk him! This principle of verbally rebuking Satan and audibly quoting Scripture was established by Christ Himself during His wilderness temptation. Christ did not rebuke Satan in His mind, but He spoke out loud saying, "It is written..." (Matt. 4:10).

THE VALUE OF YOUR FAITH AND PATIENCE

Remember, Christ's temptation extended an entire forty days during His isolation in the Judean wilderness (Luke 4:2). In this rocky, desolate solitude there is no one to speak to other than God. At times a faint echo was heard when Christ verbally quoted Scripture or perhaps sang a spiritual song to edify Himself (Eph. 5:19). Both Matthew and Luke reveal that Christ verbally expressed Scripture when resisting the adversary, demonstrating that the temptation was more than a thought in the mind; it was a literal, audible assault by Satan himself. Satan spoke to Christ, who in return rebuked the tempter by using revelation from the Torah (Luke 4:2–12).

Forty consecutive days of fasting in a desert require two important biblical virtues that are the "power twins" undergirding a believer's life: faith and patience. Faith can *start* you on your long journey, but patience will *keep* you walking on that journey through the potholes, delays, and possible roadblocks. Faith can *motivate* you to engage in the battle to see, but patience will *undergird* your faith during times of failure, wounds, and sudden conflicts. Faith can *lead you* down a road of healing, but patience *will keep hope alive* while you are waiting for the manifestation of your healing to emerge. We hear great teaching on faith but little on faith's twin brother, patience.

The Greek word for "patience" is *hupomone* and exemplifies the virtue of "happily and hopefully enduring in a steady and consistent manner—in faith." The key word is *consistent*...meaning to *not waver in unbelief* or in your determination. There are many reasons why patience is a must virtue for every believer to carry in the battle arsenal and strategy.

As I mentioned previously, all spiritual testing is for a set time period. When we as believers are in the heat of a major testing or temptation, our desire is that the crisis and conflict will cease soon, that it will depart from us as quickly as it may have suddenly appeared. However, when the test continues for months, or even years, without patience we will make unwise decisions attempting to escape the struggle.

One of the unique examples is in 1 Samuel 26 when King Saul was unexpectedly given into David's hands as the weary king and his soldiers slept. Instead of slaying Saul, David crept into the cave and seized Saul's spear and water bottle. The following morning David yelled from an opposite hill, rebuking Abner, Saul's bodyguard, for not protecting the king (v. 15). Saul was stunned, humiliated and humbled, and in fear of what could have been. He promised David that he would no longer do him harm as he had been a fool for chasing David (v. 21). Saul planned to return to Jerusalem and leave David alone. Checkmate: David won, Saul lost—time to send the king home for good. From that moment Saul *did* go home and never pursued David again (v. 25).

But read how 1 Samuel 27 starts out:

> And David said in his heart, "Now I shall perish someday
> by the hand of Saul. There is nothing better for me than
> that I should speedily escape to the land of the Philistines;
> and Saul will despair of me, to seek me anymore in any
> part of Israel. So I shall escape out of his hand."
>
> —1 SAMUEL 27:1–2

Saul had pursued David for many years, chasing him like a hunted animal throughout the wilderness. However, like a cunning fox, David continually escaped entrapment, and Saul was unable to lay a finger on him, the future king of Israel. In this narrative Saul is gone for good, yet it seems David has run out of patience and thinks Saul will be back (as he always was) and eventually kill him! Just when David experienced his most important breakthrough in dealing with his adversary, he gave up and chose to hang out among God's enemies in the heart of the Philistines territory, where eventually his decision almost cost him his life—not by the hands of Saul but through the hands of his mighty men. (See 1 Samuel 30.) David actually lost faith in God's future promises, and his patience wore thin; thus he made a bad choice.

Often our simple conception of faith is a spiritual force that creates what we see from what we cannot see and gives us confidence it will happen before we see it (Heb. 11:1). This fact gave expression in the charismatic circles that if you have "right-now, active faith," the power and level of your faith can form a supernatural shield that exempts you from opposition and trouble. The assumption is that if we fast long enough, pray loud enough, and believe strong enough, our problems will go away almost immediately and we can shout a praise, say "Thank You, Lord," and move on to the next level of success and prosperity.

However, the virtue of patience is significant for several reasons. There are times when prayers are delayed (Dan. 10), battles are long (2 Sam. 3:1), and temptation doesn't immediately go away but comes and goes in seasons (Luke 4:13). Patience assists in lighting a spark of hope in the midst of the darkness, a surge of new life in the midst of the weakness, and an invisible strength during the testing as faith and patience whisper, "Hold on; God will work it all out."

In the struggle with our spiritual adversary, patience is a very important virtue. The attacks of Satan are assigned in seasons and will expire at certain times, based upon the reaction, response, and scriptural knowledge of the believer. When a believer exercises patience during a test, the ability to endure testing for an extended season enables a believer to outlast the opposing attack, as the adversary does not have the patience to endure beyond a certain season. This is what Paul meant when he said, "Our light affliction, which is but for a moment" (2 Cor. 4:17). The enemy's success is gained from a hit-and-run strategy. He hits and retreats, hits and retreats, and hits again—all to wear you down.

When Paul spoke of having a "thorn in the flesh...a messenger of Satan" coming against his ministry, he stated this satanic agent was "buffeting" him (2 Cor. 12:7). The Greek word for "buffet" is *kolaphizo* and means to steadily beat with the fist, or to take one hit after another hit and one blow after another. There is an implication in this word of a person who is knocked down, gets up and is knocked down, gets up again and is knocked down again in a repeated cycle of "ups and downs." This "thorn in the flesh" was a satanic messenger that motivated people in cities where Paul ministered to verbally, physically, and publicly come against Paul, creating difficulty for him in his regional ministry and Asian journeys. Paul wrote a list of opposition he faced in 2 Corinthians 11:23–27:

> ...in stripes above measure, in prisons more frequently, in deaths often. From the Jews five times I received forty stripes minus one. Three times I was beaten with rods; once I was stoned; three times I was shipwrecked; a night and a day I have been in the deep; in journeys often, in

perils of waters, in perils of robbers, in perils of my own countrymen, in perils of the Gentiles, in perils in the city, in perils in the wilderness, in perils in the sea, in perils among false brethren; in weariness and toil, in sleeplessness often, in hunger and thirst, in fastings often, in cold and nakedness.

The stress and difficulties Paul faced make it clear that these trials and tribulations required him to exercise patience, or as some biblical translators say, "endurance." Paul did not faint or give up in the midst of the crisis. James points out the link of patience and faith:

My brethren, count it all joy when you fall into various trials, knowing that the testing of your faith produces patience.

—JAMES 1:2–3

James later in his epistle mentions Job as an example of a man who, during a crushing series of trials, endured to see a breakthrough at the end of the testing cycle. In James 5:11 the King James Version speaks of the "patience" of Job, and the New American Standard Bible uses the word *endurance*. Thus Job patiently endured using inner spiritual strength to stand in faith and not sin with his mouth against God. Patience provides the spiritual stamina to endure the pressure of the test and the flames of fiery trial until the weight is lifted and the fire is quenched. As James wrote:

Indeed we count them blessed who endure. You have heard of the perseverance of Job and seen the end intended by the Lord—that the Lord is very compassionate and merciful.

—JAMES 5:11

As a believer, your greatest concern during a test is the tendency to "give up" before the cycle of testing is completed. When it feels that your faith is wavering and weakening, it requires your spiritual, emotional, and at times physical determination and the arms of patience to undergird your beliefs and thoughts that a good outcome will be the end of the test. You cannot have a testimony of overcoming it there is not a test you must overcome!

One of my favorite passages related to patience is found in Hebrews 10:35–36 (KJV):

> Cast not away therefore your confidence, which hath great recompense of reward. For ye have need of patience, that, after ye have done the will of God, ye might receive the promise.

Patience breeds confidence, and holding to your confidence brings a great "recompense of reward." The Greek word for this phrase is *misthapodosia* and is similar to saying a "reimbursement in pay." A good imagery for this would be you taking a business trip that required you purchasing gas, food, and lodging. After returning home, you give your boss the receipts for expenses from the trip, and in turn he or she pays you back the amount you spent. The idea behind Hebrews 10:35–36 is if you will be patient and keep your confidence (trust, assurance), eventually you will receive a great reimbursement for your faithfulness! God is a "rewarder" of those who diligently seek Him (Heb. 11:6). The word *rewarder* here is the same Greek root word used for "recompense" in Hebrews 10:35. The benefit of exercising faith and patience is that a good outcome can be expected from waiting upon the Lord.

When you understand that the adversary has limitations and is running out of time, that your own test has a set cycle that must come to a climax at some point, and that your faith and patience can outlast the attack, then you have exposed another area of spiritual warfare that the enemy hoped you would never find out!

THE ONE DAY SATANIC POWERS CANNOT TOUCH YOUR LIFE

YEARS AGO SOMEONE asked the question, "When will the enemy ever leave me alone?" Someone seated nearby replied, "The day you arrive in heaven, because then you are out of his reach!" While it is certainly true that at the departing of the soul and spirit at death or the gathering together of the saints at Christ's return, the believer will be released from the influence and grimy hands of the adversary, there is another powerful truth that you should understand: *there is one day on earth when neither the enemy nor any of his cohorts are able to touch your life*!

I first discovered this interesting nugget while studying how the letters of the Hebrew alphabet can be exchanged for numbers. This system, called *gamatria*, is not a new system but is used in the Hebrew and Greek alphabet. It was commonly used among the

Hebrews after the Babylonian captivity. It is also one of the methods considered in Rabbinical Judaism for discovering remarkable mysteries encoded within the Hebrew text itself.

There are two aspects to this concept. The first is the name of Satan in the Hebrew language. In the Bible it would read *Ha Satan*, or "The Satan." The reason "The" is used to identify Satan is because the word *satan* in the Hebrew can simply translate as an adversary, but when saying "The Satan," it can specifically identify the person of Satan.

Each individual letter of the Hebrew alphabet has a number equivalent. For example the first letter, *aleph,* has a numerical value of one, the next letter *beit* has a value of two, the third letter *gimmel* is three, and so forth. This continues to the twenty-second letter of the alphabet, *tav,* which has a value of four hundred.

The numerical values of the Hebrew letters used for *The Satan* are as follows:

Hei	ה	=	5
Shin	שׁ	=	300
Tet	ט	=	9
Nun	ן	=	50
			364

The Hebrew phrase "The Satan" has four Hebrew letters totaling 364.

The rabbis note that the name of Satan totals to a numerical value of 364. It has been pointed out that in a complete solar year there are slightly over 365 days in a year. The name of Satan falls one short of the 365, when subtracting 364 from 365. This is interpreted as meaning that there is one day in a year when Satan cannot touch your life or hinder the progress of God in your life, and that is the Day of Atonement.

In ancient times this was the most important of the seven appointed seasons for Israel. The feasts of Passover, Unleavened Bread, and Pentecost, and even the Feast of Tabernacles, were celebrated yearly, but they were based upon major *past events* commemorated in Israel's history. However, the Day of Atonement looked into the past sins of Israel and determined if they would be forgiven, and the favor of God would be granted to the nation *for the coming year.*

From a New Testament perspective, this concept has a parallel truth. When you hear the gospel of the kingdom and understand that the redemptive covenant is available to you, then the day you make up your mind to enter that covenant through confessing Christ and turning from sins, there is no power of darkness in any form that can prevent God's power from reaching out to you! This is because there is a mysterious power in the blood of Christ, and Satan understands this authority that stripped him of his own authority over a redeemed man.

No doubt Satan saw when God cut the skins of two animals to cover Adam and Eve in the garden (Gen. 3). Generations later he witnessed an amazing event when the blood of a lamb on the outer post of the doors of the Hebrew homes in Egypt prevented the death angel from entering. In the wilderness he further observed the establishment of an elaborate system of ritualistic offerings and blood sacrifices, demanded by God for sin and transgression. He would have also known of how the sacrifices of David on an altar on Mount Moriah stopped a destroying angel from slaying the men in Jerusalem. The final blow came when Christ's blood was given total authority to overcome all the powers of the enemy!

It is your confession of the power of Christ's blood that the enemy knows he cannot prevent!

When a sinner makes up his or her mind to turn from sin and receive Christ as Savior, there is nothing that can prevent that person from receiving the redemption covenant of eternal life. Paul summed it up well when he wrote:

> Yet in all these things we are more than conquerors through
> Him who loved us. For I am persuaded that neither death
> nor life, nor angels nor principalities nor powers, nor things

present nor things to come, nor height nor depth, nor any other created thing, shall be able to separate us from the love of God which is in Christ Jesus our Lord.

—Romans 8:37–39

In conclusion, the freedom and spiritual authority freely given to a believer come through receiving and walking in the redemptive covenant provided by Jesus Christ. The Word of God, the blood and name of Jesus Christ, and being in right standing with God (righteousness) are the inner weapons provided to win battles, conquer the strategies, and defeat all of the powers of the enemy. A believer must walk in faith and the knowledge of God to maintain a life of victory. Once you know the playbook of the enemy, you then have the advantage in the battle! You are now armed with that spiritual knowledge as we have exposed the playbook of Satan. Now fight a good fight!

NOTES

CHAPTER 1
WHEN A PROPHETIC WORD BECOMES A WEAPON OF WAR

1. As related to the author on May 28, 2011, while ministering for Pastor Kimberling in East Point, Florida.

2. Biblesoft's *New Exhaustive Strong's Numbers and Concordance With Expanded Greek-Hebrew Dictionary*, copyright © 1994, Biblesoft and International Bible Translators, Inc., s.v. *"deilia."*

3. *Barnes' Notes*, electronic database, PCStudy Bible, copyright © 1997, Biblesoft, s.v. "2 Timothy 1:6."

4. Rick Renner, *Sparkling Gems From the Greek* (Tulsa, OK: Teach All Nations, 2003), 588.

5. Ibid., 555.

CHAPTER 3
LEARN HOW YOUR ENEMY THINKS

1. Flavius Josephus, *Antiquities of the Jews*, book 1, chapter 1, Christian Classics Ethereal Library, http://www.ccel.org/j/josephus/works/ant-1.htm (accessed May 11, 2012).

CHAPTER 4
CAN SATAN READ MY MIND?

1.   This incident literally occurred at an "evangelistic crusade" in Knoxville, Tennessee, several years ago. This story was related to the author personally by an attendee who knew the woman and observed the situation as it occurred that night.

CHAPTER 5
SATAN'S WARFARE BY DECEPTION

1.   "Timeline of Houdini's Life," PBS.org, http://www.pbs.org/wgbh/amex/houdini/timeline/index.html (accessed May 16, 2012).

2.   Ibid.

3.   "Houdini's Jail Escapes," Houdini: His Life and Art, http://www.thegreatharryhoudini.com/jailescapes.html (accessed May 16, 2012).

4.   This story was related to me in a personal conversation with my Israeli tour guide, Gideon Shor. More information about this attack and other similar ones during World War I may be found in Scot Macdonald, *Propaganda and Information Warfare in the Twenty-first Century* (New York: Routledge, Taylor, and Francis Group, 2007), http://athens.indymedia.org/local/webcast/uploads/propaganda_and_information_warfare_in_the_twenty-first_century__altered_images_and_deception_operations.pdf (accessed May 16, 2012).

CHAPTER 7
THE IMPORTANCE OF FIGHTING PRIVATE DEMONS

1.   Renner, *Sparkling Gems From the Greek*, 553.

CHAPTER 10
WHAT IS THE GREATEST WEAPON SATAN USES AGAINST A BELIEVER?

1.   *Barnes' Notes*, electronic database, s.v. "Hebrews 12:1."

2.   Ibid.

CHAPTER 11
WHAT IS THE GREATEST WEAPON
SATAN USES AGAINST A SINNER?

1.　Barna Group, "Teens Evaluate the Church-Based Ministry They Received as Children," July 8, 2003, and Barna Group, "Twenty-somethings Struggle to Find Their Place in Christian Churches," September 24, 2003, cited in "Transitioning to College," Baptist Campus Ministry at Northern Kentucky University, http://www.nkubcm.org/beprepared (accessed May 18, 2012).

CHAPTER 12
THE TRUTH BEHIND SO-CALLED HAUNTED HOUSES

1.　Although this was a television program I saw, I will not give specific information about the program as I do not desire for people to go online in an attempt to contact a false person operating with a false spirit.

2.　Linda Lyons, "Paranormal Beliefs Come (Super)Naturally to Some," November 1, 2005, Gallup.com, http://www.gallup.com/poll/19558/paranormal-beliefs-come-supernaturally-some.aspx (accessed May 18, 2012).

CHAPTER 13
CAN SATAN PUT A GENERATIONAL
CURSE UPON A BELIEVER?

1.　Biblesoft's *New Exhaustive Strong's Numbers and Concordance With Expanded Greek-Hebrew Dictionary*, s.v. "*paqad.*"

2.　Ibid., s.v. "*episkope.*"

CHAPTER 15
PORNOGRAPHY—THE SEDUCING SPIRIT
BEHIND THE HINDERING SPIRIT

1.　Wikipedia.org, s.v. "pornography," http://en.wikipedia.org/wiki/Pornography (accessed May 22, 2012).

2.　For more information on how images are implanted in the brain, including more about axons and dendrites, see National Institutes of Health, "Information about the Brain," Teacher's Guide,

http://science.education.nih.gov/supplements/nih4/self/guide/info
-brain.htm (accessed May 22, 2012).

3.   W. E. Vine, *Vine's Expository Dictionary of New Testament Words* (n.p.: Riverside Books, 1999), s.v. *"poneros."*

4.   Sandra Galeotti, "Dopamine Receptor Agonists," Healthline .com, http://www.healthline.com/galecontent/dopamine-receptor -agonists (accessed May 22, 2012).

5.   A detailed study is found at Elaine M. Hull, John W. Muschamp, and Satoru Sato, "Dopamine and Serotonin: Influences on Male Sexual Behavior," *Physiology and Behavior* 83 (2004): 291–307, http://www.psy.fsu.edu/faculty/hull/DA%265HT_pdf.pdf (accessed May 22, 2012).

6.   Vine, *Vine's Expository Dictionary of New Testament Words,* s.v. *"hamartia."*

7.   Biblesoft's *New Exhaustive Strong's Numbers and Concordance With Expanded Greek-Hebrew Dictionary,* s.v. *"anomia."*

8.   Ryan Singel, "Internet Porn: Worse Than Crack?", Wired f.com, November 19, 2004, http://www.wired.com/science/discoveries/ news/2004/11/65772 (accessed May 22, 2012). There are also numerous articles and studies on this subject.

CHAPTER 16
BREAKING HABITS THAT CREATE HINDRANCES

1.   Biblesoft's *New Exhaustive Strong's Numbers and Concordance With Expanded Greek-Hebrew Dictionary,* s.v. *"apollumi"* and *"phtheiro."*

2.   Renner, *Sparkling Gems From the Greek,* 114.

3.   American Cancer Society, "Secondhand Smoke," http://www .cancer.org/Cancer/CancerCauses/TobaccoCancer/secondhand-smoke (accessed May 23, 2012).

4.   Centers for Disease Control and Prevention, "Health Effects of Cigarette Smoking," http://www.cdc.gov/tobacco/data_statistics/ fact_sheets/health_effects/effects_cig_smoking/ (accessed May 23, 2012).

5.   Tri-County Health Department (Colorado), "What You Should Know About Tobacco," fact sheet, Section 2: Health Effects, http://www.tchd.org/pdfs/02_health_effects.pdf (accessed May 23, 2012).

6.   Terry Martin, "Understanding Nicotine Addiction," About .com, http://quitsmoking.about.com/od/nicotine/a/nicotineeffects.htm (accessed May 23, 2012).

7.   Regional Transportation District (Denver), "Tobacco Cessation—Why Quit!", http://www3.rtd-denver.com/content/ Wellness&Rehab/Content_Mgmt_Files/tobacco_cessation/ Tobacco%20Cessation%20Why%20Quit.pdf (accessed May 23, 2012).

8.   Martin, "Understanding Nicotine Addiction."

9.   National Cancer Institute, "Secondhand Smoke and Cancer," fact sheet, January 12, 2011, http://www.cancer.gov/cancertopics/ factsheet/Tobacco/ETS (accessed May 23, 2011).

CHAPTER 17
WHY AM I STILL TEMPTED—EVEN
AFTER I RECEIVED CHRIST?

1.   Middle Tennessee State University, "Differences Between Left and Right Hemisphere," http://frank.mtsu.edu/~studskl/hd/hemis .html (accessed May 23, 2012).

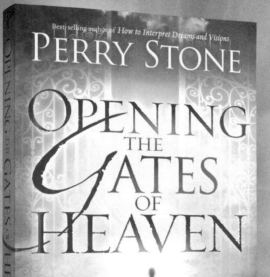

MORE FROM BEST-SELLING AUTHOR PERRY STONE

Perry Stone brings his unique blend of Bible knowledge and spiritual insight to every topic he covers. If you enjoyed *Exposing Satan's Playbook*, you will love these…

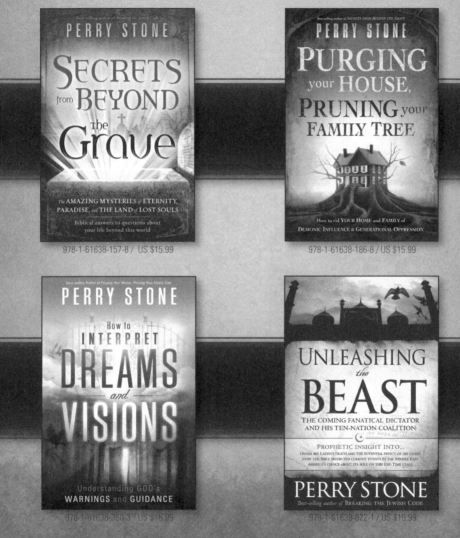
Visit your local bookstore

www.CharismaHouse.com
www.facebook.com/CharismaHouse

CHARISMA HOUSE
10930A